The Complete Guide to Mac
Backup Management

LIMITED WARRANTY AND DISCLAIMER OF LIABILITY

The Complete Guide to Mac Backup Management

Dorian Cougias · Tom Dell

AP PROFESSIONAL

Boston   San Diego   New York
London   Sydney   Tokyo   Toronto

Copyright © 1996 by Network Frontiers, Inc.
Copyright © 1994 by Network Frontiers, Inc. and Dorian J. Cougias

AP PROFESSIONAL
1300 Boylston Street, Chestnut Hill, MA 02167
World Wide Web site at http://www.apnet.com

An Imprint of ACADEMIC PRESS, INC.
A Division of HARCOURT BRACE & COMPANY

United Kingdom Edition published by
ACADEMIC PRESS LIMITED
24–28 Oval Road, London NW1 7DX

ISBN 0-12-192562-5

Printed in the United States of America
95 96 97 98 IP 9 8 7 6 5 4 3 2 1

CONTENTS

Dorian's Dedication:

To my dad,
Gust Cougias.

My Hero.

FOREWORD

by Larry and Richard Zulch, Cofounders of Dantz Development Corporation

As you might imagine, we get asked about backup quite frequently. Our response is often a question: "How much is the data on your computer worth?"

"Oh, I don't know, perhaps $500," is a typical answer.

Typical, that is, of someone who has never lost everything from a major hard disk crash without a backup. People who have gone through that experience answer differently.

"Priceless, absolutely priceless," they say.

Or "$20,000, maybe more—maybe a lot more."

People who have lost everything realize the amount of disruption a crash can cause. They realize that the hours they spend each week creating and modifying documents really add up. They know how often they refer to work they'd already created. And they find out from practical experience that, like a house burning down, there are valuable things they will never, ever get back.

We wondered if there was a way to communicate this more realistic value to people who haven't gone through the experience of losing everything. We tried asking people to estimate how much time they'd spent creating documents they'd stored in their computer. But, just like estimating value, they estimated very low.

We then had a survey performed that represented 600,000 Macintosh users. We were gratified to see that almost half placed a realistic value on their data. When we correlated that question to another we found that almost half had lost data in the last year. It was not a surprise that it was the same half who valued their data more highly.

Losing data seems like a harsh way to learn the true value of the files on your hard disk. But perhaps it is the only way. If that is correct, and since you're reading this, you most likely have lost data and have your own stories to tell.

In our survey, we asked those who valued their data but weren't really backing up (over 40%!) why they weren't. The most common reasons were "I don't know the best way to back up" or "backing up is too complex."

It is fortunate that a specialized firm was asking the survey questions, and not us, because we wouldn't have been very productive. We would have felt compelled to offer advice-after all, we've been in Macintosh backup for ten years and whenever we hear about potential data loss, we get rather animated.

Actually though, there is one way we could have stayed productive and given great advice: Tell the survey respondents to do what you have and start reading this book. We don't know of anyone even half as qualified to give advice in this area as Dorian Cougias. Dorian knows as much about backup as we do, and a lot more than we do in how to teach it and present it. After all, he's written the book on it!

There are two classes of people who should get *The Complete Guide to Mac Backup Management:* Those who have lost data and those who are going to lose data. If you're in the first class, you're probably backing up now, but knowing the best way will increase the security of your data and save you time and money. If you belong to the second class, which is everyone who isn't in the first one, starting to back up the right way before your disk crashes will make that experience as painless as it can be.

The second edition of *The Complete Guide to Mac Backup Management* is not only the very best book on keeping your data secure ever written, it is one of the most useful, amusing, and definitive books available on any aspect of using, and managing, Macintoshes.

Remember, there is probably nothing else in your life that contains so much time in such a concentrated form as your Macintosh hard disk. Concentrated data, yet concentrated risk. Fortunately, you can use your computer itself to safeguard your achievements. *The Complete Guide to Mac Backup Management* tells you how.

Craig Isaacs'
Top Ten Backup Tips

When Dorian first asked me to write my Top Ten Backup Tips, I couldn't stop thinking about my late night friend, Dave. Maybe it was the way Dorian asked me; then again, maybe it was just Dorian. So, before I share my Top Ten Backup Tips with you, I thought you would enjoy . . .

My Friend Dave's Top Ten Reasons to Back up Your Macintosh

10: New network administrator is named Kevorkian.

9: Afternoon coffee shakes keep crashing the hard drive.

8: Elvis last seen snacking at your computer.

7: Thinking about upgrading to Windows 95—today.

6: Kato responsible for computer lease payments.

5: Chernobyl to become your local energy supplier.

4: Beavis and Butthead given "Administrator" access to network.

3: Just installed 20 new INITs downloaded from the Internet.

2: Your boss is a proctologist, and yes, he really is anal.

1:      Just hired new employee named Buttafucco.

Of course, my *real* Top Ten list is a little different. It's based on discussions with thousands of you from all around the world. My list answers the question: What made some of you succeed while others failed? So, without further ado, here are...

Craig's Top Ten Backup Tips

10:      Develop a backup plan.

At a minimum, plan to back up daily using removable media such as DATs. Rotate backup sets off site weekly.

9:      Automate your backups.

Get a backup device that holds about twice as much as your hard disk(s) so you can schedule backups for times when you're not there.

8:      Back up every hard disk.

Every hard disk contains critical data, so don't just back up servers. And make sure you include portable computers.

7:      Back up more than just documents.

Don't limit backups to just certain files—you'll inevitably need one that wasn't backed up. Good backup software only backs up files that are new or modified.

6:      Make several copies of your data.

Make at least three different sets of your data. Even an old copy is better than no copy at all.

5:      Keep a backup set off site.

You never know when a fire, flood, theft, or earthquake makes your off site copy your only copy. One idea: Create a backup set weekly and send the previous week's backup to a secure off site location.

4:      Verify your backup.

You need confidence in your backups. Make sure that your backup software has full read-back verification. And try restoring files yourself—just in case you actually need to use the backups.

3:      Implement a network backup strategy.

If you're on a network, network backup software lets you share a storage device and ensures that every Macintosh is backed up.

2:      Use Retrospect or Retrospect Remote.

These award-winning products make it easy to do just about any backup strategy you can conceive of to any storage device you can connect to your Macintosh.

1:      Don't procrastinate.

Far too many new Dantz customers are people who recently lost data. Read this book and do what you need to do in order to protect your data. Don't wait until it's too late.

An Added Tip from Dorian:

If you haven't backed up your computers yet, follow Retrospect's EasyScript setup and do one *now*, before you read this book. You can find it starting on page 247.

PREFACE

First, about Network Frontiers . . .

Network Frontiers is a consulting, training, and writing company. We work on networks of all sizes. We've built networks that are *huge*, and we've built networks that are small. One thing all of them have in common is that they are *manageable* by normal, everyday network administrators. The kind who might, or might not, *do* network administration on a full-time basis. Another thing all of them have in common is that they have Macintoshes *somewhere* on the network. They don't have to be all-Macintosh networks, but there must be some Macintoshes on the network. We like Macintoshes best, and yes, we like Mac clones as much as we like the Real McCoy. They are fun, or at least they are supposed to be fun. We've built networks in this country and other countries as well.

In the last book we wrote that we conduct training courses in various networking topics. Now we are proud to say that we are the authors of the Apple Certified Server Engineer (ACSE) certification program, which, hopefully, will be equal to Certified NetWare Engineer (CNE) in the Macintosh networking arena. Don't let the title fool you—this program is backed and endorsed by a *slew* of third party vendors and is much more than server-centric. It is about how to go about designing and managing networks, whether you are a network engineer, network manager, dealer, consultant, or trainer.

To that end, we have created several books in a series, of which this is one. The first book in the series is *Managing AppleShare & Workgroup Servers*. It's about how to buy, set up, and manage one or several of the Apple Workgroup Servers. It also covers the third party software that ships with the servers and Santorini and AG

Group management tools. You'll learn what *this* book is about as you read it. It is the second in the series. The third in the series is a book about AppleTalk network design. It is not just a theory book, but a how-to-book as well. The fourth book is about managing AppleTalk networks. It covers what you should be doing by way of performance, accounting, security, and configuration management. The fifth book (and, we think, the final book) in the series is about that fifth category of network management defined by the ISO committee: fault management. The book is called *Troubleshooting AppleTalk Networks.*

And yes, we have courses that cover all of these books—so if you don't want to read the books, come to the class.

Finally, because we know that books go out of date fairly quickly, we've created a product that we think you will really like. It is called *Frontiers in Networking,* and it is a CD-based quarterly update to the books. It will cover all of the new areas of networking in the five categories of the books, as well as new and interesting networking tips and topics.

About this Book

This book is in its second edition, and is now the second title in a set of books aimed directly at those of us in the field doing AppleTalk network management and design. The title for the series was given to me by Andy Gore, one of the authors of the Digital Nomad series of books, and a good friend, I am glad to add. He summed it up when he said, "These books are really aimed at doing things on the network; at real-world application." He's right, as usual. Whether he thought of calling the series the "field manual" series because I spent about a dozen years with the U.S. Army Special Forces or because field manuals are written for people who *do* things instead of curl up with a book and read about them, it doesn't matter—the title applies. These are the books you'll want to have when you need to get something done.

Andy asked me if I think of myself as a writer of books who *does* networking, or a networking person who *does* writing. I'm not a writer. I'm an *explainer.* I'm here to act as a guide, teaching you how to do what I know how to do, and the way I do it. I don't believe that my way is the right way. I believe it is *one* way, and that *somebody* around here has to explain it to the rest of us so that we can all get something done. If you think you have a better way, tell me about it. We will be coming out with the *Frontiers in Networking* CD quarterly. If your way *is* better, we'll even pay you to write an article for it so that we *all* can share in the knowledge.

I wanted to do this book because when I get started talking about network backups I get all nutso, long-fanged, wild-eyed and crazy when I find out that people aren't doing them. Tom wanted to help with this book because he has seen a lot of good work go down the proverbial tubes through bad or non-existent backup management practices.

About Dorian J. Cougias, Author

I build networks. Clean, smooth, dynamic networks. Simple networks with great impact and ability. It doesn't have to be unmanageable if it's big. I believe in doing backups. I'm nutso about backing up. I'm nutso about *all* good network management practices. And I believe that networking should be explained in the simplest way possible. That's what I'm trying to do here.

About Tom Dell, Author

I never planned to become a network administrator, let alone a network consultant. I was a journalist. That's what I wanted to be. Trouble was, there were always problems with the computers and networks I depended on to get the newspaper out. Guess who was made responsible for them? Me—less because I was the editor and more because I was the guy who "knows something about computers." Lots of people found themselves in the networking field this way. (Get drunk at *Mactivity* sometime and you'll see what I mean.) These are the people I like to think I'm writing for. These are people who aren't thrilled by the results of a packet trace, but might like to know what one is if it'll make their jobs easier. If you're one such person, read this book. Backup management *will* make your job easier. I promise.

Getting in Touch with Us . . .

For those of you who want to tell us how great—or how pathetic—we are, here are our e-mail addresses. Remember your netiquette; yelling is in ALL CAPS.

Dorian Cougias:	dorian_cougias@netfrontiers.com
Tom Dell:	tom_dell@netfrontiers.com
Brando Rogers:	brando_rogers@netfrontiers.com
FAXes are good, too:	(415) 896-1573

We have decided that, as a policy, rocks with notes attached and thrown through the window are not to be accepted. Sorry, Andy.

ACKNOWLEDGMENTS

The original edition of this book wouldn't have been published if Paul "Doc" McGraw of APS hadn't given it his muscle. We will be forever grateful for his support and counsel.

This, the second edition, would not exist if not for our publisher, Chuck Glaser of AP PROFESSIONAL. Hopefully this, along with our other books, justifies his faith in us.

The series title, as well as the book's title, was suggested by Andrew Gore, a true gentleman and a good friend. If you don't read his articles in *MacWEEK,* you should. They are full of insight and humor.

The "Don't Bore Me with the Details . . ." summaries are dedicated to Moon Mullins, a long-fanged, war horse, administrator extraordinaire.

Thanks to our editing goddess Cassandra Kovel, who had the nifty "opportunity" to learn an entirely new page design program to put this book out—and did!

Thanks to our dedicated support team of Maizie Gilbert and Brando Rogers. You, the reader, also owe Brando one. She revised the important chapter on electricity and UPS systems.

Thanks to our beta readers, especially Tom Beardmore, Terry Beloin, Walter Fry, Earl Gerfen, Gary Mullins, Frank Plaistowe, Kathy Rose, Vernon Rose, Paul Shields, and Dean White. Special thanks to Marcelo Vergara for the best backup story in the book.

Acknowledgments

Monte Lewis is our cover artist. Isn't he great? He's also a network administrator. You gotta love that. He worked hard on the cover design and everything he has done for us. We owe him a lot.

Thanks to our amazing indexer, Steve Rath, who always comes through, even in a crunch. Like our publisher, we love a good index!

Thanks to APS, and in particular, Tom Beardmore.

Thanks to MicroNet, especially Barry Wong, Alex Grossman, and Morris Taradalsky. Your products are fantastic!

Thanks to Dantz, in particular Joanne Kalogeras, Leslie Shafer, Lars Eric Holm, Walt Hays, Pat Lee, the Zulch brothers, and Craig Isaacs.

Thanks to Cheyenne, Elmer Liam and staff in particular.

Thanks to Phil and Dimitri Zarboulas at Santorini Design & Consulting for Server Sleuth (on the CD). Read more about their great software products in our other books.

Thanks to Sassafras Software, who gave us the useful HTML Viewer application for the CD. Read more about them in *Managing AppleTalk Networks*. Thanks to AEC Software for updating FastTrack Schedule for us, especially Kurt Wyckoff.

Thanks to Elise B. Hammann at APC.

Thanks to Eastman Kodak, especially Ken Lien.

Thanks to Rip-Tie and its innovative owner, Michael Fennell. Thanks to Leslie Purmal at Kensington and Gary Torres of Qualtec DataProducts. Thanks to Keir Leiberman of DataSafe for a great interview.

Thanks to Mike Rosenfeld for always believing in backup.

Thanks to Bob Fair of Apple for letting us keep the servers to finish this book.

Thanks to all those who e-mailed comments on the first edition of this book— you have helped make this one better

—the writing team of Dorian and Tom

PART ONE:
INTRODUCTION TO
BACKUP AND RECOVERY
PLANNING

This is the second edition of *The Complete Guide to Mac Backup Management*. It has been completely overhauled, from top to bottom. That doesn't mean there was anything wrong with the first version, which was a pretty darned good book. Still, this is the "grown-up version." We learned a lot from the readers and students who used the first edition in classes we taught around the country. More than anything, though, we learned that while the first book was a great introduction to backup management and taught what to do to create a backup, it didn't go far enough into disaster prevention planning. Therefore, as the primary author, I felt it was our duty to take this version of the book, the second edition, to the next step—integrating backup into a departmental disaster prevention plan.

I say *departmental* rather than *company* plan, as I don't think many readers would want to tackle the entire *company's* plan. Some of them, like Northern Telecom, Eli Lilly, Hughes, Oriental Trading Company, and Payless Cashways, have *gizillions* of Macintoshes and a host of other computers, including mainframes. I don't think theses readers are going to run around saying, "Dorian says we have to do 'x'." They could get away with it in a limited sense, but if they said they had to buy time at a hot site and practice the company disaster recovery plan twice a year at the cost of *bizillions* of dollars, their bosses would elect to throw my book out the window rather than carry through with the plan—not that all that stuff doesn't eventually need to happen. I just don't think many companies are truly ready to follow through with an entire disaster prevention and recovery plan the *right* way. Because of this, the best we can do is to teach you how to recognize certain potential problems, how to guard against as many of these problems as possible, and how to protect your data so you can restore it when needed.

Tip: If you are really itching to get started and think that you know most of this "planning stuff" already, start with "Chapter 8: Da Budget for da Risks and da Implementation Plan" on page 129. That chapter will walk you through the creation of a budget and has links back to important pages you might want to review.

CHAPTER 1:
SO, WHAT'S A DISASTER?

The term "disaster" as I use it in this book isn't really the same thing as a disaster in the sense of an earthquake or a tidal wave or your mother-in-law coming to visit. I find that Jon Toigo, in his book *Disaster Recover Planning: Managing Risk and Catastrophe in Information Systems* (Tourdon Press, Prentice-Hall, Englewood Cliffs, New Jersey: 1989), best defines disaster in the way we will be using it:

> The term disaster . . . means the interruption of business due to the loss or denial of the information assets required for normal operations. It refers to a loss or interruption of the company's data processing function, or to a loss of data itself. Loss of data can result from accidental or intentional erasure or destruction of the media on which data is recorded. This loss can be caused by a variety of man made or natural phenomena.

If I have learned anything from my past consulting experiences, it has been this: Anything can happen at any time and you must be prepared for it. Remember Murphy, of Murphy's Law fame? Well, Mr. Murphy usually comes to visit when you are least expecting him. I don't know a network administrator who has been working in the field for over a year who hasn't experienced a Murphy phenomenon at least once or twice. I know more than one administrator who experienced Murphy at one job, had been unprepared, and then was more prepared at the *next* job—I hope you get the not-so-subtle hint there. With that in mind, you need to evaluate your current situation. Ask yourself some important questions about the stability of information on your network, and determine what needs to be done to protect that information.

What Do You Have That You Might Lose?

The answer to this most important question is data and productivity. Many computers on networks store information that is far more valuable than the actual computer the information is on. Think about how much a Power Macintosh 6100/66 costs in a SuperStore—about $1,800. Now think about a salesperson using that PowerMac to store your current client database—the only copy you have. How much more is that database worth to your company than the PowerMac? How about your bookkeeper's Macintosh that cost about $1,250? How much are your internal billing statements, cash balances, and accounts receivable documents worth? What you need to understand, from the very beginning of the process, is that you aren't in the game to back up your data; you are in the game to ensure that your users have *constant access* to necessary data.

With this in mind, don't plan for backing up your data—*plan for the restoration of it.* Think about that statement. You aren't backing up your data so much as you are planning to restore it in case of data loss. This means not only whole volumes and whole backups are going to be restored but also individual files themselves; replacing files that have been lost or corrupted. You must do everything you can to train your personnel to restore files in case of damage. This means they have to be able to carry out both your backup and your restoration plans in your absence. In other words, keep your backup and restoration plans simple.

What Can Go Wrong?

How about anything and everything! If you don't think anything can happen to your systems, the following stories are true. I have accumulated these stories in the last few years doing network consultation, and they aren't the only stories I know. If I told them all, we'd have to kill a forest to publish this book. (I'm not vouching for any of these, and I've left out the names to protect the guilty.)

Water, Fire, and Air

Flood   Nobody in Chicago ever planned for emergencies caused by floods. What could flood in Chicago? The lake has never risen above normal levels and the Chicago River is fully regulated by the locks and dams of the Chicago River Trade Authority. Nevertheless, in 1992 Chicago did flood. Somehow the river leaked into the old coal tunnels that run beneath most of Chicago. These tunnels were used back in the early 1900s to deliver coal for furnaces in the larger buildings and had since been abandoned. When the river poured into these tunnels, it was able to also pour into the basements of most of the downtown buildings. This caused the electrical systems to send high-voltage energy throughout the buildings before being destroyed. Many companies had to temporarily relocate while the entire electrical system for these buildings was rewired. Some companies survived; others did not.

Cuban Cigars Lighted tobacco products are on fire, even though the burning is usually contained to the end of the cigar or cigarette. The smoke can be a potential hazard, too, as was the case in this story I heard. The wife of a rather well-liked corporate MIS director had just had a baby. Being an excited new father, and being that he had just come back from overseas with a stash of smuggled Cuban cigars, he passed out cigars to everyone in the office. A few of the "old boys" gathered at one of the desks and lit up at the same time. Now, I don't really know how this happened, but supposedly it was the combination of all eight men smoking in one small space that caused the sprinkler system to activate. Being an old building, water shot out of the sprinklers, instead of Halon. The water went right in to the tops of the two computers on the desk and caused the monitors to blow out. As the monitors had their power cords connected to the backs of the computers, one of those was lost, too.

Construction Dust I had a client call me one day and ask me about the reliability of a certain type of hard drive. It seemed that half a dozen of them at his site had broken recently. I told the client that the optical drives were normally very reliable, but all things wear out over time. I asked how long the client had owned those hard drives, thinking that the mean-time-between-failure rate might have been reached. Two were new and the rest hadn't been around for long. After further questioning, I found out that they were doing construction in their area. When the drive manufacturer's service representative opened the hard drives, he found they were caked with construction dust and that is what caused the problems.

Plumbing Leaks Check who your upstairs neighbor is if you are in an old building. In Chicago, there are a great many buildings that are old and have been "rehabbed." I worked in one of these. In my office, there was a hole in the floor big enough for a ping-pong ball to drop through. Next door to us was a service bureau operating several film processing devices. Often, as they were changing the highly acidic fluids in these devices, some of those fluids would spill onto the floor and consequently down to the office below. I'll leave the rest up to your imagination.

Power

Too much power creates electrical surges. Too little power creates brownouts. No power is a blackout. None of the three are welcome. Here is what can cause them:

Transformer Failure

Remember the Chicago flood story? The flood caused transformer failure. This failure first sent a huge surge through the power systems and then caused an immediate blackout.

Lightning Damage

This is a big problem in the Midwest in the summer and fall. Lightning can cause a power surge to be sent throughout a building.

Utility Company Failure

This one happened in a small town in Missouri. A contractor decided to upgrade his sidewalk area. As he was digging up the street in front of his building, he hit a utility company branch line. He took out eight square blocks of power immediately.

Inadequate Power Handling Capacity

This can be caused either by the building's electrical distribution or by the user attaching too many computing devices to one electrical outlet. More than once I've seen clients blow fuses in their buildings when they have overloaded their circuits.

Small Brownouts, Sags, and Surges

Over 90% of all electrical problems can be associated with power fluctuations that drop (brownouts and sags) or rise (surges) too much and too quickly for the computer system to adapt to them.

Disk Failure

Disk drives fail—no *ifs, ands,* or *buts* about it. One day, your hard drive will fail and you won't be able to do anything about it. Unless you have planned for this event, you will lose all your data. If you didn't plan, there is nothing you can do— the data is gone forever. The following illustrations depict a few of the problems your drives can encounter. Although some of these problems relate specifically to drives with "open" formats, such as SyQuest, Bernoulli, and Magneto Optical cartridges, others are universal.

Hard drives, including to certain degrees SyQuest, Bernoulli, and Magneto Optical cartridges, are basically racks of spinning aluminum platters that are approximately .075 inches thick. These platters have a 50-microinch-thick coating of oxide for the reading and writing of information. Information is written to these platters by small read/write heads that pass over the drive platters but do not touch them. Information is passed back and forth via electrical current and magnetism.

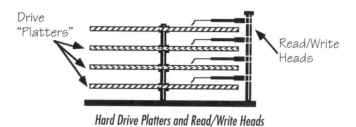

Hard Drive Platters and Read/Write Heads

In the following picture, we show a drive platter and read/write head along with various particles that can cause problems.

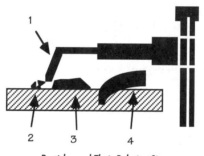

Particles and Their Relative Sizes

1. This is the read/write head of the hard drive mechanism, and it isn't supposed to touch the disk. This allows very small dust particles to fit between the disk's surface and the read/write head without causing any problems. Sometimes, however, it just doesn't work that way.

2. This item shows the relative size of a smoke particle. These are usually 250 microinches thick—large enough to cause interference between the read/write head and the disk's platter.

3. These items show the relative sizes of fingerprints and dust, which can cause even more interference problems.

4. A human hair is 3,000 microinches thick (yes, even you folks with "thin" hair). A hair causes extreme problems *immediately.*

Even if your disks are kept free of these hazards (that is, they are hard drives and are therefore sealed), general usage over time causes the disk to fluctuate and begin to have problems.

Normal Operation   Contamination Buildup   Head Crash

Simulation of a Head Crash

Performance is at its best when the read/write head is hovering over the disk at 100 microinches. Over time, "stuff" will build up on the disk's surface, and the read/write head will begin to hover higher in the areas of more buildup and lower in the areas of less buildup. Thus, the read/write head hovers in an erratic pattern. Sooner or later, the head comes in contact with the recording area of the disk and a head crash results.

People

People do the dumbest things to their computers. While some people treat them with kid gloves, others treat them like footballs. Here are a few more "stories from the front."

Coca-Cola Receptacle More keyboards have been ruined by the acidic nature of soda drinks spilled on them than anything else. I know of some monitors and CPUs ruined in the same way. (Want to know how to clean them out? See page 90.)

Baggage Handlers I once watched a baggage handler (*mauler* is a better word) toss my computer onto a ramp when an air carrier forced me to check it because of limited storage space. It was gone forever. Even worse, I had to wait to put my drive in a new container.

Now that you know what can go wrong, you need to know how to get ready for it when it happens. The question now becomes: How much loss can your organization tolerate?

WHAT DO I NEED TO KNOW ABOUT DOWNTIME?

Now that you know things are going to go wrong, there are a few additional things you need to consider before you can really begin to plan for when a disaster strikes. What exactly will happen? How well equipped are you to cope with such a situation? When I ask how well equipped you are, I'm *not* talking about how quickly you can restore your server's data or rebuild a hard drive. What I mean is how *tolerant* is your company to data being unavailable? The ability to cope with the loss of use of data and the amount of data that can be lost is called *tolerance*. Tolerance can be expressed in dollars. It is the loss of revenue, or cost of downtime, to a company during the duration of the system outage or data loss.

If there is a very low tolerance for downtime or loss of data—that is, everything has to be done yesterday and you can't afford to have people sitting around without computers—then the dollar value associated with downtime is high. On the other hand, if there is some tolerance for downtime, as users can do other things until the data is restored, then the dollar value of downtime will be lower. Software applications and data the loss of which would cause a high dollar value in lost resources or revenues should be labeled *Essential*. Conversely, those applications and data the loss of which wouldn't be as significant are termed *Noncritical*, or in my verbiage, *Cool*. Of course, there isn't a solid line dividing Essential and Cool applications and data. As with most things, there is a gray area between the two.

Cost of Downtime

I've been teaching a backup planning class on a national basis for over three years now. The recurring question seems to be, "What does cost of downtime mean?" Well, first of all, cost of downtime is not a fixed set of numbers. To one client, 100% loss might mean losing a sale because the bid wasn't sent to the client in time. To another company, 100% loss might mean that because an ad slick wasn't received by the publisher on deadline, the ad could not be placed. That single ad could have generated a great deal of money, but now it won't. For us, if the master files to this book were ever lost, it would mean over two years of research and writing down the tubes. It would mean that the person in my office who was responsible for the backups would be fired if this book couldn't be restored. Because you are reading it, that didn't happen. Some of my clients have their "loss factor" spelled out for them in terms of liability to their clients. What I want you to know about the cost of downtime is this:

You will probably lose your job if you cause the company 100% loss on a project because you didn't protect the data well enough to be able to restore it.

I hope I woke you up with that statement. In the last year alone, I have watched as two friends were fired from their jobs because of significant data loss. One lost a company's client database. The other lost a major ad campaign and cost the company almost a million dollars in lost revenue. Both were asked to leave within a week of the incident.

Originally, everyone seemed to agree on the amount of time a company could take to restore the data. Then, as luck would have it, the readers of the first version of this book showed us that although most of our timing was dead right, we allotted too much time to restore one of the categories of the files. Our goal is to help you understand how soon some of the data must be restored in the event of an emergency and how to explain that to your users.

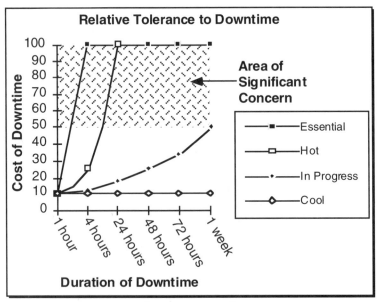

Tolerance to Downtime Chart

Time Frame

By looking closely at the previous chart, notice that the time scale starts at the one-hour mark and then has a few timed intervals after that. I'll cover these timings one at a time.

One-Hour Mark

Everything starts at the one-hour mark. This represents the time it takes a network administrator to, first of all, hear that there is a hard drive problem; second, to figure out that "Norton" isn't going to be able to fix it; and, finally, to get a new drive ready to go and the computer ready for restoration. After working with countless network administrators worldwide, I have found that the average "start time" before restoration can take place is one hour. Frequently, it takes much longer. Only those who are prepared in advance are able to get going in that, or an even shorter, amount of time.

Four-Hour Mark

The four-hour mark is one of the most important intervals in the recovery of information, as it represents data that must be restored by that point in time. In other words, this is data that, if lost, must be restored *immediately*. This data, if you have the budget, should not be stored off-line but backed up and either stored on-line—such as the case with mirrored systems—or stored near-line in Finder format on a drive that is ready to plug in and use. For some of you, that might not be possible, due to monetary constraints, and may have to be a future goal to set for your system. Whether or not you have mirrored drives or data being backed up to a spare drive does not alleviate the fact that there is going to be some data on your network that, if lost, you will need back without delay.

The reason for the four-hour mark is that most data can be gone for a short period of time. However, Essential data, which I'll identify later, must be restored within four hours, meaning by the end of the business day, or by, say, a 2:00 P.M. deadline that same day. I have found that most people are willing to wait a couple of extra hours for a very important file or a very important project. Users will stay late at night to finish a project, but only if the data for that project is restored and ready to be used within a relatively short time span. If the administrator can't restore the data necessary to finish a project or deliver a report within four hours, the next reasonable time users will expect it is the next day, or the 24-hour mark.

In a practical sense, this means you can restore around 4 GB locally, 2 GB over an EtherTalk network within four hours, or 240 MB of data over a LocalTalk network within four hours. This means restoration time, not the time it would take to search for files one by one and restore them. It presupposes that you have practiced restoration and can click the **Restore** button with your selectors in place to begin the restoration project quickly and smoothly. So, if you haven't practiced this, or don't know where your information is, you won't even come close to being able to restore that amount of data in four hours.

24-Hour Mark

Client: "Where's the report?"

Salesperson: "Our server crashed and we can't get it to you today."

Client: "Can you express mail it here by tomorrow morning?"

Salesperson: "You'll have it on your desk by 10:30 A.M."

Have you ever heard that conversation? If you haven't, stick around and you will. Clients, vendors, and others are sometimes willing to forgive a deadline for technical difficulties. But forgiveness lasts only until tomorrow morning. That is what the 24-hour mark is all about. This doesn't mean if your data goes down, you can take 24 hours to restore it. It means that if your data goes down, it has to be back to its intended state *within* 24 hours.

48-Hour Mark

If you have hard drives that are larger than 2 GB capacity on your servers, or specialty drives like the Wren or Raven drives, and you don't have a replacement unit on site, you won't be able to begin the restoration process for at least 24 hours. Why? Because you can't even *get* a drive express mailed to you any sooner than that. Dealers don't make a habit of stocking these drives, because they don't sell too many of them to customers who walk in off the street. I live in San Francisco, one of the more technologically advanced cities in the country. In my city alone, there are three Mac-only dealers of great importance and national reputation.

They are all within walking distance of the classroom where I teach our backup course. For fun one day, I took my class to each of the dealers and, with check in hand, offered to immediately purchase any hard drive they had in stock that was 2 GB or larger. That would have been a nice sale and commission for any salesperson on the floor. Each of them hurriedly scurried to the back of the office storeroom, looking frantically for drives. Not one drive amongst them. I made believers out of my students and got a free lunch because they collectively lost the bet. Take their loss for your gain—don't bet your dealer has a drive in stock when you need it. Keep a spare drive on your shelf.

Cello's Rule:

For every drive type and size you buy for live usage over 1 GB, budget for a backup device of that type. Buy it and have it ready to go on-line while on the shelf. It doesn't need to be a one-to-one ratio, though.

One-Week Mark (or Longer)

If it isn't back in a week, and nobody notices it, don't worry about it. It probably should have been archived years ago, or should have been trashed, but nobody got around to it.

Area of Significant Concern

Look back at the Tolerance to Downtime chart again. Notice that area on the chart called the "Area of Significant Concern." This is the time span wherein data has been lost by people who normally can't remember your name and now they are standing outside your door offering to send someone over to "help" you. You are now noticed within your organization. This kind of notoriety you can live without. By this time people are in a panic, the users are complaining that the network "has always been a pain," and there is talk of all the other problems about which you probably never heard before. At this point, your boss wonders what it is you *really* do, and significant time has to be made up to put the project back on track. Between now and when you restore the data, it's hero or heel time.

The Labels

We used the normal labels found on every Macintosh to delineate the differences between Essential, Hot, In Progress, and Cool data. We don't suggest you change these names, as they come with every Macintosh on the market, and thus every user automatically will have the same labels.

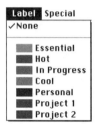

Mac Labels We Use to Define Data

Essential Data

Essential data must be restorable within *four hours* of losing it. That means that realistically you have three hours to restore a server, as the first hour is lost to figuring out that the drive isn't going to come back and that Norton should have remained a character on an old sitcom. Not being able to replace this data within a four-hour time frame, or at all, will cost the company dearly. "Catching up" on this data could either bankrupt the company or cause it to lose a major account. You, the administrator, probably will be fired, or at least won't receive that hefty raise you were planning on, if the data isn't restored within the appropriate time frame, especially if the client or project is worth twice your salary.

Hot Data

Hot data is data that must be recovered, but that allows you a certain amount of time (usually 24 hours) when recovering it. You won't lose any accounts today because the data is lost and must be recreated unless, of course, you can't recover it at all. However, if you take too long recreating the data, or if recovery becomes impossible and recreation becomes improbable, you will be in serious trouble. You will hit that ever-present 100% worthlessness point wherein the data doesn't need to be recreated because what it was being created *for* no longer matters. You have missed the deadline. When we first wrote the backup book, we figured you have up to three days to recover this information. What we discovered is that most users need their information back within 24 hours, or they can wait at least a week or so. It seems to be one or the other.

In Progress

This data can be recreated or recovered within a longer time period. It would take a week or more of the data being inaccessible for it to become vitally important. This information is important to your company, as it is always being drawn from for other projects and proposals. Users tend to notice when those old files are gone but don't need them back right away, as they can go on and do other things. However, after going back and looking for them repeatedly and not being able to access them, they begin to be noticed and greatly missed.

Cool

Cool data is information that, when lost, nobody even notices for a week or more, if at all. This information being lost would probably cost your organization very little. Sometimes what is lost should stay lost. I'd say about 35% of the information on AppleShare servers across the country could be classified in this manner.

How Group Work Affects Tolerance

We work in networked environments. Thus, to some extent, each workstation is probably sharing information with at least one, and possibly many, others. Tolerance to data loss and system failures has to be examined not just in light of individual workstations but also as it concerns workstations that share information on any given project. What aspects of ongoing projects are interrelated? What aspects of ongoing projects rely on *all* the data being available at *all* times?

Take, for instance, a page from a catalog. If, while the page is being designed, one of the artist's workstations goes down and some of the illustrations for that page are lost, the rest of the page can be designed by using mock illustrations while the data is being recovered. Immediate tolerance is sensitive but will increase over time. Another example is an annual business report. Missing information, such as projected numbers or associated projected goals, may not be that noticeable. However, if the original assumptions are irretrievable, the loss may be critical.

PLANNING TO REDUCE THE EFFECT OF DISASTERS

You can't stop them. As the saying goes, "shit happens." Therefore, we will work with you in this book to create a system by which you can effectively plan for reducing the effects of disasters and other things that go bump in the night, and then carry out the plan. We will be using more than Retrospect or ARCserve to create the backup plan you need. We will also be using one of my favorite network management programs, FastTrack Schedule. Now before you go nutso jumping up and down saying this isn't a networking program, don't worry, I know it isn't. However, it is one of the best tools to help you *buy time* and *acquire the funding* you absolutely need to create your backup and recovery plan. It's a wonderful tool. I should know. I've been critical of it since it launched (isn't that right, Mike?), and now I swear by it. We cover FastTrack Schedule in more depth in our design and management books, as well as in our primer on AppleTalk networking.

Activity Name	Responsible	1	2	5	6	7	8	9	12	13	14	15	16	19	20	21	22	23	26	27	28	29	30
Risk Analysis																							
Recovery Strategies																							
Budget and Implementation																							
Procedure Development																							
Testing and Training																							
Plan Maintenance																							

FastTrack Schedule File for Disaster Prevention Plan

On the left of the preceding schedule is the basis of your disaster prevention plan. There are six easy steps for planning your system. Yes, yes, you receive the schedule itself on this book's enclosed CD. You can purchase FastTrack Schedule from MacWarehouse or your local dealer. Here are the major steps, some of which serve as major chapter headings farther on in this book.

Risk Analysis

This involves figuring out your tolerance to data loss. It also involves figuring out how much you have to lose and where it is located. This means you will be going on a little hunt for computers and information in your office, and maybe *outside* your office, if you can't find your computers like *some* clients of mine (Katie). In short, risk analysis is preparation for the worst exposure to danger you can imagine. Don't bother determining what percentage of risk you face. Either you have a disaster or you don't. Risk analysis is preparing for the fact that you *might.*

Risk Elimination and Recovery Strategies

This involves examining the findings of the risk analysis and determining which risks can be completely eliminated and which risks must be "lived with." It will be the risks you have to "live with" that you must continually guard against. This is where backup and recovery planning comes into play. If you can't eliminate the risk entirely, you will have to plan for recovering from it.

Budget and Implementation

With planning comes *budgeting,* that all-important word, and tool if used properly. No plan is complete without an owner, a budget, and a timetable for implementation. This is where most companies go wrong. While they plan recovery strategies, they never budget for them or test their implementation. Hence, you will see that we are *serious* on this subject.

Procedure Development

Once you have your budget and your time line set, you can begin to develop your procedures. Notice we put this part *after* the budgeting part. That's because your budget will dictate your procedures. You can't develop your procedures and say, "Put the files from this computer on that DAT drive," and "Store the tapes in the safety deposit box," until you have budgeted for all of these items. In this book, procedure development is covered in the chapters on how to use Retrospect and ARCserve.

Testing and Training

After the procedures have been created, *you need to test them.* Did you read that last part? Go back and read it again until it has sunk in. Then, once you fully believe in it, make your boss understand it as well. This is the other place where corporations often go astray. I know many students who have never passed our backup class because they didn't go back home and test the procedures on their own networks. That amounts to a waste of time and effort. Although testing and training are not specifically covered in this book, they are highly recommended. We can't force you to test or train your plan, but we highly suggest that you do.

Plan Maintenance

As time passes, so will the applicability of your plan. Disaster prevention plans are not static. They should change as your networking and needs change. They should be revised as your view of the world of information management is revised. Notice that this is the *second* edition of this book? Our attitude on backup planning has been revised since the original version of the book. So, too, should your vision of backup planning for your office or corporation. Again, we can't force you to maintain your plan throughout the year or work on upgrading or changing your plan as necessary, but we highly suggest that your plan does not become static. Your plan should change with your business needs and the technology that you possess.

PART TWO: RISK ANALYSIS

Loss of Life

Loss of Business

Loss of Critical Applications

Loss of Critical Employees

Loss of Revenue

Loss of Competitive Position

Loss of Customer Goodwill

Loss of Communications

Loss of Building Facilities

Loss of Power

Loss of Security

Loss of Information

In short, risk analysis is continually asking the question, To what degree can the company tolerate the loss of information or networking systems ordinarily provided? To the left is a pyramid I really like, which I found in Regis J. Bates Jr.'s book, *Disaster Recovery Planning: Networks, Telecommunications, and Data Communications* (J. Ranade Series on Computer Communications, ed. J. Ranade, San Francisco, CA: McGraw-Hill, Inc., 1992). Basically, it shows a "computer-centric" view of Maslow's hierarchy of human needs. However, this one shows the hierarchy of loss, or as seen differently, potential risks. It is these risks, or some of them at least, that you will analyze during this phase of the planning process.

The gist of this section is that your first step in planning is to find out what on the network you have that you can't live without or to find out what you can't live without for long before everybody wants to lynch one another—not like that would happen around *my* office or anything . . . .

DON'T BORE ME WITH THE DETAILS . . .

- Conduct an internal audit of your systems. There is no way around this.

- Find your floor plans and figure out which computers are your responsibility. While you are at it, figure out who is in charge of the computers for which you aren't responsible. This is like being in the roofers' union—everything gets covered. (So it's a bad joke. Blame it on my dad; it's one of his favorites.)

- Once you have found everything, prioritize what needs to be restored first if something croaks.

- Walk the network and make sure you aren't backing up somebody in a foreign country. That concept was quoted once in a magazine, pretty much taken from one of my books even though the guy swore he didn't steal it. Do you think I should consider it an honor that he couldn't come up with something better on his own?

- Monitor your network for new services for a week or longer. If you scan the network once, the chances are good that you will miss something important. The best software to do this is from AG Group.

CHAPTER 2:
DEFINING CRITICAL SYSTEMS

In this chapter, we will show you how to define your critical systems. You won't find anything new here if you have taken our network management course or read our network management book (heretofore privately published but now, with the help of good ol' Chuck "we-love-this-guy" Glaser, to be published by AP PROFESSIONAL). A few years ago, I ran around the country with Mike McCarten, Pat Hurley, and others in the JWP crew doing for large corporations what I am about to teach you. Here is the lowdown on this chapter:

- First, scan your network to find out what you have.

- Once you have scanned your network, determine whether you are going to be concerned with off-site computers or just the ones on your LAN.

- Next, pay your users a visit and count computers. While you are at it, install information agents on the computers, such as SaberLAN's responder or SNMP from Apple.

- Finally, create databases of the information you have gathered so you can determine what needs to be protected and what, if anything, can fall by the wayside in the event of an emergency. Tom created such a helpful database for the *Managing AppleTalk Networks* book. You might want to buy the book just for that database. It even looks great!

FINDING WHAT YOU HAVE (AND WHERE IT'S AT)

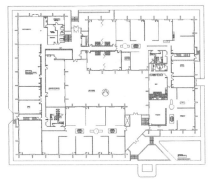

Having a network that fits into a single building, like the one on the left, is completely different from having a network that spans several buildings, cities, or even states, like some of my clients. The map on the left would have 200 or fewer nodes to include in your disaster prevention plan. That is fairly manageable by most standards.

However, the map in the next picture shows one of our client's sites in Los Angeles. It's a school system with *many* networks spread across a vast amount of space. If you were one of the network administrators on *this* network, a scan of the network would find a bunch of stuff located around the rest of the county with which you probably wouldn't want to be concerned.

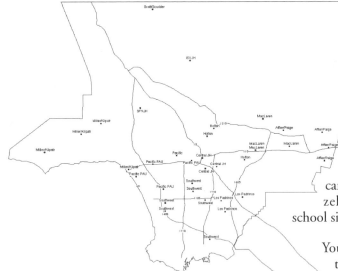

The point I am trying to make is that *before* you do any network scanning and searching for computers, make sure that you have a handle on what your *geographic* regions of operation are going to be. Your geographic region could be simply the third floor, or it could be Buildings A–E of your campus system, or it could be Munzel, Funzel, Zerbel, and Gerbil school sites. (Did I get it right, Frank?)

Your geographic regions of operation are going to be a determining factor in your backup planning process. Once you know where you are operating, you then need to tie that information into the locations of the network zones and network numbers. Somehow, you have to come up with a floor plan or physical plan that matches your network plan. It's one thing to understand how to read a floor plan and another to understand how to read a network plan. You have to understand *both* and tie them together when figuring out where your systems are located in the real world and on your network.

The following graph shows a work plan for this segment of risk analysis. This should give you a good idea of how long it would take someone to finish this portion of the analysis.

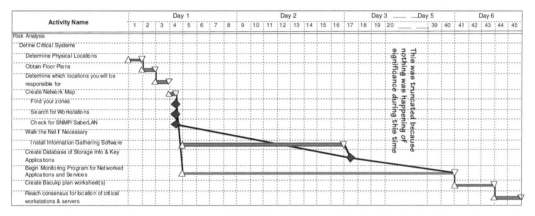

Work Plan for First Part of Risk Analysis

The necessary steps we found are shown and in the order in which they should occur. The amounts of time we figured each of these steps should take are generalized and may or may not apply to your individual situation. The one step about which we haven't the *faintest* clue is the time it would take you to physically reach each computer and install a reporting monitor like SNMP or SaberLAN. We don't know how many computers you have and where they are on your network or in the physical world. As we can only guess at the number of days it should take, we set it at two days overall. Of course this isn't realistic if you have 10 computers just as it isn't realistic if you have 10,000 computers, but I had to put something in here for the book, okay?

There are many ways you can find existing file and print servers on your network. One of them is to know about each and every server you have. This is admirable, if you can do it. However, if you are a network administrator with more than 200 computers, you won't know who is and who is not regularly publishing folders with System 7's Personal File Sharing, who is running software that uses special network serialization techniques (like Quark), and what other mission critical software is on the network—unless you regularly use a monitoring program. Remember, the goal here is to define critical network services, such as file servers, print servers, and groupware servers. We are using network scanning technology so that we can quickly and easily identify those services on the network. You will still have to find out where the computers are physically located on the network—as in, what room and building—so that you can examine the type of hard drives or find out anything special you need to know about the devices when backing them up.

What Does a Monitoring Program See?

When people look at networks, what they physically see is the cabling system and the computers connected to the cabling system. They look at the cables and the computers and say (hopefully, only to themselves), "This is our network." It's only a small part. There are many layers to a network—seven, to be exact. The bottom of the seven layers is the physical layer, where the computers and cables reside.

The cables you see are called the network *media.* Hardware on an AppleTalk network includes physical devices, such as Macintosh computers, printers, and Macintosh computers acting as file or print servers. These devices are all referred to as *nodes* on the network. So, what people actually see are only the very bottom parts of the network: the media and the nodes attached to the media.

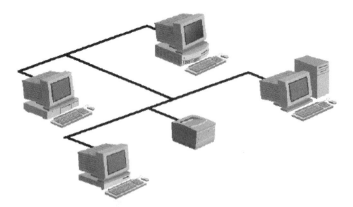

Devices Shown Are Nodes on the Same Network

Looking at the previous diagram, you might say to yourself, "Yes, this looks like my network" (or at least a portion of it). "Again, Watson, you look but you do not see. You do not observe that which is so plainly evident in front of you," to paraphrase Sherlock Holmes. When you are sitting at your computer, what you see on the network through the Chooser is something completely different. What you see are the network *services,* as in the software running on those nodes. You see file server software, such as AppleShare; printers and print spooler software; electronic mail; SaberLAN responders; and maybe even Timbuktu. The next diagram is how the network might appear if you were looking through the Chooser or working with a program like AG Group's Net Watchman or Neon's LANsurveyor.

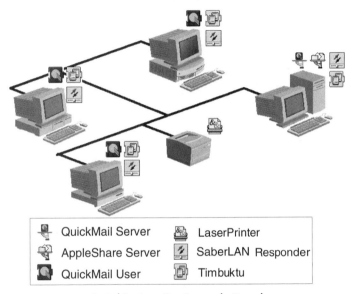

QuickMail Server		LaserPrinter	
AppleShare Server		SaberLAN Responder	
QuickMail User		Timbuktu	

Typical Services a User Sees on the Network

Now that's a network! Nodes themselves don't do much. Think about when you look through your Chooser. Do you see every computer on the network? Unless the Macintosh is running Personal File Sharing or is configured as a dedicated file server, you probably do not see it at all. What you see on the network are different services, such as printers, file servers, and mail servers. Thanks to the designers of AppleTalk, more than one application using AppleTalk may be running simultaneously on any given node. Think of how many computers we would need if we could run only one network service at a time. We'd need separate servers for mail, file service, backup service, print spooling, and our ever-present databases.

When a computer is running software that can be "seen" by other computers on the network, that software becomes a *network visible entity* (NVE) and is registered as a socket on the node. This socket becomes an addressable entity on the node, and these sockets have numbers associated with them. In the next chart, I show an NVE export with the CPU name, zone, and type of network software visible to any network software that can gather this type of information.

Name	Zone	NVE Name	NVE Type	Net	Node	Socket
Dorian Cougias	Acme Production	D's Computer	PPCToolBox	10	47	245
Dorian Cougias	Acme Production	123456	Timbuktu Serial #	10	47	244
Dorian Cougias	Acme Production	D's Computer	Timbuktu Host	10	47	244
Dorian Cougias	Acme Production	Dorian	Retrospect Remote	10	47	246
Dorian Cougias	Acme Production	Dorian Cougias	netOctopus II	10	47	247
Dorian Cougias	Acme Production	D's Computer	Workstation	10	47	4
Dorian Cougias	Acme Production	Cougias|Dorian	QuickMail	10	47	250
Dorian Cougias	Acme Production	D's Computer	Macintosh IIci	10	47	253
Dorian Cougias	Acme Production	Dorian Cougias	GraceLAN	10	47	249
Dorian Cougias	Acme Production	123-4567	Retrospect Remote	10	47	246
Dorian Cougias	Acme Production	Dorian Cougias	Canvas 12345678	10	47	0

Network Monitoring Software Export Showing NVEs

The set of three numbers is the network address of the software, including the network's number, the node or computer's number, and the socket number for the software running on the node. If you don't know where those numbers come from (no, they aren't issued by Apple or the Router Fairy), you should buy a good book about AppleTalk or take our course on AppleTalk. By the way, if you are wondering, it is very typical to have a single workstation running this much network software at any given time.

Creating a Network Report with Apple's Inter•Poll

Inter•Poll was probably one of the first, if not *the* first, network tool for AppleTalk networks, and it is still a viable tool today. You can use it to run a check on your network and locate computing devices, as well as to send test "echo" packets to computers, recording how long it takes for them to reply. There is really not much to teach you about Inter•Poll, but I'll show it to you anyway.

In the next picture, we show the basic Network Search window for Inter•Poll.

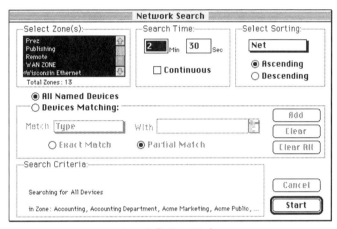

Inter•Poll's Main Window

In the top left are all the zones on your network. In the middle is the search time, or the amount of time that the application should spend searching your network's zones for devices. The middle portion of this window is the section that will interest you the most. This is where you can do one of two things. Your first option is to have Inter•Poll find every last network visible entity in the world (which will give you multiple listings for every computer). Your second option is to click the pop-up menu for a listing of each of the services it has found. If you do that, you can select the services for which you want Inter•Poll to search and can click the **Add** button to add to the list of services or computer types you would like found. It is always best to start by looking for everything and then to narrow down the search from there.

Once Inter•Poll has begun its search, it displays the information in the Device List window. You will be able to see each computer's **Net**, **Node**, **Name**, **Type**, and **Zone** information.

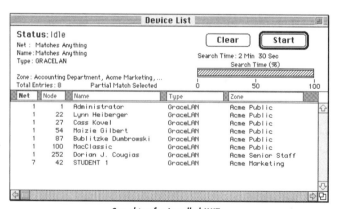

Inter•Poll's Device List

You can then export this list to a tab-delimited text file. If this is sufficient as your "network map," this is all you need for this portion of risk analysis. You can then move on to checking whether the computers have either the GraceLAN/Saber-LAN INIT or the SNMP INIT installed. You need to figure out some drive-size information to help you plan how many backup tapes and how long it will take for the backups to run.

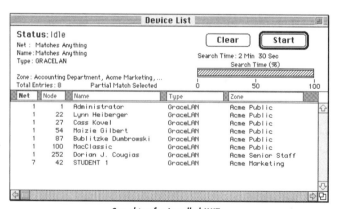

Searching for Installed INITs

Also, make note of all the different services that are running on your network. This is going to be important to you as you begin your planning phase.

On the right, I show a listing created by Inter•Poll showing the different network services it found on our network. This gives you a good idea of the different networking services that are running. Some of them, like e-mail and AppleShare servers, will be critical in the risk analysis you are conducting.

| Macintosh |
| Macintosh PowerBook |
| AFPServer |
| Canvas |
| Canvas |
| GraceLAN |
| LANsurveyor® |
| LaserWriter |
| MacInit |
| MacInit-2 |
| Macintosh IIci |
| Mail*Link® PMSAM |
| MsgReceiver |
| NameServer |
| NokNokNum |
| NS File Based |
| Power Macintosh 8100/80 |
| PPCToolBox |
| QuickMai |
| Q_Online |
| Q_Server |
| Remote location type |
| Retro A/C |
| Retrospect Remote |
| RISC•Router 3000E |
| SNMP Agent |
| Timbuktu Host |
| Timbuktu Serial |
| Workstation |
| WS 6150/66 |
| WS 8150/110 |

Creating a Network Map with LANsurveyor

We just covered how to generate a very simple network plan using Apple's Inter•Poll. In this section, I show you a more detailed plan using Neon Software's LANsurveyor. Although Inter•Poll works well for network administrators with small- to medium-sized networks, I don't recommend it for networks larger than 100 nodes and with more than one router. If you have more than 100 nodes and several routers, run LANsurveyor to acquire a more detailed picture of your network's logical layout. LANsurveyor shows you, in what I call a network organization chart, how your network is laid out. This is particularly useful when planning where to place network services, such as printers and file servers. By helping you understand how your network is laid out, LANsurveyor is extremely helpful for planning your network backup strategy. There really isn't another piece of software that can perform this function.

Basic LANsurveyor Usage

When LANsurveyor is first opened, it shows a blank canvas area where the network will eventually be drawn. To create a new map, select **New Map...** from the **File** menu. A dialog box appears listing all zones in your network. Select the zones you wish to scan and click the **Add>>** button. Once you have all the zones selected, click **OK** to continue.

3512
3511
3501 - 3510
500 - 500
300

After you give LANsurveyor the parameters for creating a logical map, it begins searching the network and building the network map. The first indication of what you will eventually see is in the form of "network blocks." These are the individual networks and network ranges set by the routers, as shown by the small diagram of blocks to the left.

Once LANsurveyor acquires the network ranges and connects the network together through the different routers, it displays the network map on the screen. Often, you won't be able to see the entire network on a single screen and need to scroll through the window to see all computers.

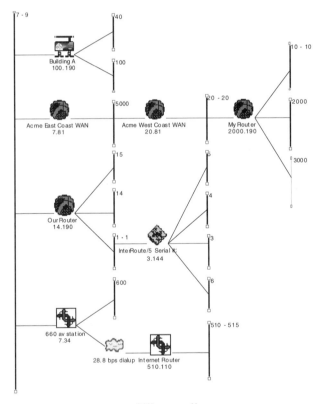

LANsurveyor Map

If you have a network picture that doesn't show any of your nodes, this doesn't necessarily mean that you don't have any computers on your network. The default for LANsurveyor is to display only the routing devices it discovers. Displaying all the computers on some networks would take too long. The network shown in the previous picture was cleaned up by us *a lot*. We did this to show you what our test network looks like. We will be coming back to this diagram quite often throughout this section. Look at it for a minute so you will remember what it looks like as we talk about it.

Some Explanations of What You See

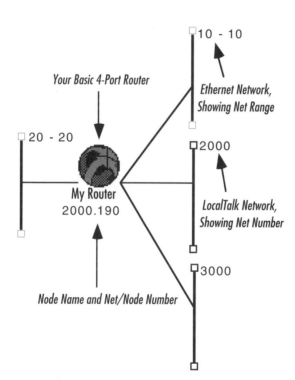

Different networks are shown as connected via routers. If there is a router product that LANsurveyor doesn't understand, it inserts a generic router icon. You can always change the displayed icon, as well as add a name to an icon LANsurveyor doesn't have in its database yet. Yes, you read that right. As LANsurveyor scans your network, it maintains a database of all network services (and their related icons) that it finds. You should see our copy. Whew, what a list! If the networks are connected together via a redundant routing system, multiple lines are drawn from each router to the corresponding network, often intersecting one another. If the networks aren't connected together using AppleTalk, such as with a WAN serial connection or through tunnelling AppleTalk inside of TCP/IP, you have to draw the connections manually. On the left, I show part of the previous map, with four different networks connected together via a Compatible Systems RISC Router 3000. This diagram shows the networks, with their numbers and ranges, and the router's name and network ID.

Now, here are tips to make your maps look like something you can understand.

Adjusting Node Framing The way the network looks on the page is mostly due to the way the drawing options are set. To change these options, select **Drawing…** from the **Options** menu. You may set these options as follows:

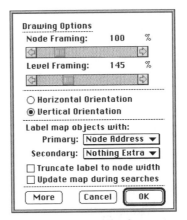

LANsurveyor Drawing Options

- **Node Framing** lets you place extra space around the network, router, and end node icons. This space is a multiple of the size of the icons. Add extra space if you want to show network numbers. Add more space if you want to see the node's entire name.

- **Level Framing** lets you place extra space between different networks.

- **Horizontal/Vertical Orientation** lets you toggle between showing the map horizontally or vertically.

- **Label map objects with** lets you select different labels to be placed below the node's icon. Your choices are no label, User Notes 1, 2, or 3 (which are not remembered between scans), or the user's network number. I strongly suggest that you display the user's network number in the primary label and then the zone in the secondary label, if you show anything at all.

- **Truncate label to node width** keeps the node's name within the framing boundaries you specify. If you don't select this box and you use horizontal layouts, the node names will run on top of one another.

- **Update map during searches** isn't good for much. When you search for end nodes, LANsurveyor rebuilds the map each time. This is very time consuming and I don't recommend it.

Navigating the Map

On large networks, it is better to use LANsurveyor's built-in searching commands than it is to scroll around the map. The **Navigate** menu has two menu items that make it much easier to find what you want. **Find Net…** presents a dialog box with a pop-up menu of all the networks present on the map.

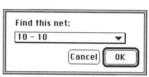

Moving to a Specific Network

Specifying Networks

Now that you have your basic network map, decide on the networks (if not all of them) with which you are going to be concerning yourself. The reason for doing this is that although some networks are local, others may be long distance.

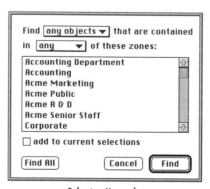

Selecting Networks

Don't concern yourself with the long-distance ones immediately. For now let's focus on the ones that are local to your building and to your department. Probably the best way to start is to look for the zones with which you are already familiar. To do this, select **Find Zone...** from the **Navigate** menu. The dialog box in the preceding picture appears. Select the zones you think are local to your network or department and then click the **Find All** button. LANsurveyor highlights those networks containing the zones you specified.

Net 1 - 1			
Name	Zone	Net	Node
Acme AWS 6150	Acme R & D	1	77
Acme AWS 8150	Acme R & D	1	56
Cass's PowerMac	Acme Public	1	27
Dell's PB 520	Acme Public	1	104
Dorian's Computer	Acme Senior Staff	1	252
Ether10-T StarContr...	Acme Public	1	154
LW Pro 630	Acme Public	1	130
Lynn's PowerMac	Acme Public	1	22
MacClassic	Acme Public	1	100
Main 8150	Acme Public	1	1
Maizie's IIci	Acme Public	1	54
One World™ ARA Ser...	Acme Public	1	202
OneWorld™	Acme Public	1	253
QM_QM	Acme Public	1	87
TribeStar005690	Acme Public	1	129

Zones Found by LANsurveyor

Note: Some networks have zones that span multiple networks. Take our network, for instance. The zone **Acme Public** appears in most of the networks making up our internetworking system. If you were to scan for that zone in particular, about seven of the total networks would be highlighted. If you are having trouble with the concept of zones and network numbers, either read our books *Designing AppleTalk Networks* and *Managing AppleTalk Networks* or talk to the overall network administrator who set up your zones in the first place.

Adding Nodes

Now that you know the networks with which you are going to be working, it is time to start finding the *computers themselves*. There are two ways you can display the computers with the LANsurveyor application. The first is to display them directly in the map window. If you select this option and have a network with many computers, things tend to become pretty messy. Instead, we prefer that you find the networks with which you are working and then display the computers in a separate window. Since this is **our** book, we are going to teach you to do it **our** way (that's like saying "because I'm the daddy," isn't it?).

With the networks already selected, Choose **Display End Nodes In Net Window** from the **Display** menu. LANsurveyor creates a separate window for each of the networks you have selected.

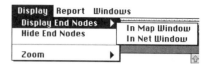

Peeking Under the Hood

Once you have set LANsurveyor to display the end nodes in the individual network windows, you'll see something like the window on the right. This shows what LANsurveyor found for the zone *Public* in Net 1-1. LANsurveyor will create a Net window for every network that has that particular zone. Although looking at the cool icons might be pleasing for a moment or two, this isn't going to do you much good. What you are attempting to do right now is to find all the computers you can and also to find some information about them.

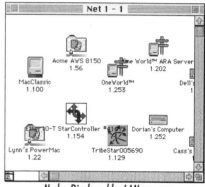

Nodes Displayed by LANsurveyor

Notice the pop-up menu in the bottom left of this window. Holding the mouse down on it will reveal that it is used to set the view of the window, much like the **Views** menu in the Finder. You'll probably want to set the view for this window to be **by Name**. We have done this in the following window.

| by Icon |
| by Name |
| by Zone |
| by Net |
| by Node |

Name	Zone	Net	Node
Acme AWS 6150	Acme R & D	1	77
Acme AWS 8150	Acme R & D	1	56
Cass's PowerMac	Acme Public	1	27
Dell's PB 520	Acme Public	1	104
Dorian's Computer	Acme Senior Staff	1	252
Ether10-T StarContr...	Acme Public	1	154
LW Pro 630	Acme Public	1	130
Lynn's PowerMac	Acme Public	1	22
MacClassic	Acme Public	1	100
Main 8150	Acme Public	1	1
Maizie's IIci	Acme Public	1	54
One World™ ARA Ser...	Acme Public	1	202
OneWorld™	Acme Public	1	253
QM_QM	Acme Public	1	87
TribeStar005690	Acme Public	1	129

Network Nodes Sorted by Name

Creating the Initial Service Listing

As a part of the risk analysis, create a listing of all the different network services running on your home network. You can do this by individual nets or do this for all the networks at once. We prefer to know what services are running on the individual networks because that is how *we* like to track things. You may think differently. To accomplish this, select one of the Net windows within LANsurveyor and type Command-A or just click and drag through the whole list to select all the nodes shown. Then select **Service List** from the **Report** menu, and a listing like the one shown in the next screen shot is created for you. This is a great list because it summarizes how many of each different type of service there are. Save this report for now. We'll come back to it later.

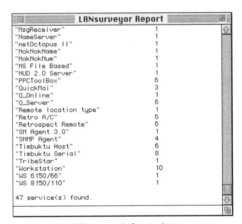

LANsurveyor's Service List

Checking for SaberLAN or SNMP on Workstations

You have one more step to accomplish to complete this first goal. That step is to scan the computers, searching for either the SNMP agent or the SaberLAN agent residing in the System Folder. You are looking for either of these agents because you will use them to gather important information about the size of hard drives, the amount of data in them, and the free space available. You will use that information to plan your backup and recovery procedures. By searching for the SaberLAN, GraceLAN, or SNMP agent services on the computers, you can quickly see which computers have the reporting capabilities already installed and which you need to go visit and install the reporting software. This *does not* mean that you don't have to physically check out these computers. You have to stop by each one anyway. Remember folks, there is no easy way to find out if the computer's drive has been mirrored or striped or partitioned in some strange way without physically inspecting it, okay?

Walking the Net

Once you have your network device list in hand, along with your backup planning chart (shown in the next picture) and a floor plan if necessary, you should walk your network. This means checking each one of these computers for the information shown in the previous chart's fields. While you are there, ensure that you have installed or updated your information-gathering agents, such as SNMP or Saber-LAN, so you don't have to gather the information manually next time.

			Macintosh Backup ThroughPut Analysis							
Computer Name	AppleTalk Connection	Zone	Volume Name	Vol. Cap	Free Space	% Change	Daily Backup	Volume Backup Date	Type	Physical Location

Portion of the Backup Planning Chart

Note: We highly recommend having a floor plan with you when you walk your network. This will help you visualize where your computers are and will give you a record of where *they should be* for your recovery plan, in case something goes wrong with one of them and you need to restore it

If you'll notice back on page 23, we allocated around two days for you to traverse your network, looking for computers. I don't know if that is the right amount of time, but what I do know is that this isn't something you are going to do in 15 minutes. For one thing, seeing a computer on the network with a search engine like those in Inter•Poll or LANsurveyor is completely different from finding it in the real world. When we teach our classes in San Francisco and across the country, I have the students get up and go find the computers they are going to back up. It takes approximately 15–30 minutes *for the entire class* to hunt for maybe two dozen computers. That's two computers per student. If it takes them *that long* to find them, think of how long it will take you the first time you decide to do this for your whole network.

Information You Need to Know

There are seven different pieces of information to gather about each piece of equipment you are going to back up. You need the name of the device as it appears on the network, the zone on which the device resides, the volume name and type, the volume's size, the physical location of the equipment, and the type of network it is on. I have created an electronic form, the *Macintosh Backup Throughput Analysis* chart, to help you keep track of this information. Two of the fields can be filled out before you go out and look at the computers. The rest should be filled out while you are performing your physical inspection of the network.

Computer Name

You should already have a list of the device names created with one of the network scanning devices, and thus you can enter this information without leaving your desk. Enter the computer's name in the first column. When you are walking the network, verify this information from the computer. The computer's device name can be found in the **Owner Name** or **Macintosh Name** in the Sharing Setup control pane. Retrospect initially takes the **Owner Name**. Therefore, that is the name you might want to check. However, AppleShare puts "Administrator" in as the **Owner Name** and registers the server on the network by the **Macintosh Name**. Be aware of this distinction.

AppleTalk Connection

In this field, you are going to enter Ethernet or LocalTalk. If you are filling out the form electronically, you are presented with a pop-up menu asking you whether the equipment is on Ethernet or LocalTalk. I did my calculations based on those network models. If you want me to add a section for TokenTalk or Fast Ethernet, send me some information and I'll send you an updated form. You'll need to know this information to calculate the throughput when backing up that computer using that type of network connection.

One of the things that we found when performing the backup calculations for throughput is that there isn't much of a difference among LocalTalk, the Digital

Ocean radio frequency Grouper, or infrared (using a Photonics device). Even though the Grouper attaches to the computer's Ethernet port, it is transferring data only slightly faster than LocalTalk speeds. Therefore, when attempting to calculate throughput speeds for computers running on either of these media, use the LocalTalk connection algorithms.

Device Zone

You should also have a list of zones for each of the devices. You can enter this information before you leave your desk, too. Walk around and look in the Network control panel—or the AppleTalk control panel for computers with open transport— for the computer's network connection. While doing this, jot down the device's zone. This is important because you will be signing on to the computer over the network later, and in order to find the computer, you will need to know its zone.

One of the readers of the first edition made another helpful suggestion. If this is the type of network that allows for multiple local zones (you can tell because the Network or AppleTalk control panel will have a pop-up menu showing all the available local zones), you may want to also log the *other* available zones. If you can't find the computer one day, it may be that the user decided to switch zones, and you will want to search those available zones for the missing computer. One of the nice things about Retrospect 3.x is that it will look through *other* zones if the computer doesn't show up in the one originally selected. However, you will have to tell Retrospect through which zones to search, so you will need to know which zones are the local zones for the computing devices versus the overall zones.

Volume Name

For each different volume (I am using the word *volume* in this context to mean an entire hard drive), enter that volume's name in the column as it appears on the desktop. If there are multiple volumes, enter each individual volume name in its own cell, adding additional volumes in the rows below. Even if the server is a non-dedicated server and the user is publishing only a folder (or series of folders), you should still enter the entire hard drive's name. It's easier to back up a whole computer than it is to find a folder or two. If this volume is a part of a partition, you might want to annotate that it is a partitioned drive and also annotate the drive's SCSI ID. By doing this you will know which partitioned volumes are parts of which physical devices.

Volume Capacity

There are two options for listing size in megabytes. The first option is to list the amount of space the user has already filled up on the hard drive—in other words, the amount of data that currently exists. The other option is to list the total size the hard drive can hold. The latter is the better of the two options, as you will avoid underplanning. When you walk over to the hard drives to check their size make sure that you determine the correct size.

Acquire information for all partitions, as well as for the currently mounted drives. You will know the server's drives because you are probably the one who set them up. However, if you aren't the person who set up the hard drives, there's only one way to find out what's really going on. You may want to write this down, as it's very technical: *Ask the person who set it up.* Gasp! Talk to a user?!? Yes, talk to the users. Talk to the other administrators. It's the only way to know whether the drive information is correct.

Another way to accomplish this is directly through the network reporting agents. They will let you know how many volumes (logical drives) the computer has and how much information is used on each of the volumes. Don't forget to check for mirrored or striped drives!

Volume Free Space

Knowing how much free space you have is just as important as knowing how much data you have in your computer's drives. Tests have shown that drives with less than 20% free space tend to fragment more quickly than drives with at least 20% free space. Once you get down to those last precious kilobytes of free space, you could be running into a lot of trouble. For more information about maintaining free space on your computers' drives, see our books *Managing AppleShare & Workgroup Servers* and *Managing AppleTalk Networks.*

Percent Change and Daily Backup

These two cells are linked together. The % **Change** cell is used to set the approximate percentage of the computer's information that changes on a daily basis. This is used to calculate how much information per computer will be backed up during the incremental backups. Most computers change only about 1–2% of their information per day.

However, database servers, because the database file is a single file, change almost 75% of their total information every day. For example, Joe Schlabotnick hits the FileMaker Pro server and creates a record. It changes the entire file. Then Sally Sue comes in the next day, finds that Joe misspelled a name, and changes it. Because *any changes* were made to the file, the entire file has to be backed up again.

File servers, it seems, change anywhere from 1–10% per day. Small offices will find that their servers change around 1–3% per day, while offices that have many users tied to a single server will find that the data on those servers changes somewhere around 5–10% daily. Of course, if you are as large a company as Multi-Ad or Payless Cashways the change rate is much higher. This is why we have given you a pop-up field in the electronic version of the form. Select a change rate, and the form will automatically fill in the **Daily Backup** field for you.

Volume Backup Date

This is the date on which the computer was last backed up. Here's a hint, folks: If the field says "Never," you are in deep you-know-what (they won't let me say doo-doo in a sentence). This backup date should be as current as your report. You can use this field to see whether the user has added a new drive. If you are using Retrospect 3.x and are backing up Remote Desktops, this is now automatic. If not, you must alert the backup software to the presence of changed or new drives. This is a manual process and one that isn't readily evident or easy to track. Therefore, one of the key weekly tasks of the backup administrator is to monitor computers for new or reformatted hard drives that need to be added to the backup list.

Volume Type

This column is a little different. For your own information, enter the type of volume being backed up. Note and remember any volume that is not a "normal" drive—that is, any removable media or other volume that could disappear when you begin your backup or archival session or one that might cause you concern when backing up and restoring. If you are using the electronic form, a pop-up menu gives you a choice of the following items:

Regular Drive   Standard hard drives, whatever size they are, pose no special problems. You need to know their capacity. You also need to know whether the disks were partitioned, as you could possibly be looking at what you think is an 80-MB hard drive and find out it is a partitioned 120-MB hard drive.

Large-Format Hard Drives   You are going to want to note any hard drive larger than 2 GB. If it breaks, it's difficult to obtain another drive that size the same day. It's almost impossible. If you need to restore one of these drives within 24 hours, it won't be possible, because no dealer will be able to sell you one on the spot.

Mirrored Drives   Other types of drives posing special problems in backing up are those being backed up through disk mirroring, or duplexing. These drives use special software that writes information to the main disk and then immediately after, or simultaneously, writes the same information to the second disk. You need to know the capacity of the main drive only and any special procedures needed during backup. Some mirrored drives, like the MicroNet line, are bundled in the same housing unit so that they look like one drive. Even though it might say 1.2 GB on the outside of the box, the drive might very well be two mirrored 650-MB drives. Make sure you don't overplan or underplan for mirrored drives. The safest thing to do would be to ask the vendor from which you purchased the drives.

Removable Drives   The most difficult types of drives to back up, in my opinion, are cartridge or removable drives, whether they are SyQuest drives, magneto optical drives, or removable hard drive systems. The reason these are difficult to back up is that sometimes when the backup is scheduled, the media itself has been removed from the physical unit and replaced by a different unit. Backup software looks only for volume, folder, or file names. If the media has been removed, it can't be backed up. However, attempt backing up the information anyway. Murphy says that the one time you just give up will be the time the media failed and the boss's presentation was on it.

People have asked me whether they could back up several of their cartridges during the backup process. I asked them whether they had multiple drives for the cartridges. They answered, "No." I then asked them how they thought they were going to make the backup system find cartridges that weren't loaded into the drives. They withdrew their question. A number of clients think this way. If users are going to put mission-critical information on removable media, especially multiple disks of removable media, they are putting themselves at risk because only one removable disk can be inserted and backed up per removable drive. If you are thinking that your users will put the right removable disks back into various removable drives around the network, think again. Murphy would just love to hear of a backup plan like that.

CD Drives I'm going to mention CD drives only because once in a while, users have read-write CDs. I once ran into a novice network administrator who had set his backup system to back up all mounted volumes on his file server. One of those volumes was a standard CD-ROM drive. He was spending a large amount of time and tape space backing up a read-only, off-the-shelf CD. It wasn't worth it. However, if you are using a read-write CD, you might consider backing it up. If so, you need to know only the size of the CD. There are no other problems backing them up.

Physical Location

You are going to want to physically find the computers and drives with which you are working. If you don't know where the computer is and you've been entering all the previous information on your form from "memory," it is now time to stand up and actually go and touch the computers you are planning to back up.

I have been to networks in which administrators were trying to back up a server they thought was in their building but was only in the same logical zone. The building just happened to be about 25 miles away and was connected with a partial T1 line running at 56 Kbps. In case you are wondering, the throughput speed on backing up across a leased line is slower than molasses in January. The throughput speed on 56K lines is one-fifth the speed of LocalTalk, or about 200 Kbps of sustained throughput per minute. It takes almost an hour to back up about 10 MB of data across a 56K line. Why did they do it? Because they "didn't know." If they had looked for the server, they might have "known" and could have made more practical backup plans for that particular server.

The information I usually enter in this field is the room in which the device can be found and, if one exists, the phone extension for the user in the room, in case of a backup problem.

Install Information-Gathering Software

While you are walking the network and gathering information from the various computers under your jurisdiction, take the time to install either the SNMP agent or the SaberLAN agent. You shouldn't have to do all of this a second time.

Some SaberLAN Settings

One of the things I like about the SaberLAN software is that the SaberLAN agent on the user's computer has some handy database fields you can fill out while you are at the user's workstation. The other handy thing about it is that you can set a password on the SaberLAN agent so the user can't change what you put into the fields. Although the user's computer may be the user's to work with during the day, it is also the network administrator's computer when it comes to being maintained and backed up. Part of the network administrator's responsibility is knowing where the computers *are* on the network, and that can be facilitated by filling in some key information in the SaberLAN agent.

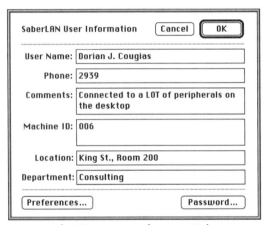

SaberLAN Agent User Information Window

You don't want the user to change this information after you have entered it. In the preceding window, we show fields that can be filled in while you are at the workstation. You will want to fill in *at least* the location section of the responder and then set the password so that end users can't change the information.

Begin Monitoring Program for Networked Applications and Services

If you are a network administrator or are a consultant who can return frequently to a single client, you might want to take a much broader look at the network than we have so far. You might want to check in on a regular basis and discover what network services "pop up" on the network. This is a much better way of finding out what is running on your network than running a program at a single point in the day. Serialized software comes and goes on the network on a regular basis; System 7 Personal File Sharing is activated and then deactivated on a regular basis. This is the kind of information you want to know. It could *really* affect your network if Fred's computer went down and you replaced his copy of Quark with Janet's copy. Now neither Janet's *nor* Fred's will run, because of serial number conflicts. Get the picture?

Net Watchman

This is the only software I know of that actively looks for new services appearing on the network. Short sentence, big difference. Get the software.

I am going to show you just a small portion of what Net Watchman can do for you. The steps aren't supposed to be a training guide or user manual. They are simply to get you up and running on your way to finding out what is appearing and disappearing on your network. The next screen shot shows the contents of the Net Watchman disk. To use the software, copy the entire folder to your hard drive.

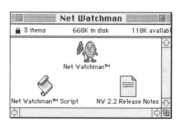

Net Watchman's Disk Contents

Setup   After Net Watchman is launched, a dialog box appears asking you to select the zones you want to monitor. Select all zones on your local area network. Make sure that you aren't looking for zones across leased lines. You don't want to back up computers in a remote location; you want to back up computers only on your own network. Thus, run LANsurveyor if you need to find out whether you have remote networks. Backing up computers in, say, Soweto from, say, Iowa isn't a good idea (and if you steal that line, buddy, I know you're lazy).

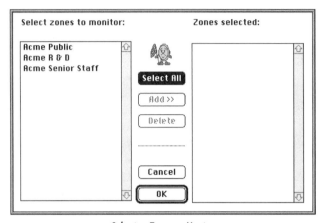

Selecting Zones to Monitor

Once you've selected the zones to monitor and clicked **OK**, a Zone List window appears. It has the zones in it with small bells next to them, showing that you are monitoring those zones.

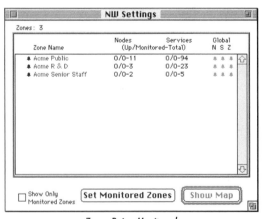

Zones Being Monitored

If you want, you can select any of the zones and have Net Watchman display a node map of that zone, showing the computers in the zone, along with the different services associated with each of the devices.

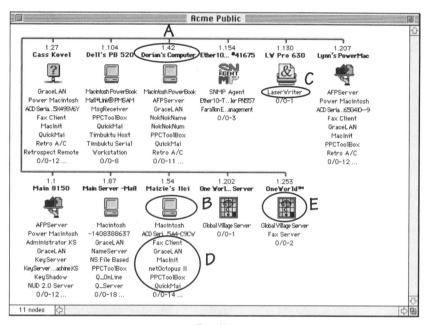

Zone Map

The zone map shows some pretty cool information. Note that this isn't the same type of map that LANsurveyor or NetAtlas displays. The cabling connecting computers represents merely that they are on the same zone.

A. This shows the network number and service name for the device. For Macintoshes, this is the **Owner Name** in the Sharing Setup control panel. For other devices, this is the name the administrator gave to it when setting it up.

B. This is the device's icon.

C. This is the device's network *type*. This is the type for which you would search the network if you were looking for this device in the Chooser.

D. This lists the services currently running on this device. They can be anything from Timbuktu, to AppleShare, to MasterJuggler. Quark, Canvas, PhotoShop, and other serialized network software display their serial numbers here.

E. If Net Watchman doesn't know what type of device this is, it displays this puzzle, although this doesn't affect Net Watchman's ability to scan this device.

Setting Net Watchman's Global Alerts

Now that you know what types of services are running on your network, it's time to start looking for the ones that appear and disappear without your noticing. Begin this step by selecting **Global…** from the **Alerts** menu.

A dialog box appears asking which alerts you would like to set, the amount of time between each network scan, and the different types of additional alerts you want. Net Watchman places the new service events in a log for you. Realistically, the alerts won't do you much good. If you are like most network administrators, you won't be sitting at your desk waiting for Net Watchman to tell you that somebody launched Quark. You probably have better things to do with your time. I like playing the sounds because they're cool, not because they do me any good.

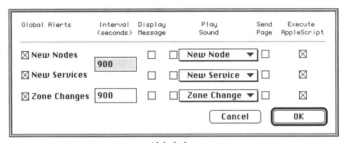

Global Alerts

By default, the alerts are set to scan every 15 minutes (900 seconds). I like to set my scan times down a bit from that. When I first begin to watch a network, I would rather it scan the network every 5–10 minutes, with 10 minutes being the maximum time between scans. Some people share through System 7 for only a short amount of time—especially if their company has something against System 7 Personal File Sharing (be realistic; you aren't going to stop it completely). Also, they might launch a serialized application for only a couple of minutes. I want to know what is happening and when, and I don't want to miss anything. Yes, scanning this much puts a little more strain on the network, but when I need to plan something as critical as a backup document, I need all the information I can get.

Once you have set your alerts, go to lunch. When you come back, check your event log. To do this, select **Event** from the **Lists** menu.

The event log appears, showing that some services have appeared (as in my window) or that services have appeared, disappeared, and then reappeared.

```
▤□▨▥▥▥▥▥▥▥▥▥▥▥▥▥▥ NFI Settings Log ▥▥▥▥▥▥▥▥▥▥▥▥▥▥□▤
  Time        Name              Service          Zone              Status
  5/4/94      –                 –                –                 –                    ⇧
  4:16:51 PM  Maize Gilbert     AHS Serial       Acme Marketing      new service
  4:18:53 PM  Cass's Computer   AFPServer        Acme Production     new service
  4:19:43 PM  Dorian's Powerbook ALD5            Acme Marketing      new service
  4:20:58 PM  Maize Gilbert     Canvas           Acme Marketing      new service

                                                                                        ⇩
                                                                                        ▢
```

Event Log

Notice in the previous screen shot of an event log that there is a total of three different users. Each user is displaying serialized applications in this list. This shows one copy of AppleShare (AFPServer), one copy of TouchBASE Pro (AHS Serial), one copy of PageMaker (ALD5), and one copy of Canvas being launched. This identifies computers running critical network services or computers running network services that would be a pain to replace, if lost.

Serialized Applications

Critical applications on users' machines are those applications that if "lost" or "destroyed" would be difficult to replace. These are usually the applications that are serialized so if the user loses it, you have to replace *that* copy and not a generic one. Some of these serialized applications make you enter the serial number *before* the installation process takes place, thus creating serialized installer disks. Some of them then use that serial number to find "illegal" copies on the network. This is the reason, more than any other, for using Net Watchman: finding applications that register network serial numbers. Trust me, it's a real drag to have to search for your installer disks to reinstall a copy of Quark or to reinstall any software that has been preinitialized.

"Up and Down" Services

When you read Net Watchman's log, notice which computers on the network are running Personal File Sharing for a limited time during the day: enough time to share files on the network with other users but not enough time to be "seen" when running your regular network scans. If your company is one of those that has the "no Personal File Sharing" policy, this is probably how most of the users who want to share files from their computer go about doing so. They share the folders, trade information, and then stop sharing the folders.

Another type of "up and down" service is networked databases, such as TouchBase Pro and FileMaker Pro. When a user launches a FileMaker Pro database set for multiple users, that database file is visible only while the application is running and the file is open. These databases are the most difficult to track for this reason alone. However, running Net Watchman for a week or so will clearly point them out to the administrator. (This doesn't account for FileMaker Pro dedicated server software or other "full-time" servers. These should have been accounted for during the critical "server" sweep you conducted earlier.)

Dealing with the Services

Once you have found the services and applications you are trying to identify, figure out what you want to do with them. If the serialized applications are lost or damaged, can you quickly and easily find the master disks with the serial numbers? Do you *know* which computer has which serial number? Many times network administrators will assign a serial number to "Joe" or "Maria," only to have Joe or Maria leave the company and Oscar or Jayne take over the computer without ever notifying the network administrator. Get the point?

So, now it's time to take the information you spent your time gathering and come up with some definitions of what is critical in your company.

DEFINE CRITICAL NETWORK OPERATIONS

Now, given all the information you have gathered, given that you have scanned the network for network services that might just be critical to your daily operations, it's time to come to a decision about which computers or servers are most important on the network, next to most important, and so on all the way down to which computers or servers are *not* important. As a guide, use the outline for defining critical systems we covered earlier:

> **Essential** workstations and servers are those computers you can't afford to have "down" for longer than four hours.

One of my clients called me in a panic the other day. It seems that the president of the company (that is who was calling) decided, all of a sudden, that the e-mail system was a critical system. No kidding. It had become a critical system about a year before, when the company decided that it would the primary means of communication within the company. Still, it had only just dawned on the president that it had become so. He wanted to know how the system was being protected. He wanted to know what would happen if the computer on which the e-mail system was running "died," as he put it. The answer was that his staff had been continuously asking the MIS department for another drive so they could mirror the e-mail system in case the primary drive went down. MIS had decided that the system wasn't that critical. After the phone call with me, they changed their minds. I wonder how that happened! I hear tell that they even put a UPS power supply on the server so it could be protected in case of a power surge. Imagine that!

> **Hot** workstations and servers are those computers you can afford to have "down" for a total of 24 hours, or one working day.

Although most of the servers in your company probably fall into the **Essential** category, there are some other computers on your network that probably fall into the **Hot** category. Computers and servers that fall into this category are ones like your print servers. Although the print server going down might cause a real pain in the rump for a lot of people, it won't halt network operations. It won't halt electronic mail traffic. It will *definitely* slow down network operations if your company is a service bureau. It will *definitely* slow down operations if you are a "print-centric" firm, like one that produces catalogs. For some people, their Web server might be an Essential or Hot server. For us, our WebSearch and AppleSearch server is crucial. We could live a day or two without our calendar server, whereas we can't get through a single day without our contact management server.

> **In Progress** workstations are those computers you can afford to have down for about a week. After that point, it then becomes important to replace or fix these computers so they are "up" and usable again.

Our backup computer is one of the In Progress computers in our company. If our server went down, we would not stop doing backups. We have multiple servers and drives for our classes and could easily shift our backup server to a class server, run the backup, and return it to being a class server when needed. However, it would be inconvenient for us to do that for a week. We could manage, but after a week somebody would start becoming angry. And is she mean . . .

> **Cool** workstations, if down, won't be noticed for *quite* some time.

This is usually your boss's machine—the one that sits on the desk and isn't ever turned on, anyway. Just kidding. This is the kind of computer that, if it died, everyone would say "good riddance" and probably wouldn't want to replace it. As is the case with one of my clients, it might be the "training" computer—an old IIcx sitting in the training room. Rumor has it that the IIcx was at one time a Quadra 700, but somewhere along the line a IIcx user swapped computers. Since nobody noticed for a month or two, the IIcx sits in the "training" cube. Nobody even knows or cares whether it works.

Here, now, is a way to apply these categories to the different network services you might find on your network.

File Services

I put servers into three categories: primary, repository, and personal.

Primary Servers

Primary servers are those servers that might have more than one network service running on them. An example of a primary server would be a workgroup server running file service, print service, e-mail service, and backup services. Many small companies have only one server. We have three servers, and yet we still have one primary server. Our primary server is where all the current information is kept. It is where the client folders are kept. It is where the server copies of this book are kept. It has the largest hard drive and the most RAM of our three servers.

Primary servers should always be classified as Essential devices.

Repository Servers

Repository servers are things like art servers, archive (CD) servers, and maybe even backup servers. These are servers that don't have common on-line information that people need to do their jobs. Yes, they might hold art needed for printing, but print jobs, or at least proof prints, can be accomplished without the primary art. CDs can be replaced.

Repository servers are usually classified as either Hot or In Progress devices.

Personal File Servers

These are computers that are used as more than just workstations. They are also being used as servers. My computer, the one in front of me right now in this stinking hotel room (never stay at the Omni Parker House in Boston; the service stinks), is also my classroom server for my students. Because I keep all the student software on an APS external drive, it wouldn't be a problem for me to shift the server portion of my workstation to another computer. However, I don't represent the typical user. Heck, my wife says that I don't represent the typical anything. The point that I'm trying to make here is that you will want to find out what *each specific user* is sharing on his or her computer and then make your determination of how critical the information is.

Now, for all you buttheads out there who think you can disallow Personal File Sharing, listen up: This is not the time to argue whether Personal File Sharing is allowed on the network. This is the time to protect important data on the network. Leave your "file sharing" biases, one way or the other, at the door. For all of you who are my students, yes, I was standing on top of the dresser in the hotel room as I wrote this. If I were writing from class, I'd be standing on the table, doing the jig to drive home my point.

Print Services

This means more than your print servers. It means your critical printers as well. A few years ago, I helped a company design its technical plan for the next couple of years. This is a catalog design and production agency—or so it thought. It turns out that about half of what it does is focused on developing a certain catalog. It also does product design, comp work, flyer design, and poster design. The wildest thing about all this was that it had only one printer as the central output printer. If it went down, it would mean that untold numbers of production hours would be held up waiting for another printer to be brought on line. The point is that you need to think about your printers *themselves* as much as you think about the print spoolers.

Not many people bother with the print spoolers, as they are so easy to set up and run. These are what I call the *forgotten machines.* They do their jobs so well and so quietly that many people forget they are there. The problem is, though, that some of them are quite active and if lost, would take a bit of work to restore. An example is the OPI (Open Prepress Interface) print server from Adobe Systems (formally from Compumation). As you print your massive color files to the printer through this print server, it logs the art files into a database on its hard drive. In that way, you don't have to spend so much time downloading art files across the network when you print. If one of these print servers goes down, it has to rebuild that database of art files. This slows the printing process, as people have to resend the original file, instead of the low-resolution version, across the network.

Database Services

We covered these when we were talking about the "up and down" services found on the network using AG Group's Net Watchman. These are databases that are more difficult to locate than corporate 4D, Ingress, or Oracle databases.

It seems that the most difficult thing to figure out when planning to back up the database servers is planning to kick the users off them during the backup time. We worked with an international law firm that had a major problem—it seemed it continuously had users who wouldn't log off the database so it could be backed up properly. The report I received showed that users from Saudi Arabia would be on at one point, then U.S. users, then users from Asia and other parts of the world, all on a continual, rotating basis. Then one day the database went down. Hundreds of records were completely lost, and a few other hundred records were corrupted. The administrator lost his job because he hadn't protected the sensitive database. My advice to you is that you protect your data no matter what, and if that means it needs to come down during the backup, so be it.

The one key thing you need to know about backing up a database is that you need to plan for more capacity than with most any other computer service you back up. A database is a single file object. If one change at all is made to the database, the *entire* database file has been changed. If one "t" or "." or space is added, the whole file is changed, and therefore the whole file has to be backed up. For example, if you have a 40-MB database, every day you will be backing up 40 MB.

E-Mail, Information, Calendaring, and Workgroup Services

With your e-mail and other information services, list your fax gateway, your Internet gateway, and any other gateway that needs to be configured, especially the Domain Name server and the Directory server for the mail system. Just because many companies are putting their mail gateways on older computers, because the older computers are still faster than their 56K Internet connection, doesn't mean that they shouldn't be backed up.

One of the biggest problems with distributed e-mail systems like PowerTalk is that all the e-mail, logs, and messages waiting to be sent are kept on the end users' computers. If you aren't backing up each of the end user's computers, you aren't backing up critical electronic mail information. Think about that.

Another thing to think about is how long you can go without e-mail or other calendaring or workgroup services. I couldn't go a day without e-mail. I could go forever without my calendar. I hate that thing. Any calendar hit-people reading this book? I'd love to hire you.

Routing and Communications

Here's one that no one thinks about—their routers and important communications devices. The reason no one thinks about them is that these devices operate 24–7: 24 hours a day, 7 days a week. "They just work," one of my clients told me the other day. Okay, so they just work, but *before* they worked, they had to be configured correctly, and when configuring them correctly, *somebody* should have saved the configuration files somewhere. That way, if the routers went down, the administrators would know exactly how they were set up originally and could return them to their original setups. It is also important to know which of the routers is the *seed router* that needs to be restarted *first* in case of a total power outage and then which routers need to be restarted second, third, and so on.

When recently upgrading a network that spanned about 100 small- to medium-sized sites around the country, I scanned the network with LANsurveyor and counted a total of 137 routers. I asked my client, "If all of them had to go down [which they did, to do what we wanted to do], then in which order should they be shut down, and in which order should they be restarted?" He couldn't even remember which ones were seeded and which ones weren't and even worse, had absolutely no copies of the configuration files anywhere to be found. That's what I call scary. Once he thought about it, that's what he called scary, too.

So, the point of this whole diatribe is that you should know which routers are configured which way and in the case of an emergency, in what order your routers should be shut down and then brought back up. Although you won't back up these routers, you should plan on backing up and archiving all the router configuration files so they can be used for restoration. You should also begin thinking about a router restoration plan in the case of a total power outage.

DEFINE CRITICAL COMPANY FUNCTIONS

The previous section walked you through what you need to consider when look-ing at critical networking systems, such as servers and routers. Now we need to talk about what to consider when looking at critical company functions. Plan for functions a little bit differently than for systems. The functions you are attempting to protect often are spread across the critical systems you are already backing up. When looking at these functions, you define the individual users and peripheral devices that need to be protected to restore critical functions after a disaster.

Accounting and Inventory Management

Okay, let's go right to the heart of a company—where the money is. I have a friend who used to work for a small company, and this person was in charge of accounts receivable and payable. One day the accounting database went down and, because it hadn't been backed up recently, $40,000 worth of billing records were lost. Guess what this person does for a living today? Well, all I'll tell you is that it isn't in the same business or the same city. In the small business in which she worked, this person was responsible not only for accounts receivable and payable but also for backing up the system.

Accounting systems usually aren't kept on a dedicated file server. They are usually kept on the accounting person's computer, which should, therefore, be listed as a critical system but often is not. Also, many medium-sized companies have more than one person in charge of accounts receivable and payable, and the systems are spread between the two or three individuals. Now you not only have to plan to back up one system, you have to plan to back up all systems and then restore all systems at the same time. The complexity of backing up those systems is much different from the complexity of backing up individual computers. Many of the accounting programs in use today, like Great Plains, Medi-Mac, or Denti-Mac, require all the files to be backed up every day. They don't allow some files to be backed up on one day and others on a different day (incremental backups). If not backed up properly, they won't be restored properly, and restoration is the key issue at hand.

Add to this the inventory tracking system for small- to medium-sized businesses. Most of the time, these tracking systems span at least two computers. A reseller we know has a centralized database for inventory management, but the daily information is tracked at the individual store level (there are five stores) and uploaded to the main server only at the end of the day. Therefore, the inventory management system is only as protected as those computers spread across a number of cities are protected.

The point I'm trying to make here is that with accounting systems as well as inventory management systems, you are beginning to look at more than one computer in the backup process—usually computers you would ignore otherwise. Your mind should now be shifting from which *individual* computers should be backed up to which *sets* of computers in a system should be backed up.

Office Resource Management

What's this stuff? This is the stuff used to run your office on a regular basis. However, since it is "stuff" that is used by the front-desk secretary, the office administrator, or the shipping clerk, nobody ever pays attention to it.

It's the Federal Express or UPS tracking software database that has a list of all the things you have sent to your clients. It's the training room schedule. It's the conference room schedule. It's the staff directory. It's the computer "node book," as Cello calls his computer tracking system he created in FileMaker Pro, which has everything from the amount of RAM per computer to the authorized software listing for everyone in the system, and finally to even the bidding process for buying new gear and software. And yes, Martha, it is *your* charting macros that Wayne uses for his Monday-morning presentations and for which he never gives you credit. It is all of the "stuff" you have created that if you didn't have at your fingertips would noticeably slow you down.

So, on what level do these items need protection? I don't know. That's for you to decide. You need to start considering that you need to protect them, or they will cost you wasted time recreating them. *I* would protect them.

Sales and Contact Management

I did a test in the office the other day. We use a distributed contact management tool called Now Contact. I "dropped" my contact database, signed on to the central repository server, and asked it to "synchronize" what I had (now nothing) with what it thought I needed (what I had before). I did this on a computer I could let run for a while. Five days later (count 'em, 5, as in 24 hours a day for 5 straight days) the database was finally rebuilt. Get the point? If you don't, then read this paragraph to one of your sales staff. You'll get the point after that.

Other Key Computerized Functions

Now that I've gotten you started, it's time for you to teach the teacher. Think up the rest of the key pieces of equipment or processes that I may have missed and send your list to me. I'll think up something cool to give you. Here's my address at which you can reach me via fax or e-mail:

FAX: (415) 896-1573

E-mail: Dorian Cougias   dorian_cougias@netfrontiers.com

           Tom Dell   tom_dell@netfrontiers.com

DETERMINING DATA PROTECTION NEEDS USING SERVER SLEUTH

Server Sleuth is a package I asked Phil Zarboulas to write for Network Frontiers. Phil is the creator of many fine applications for managing AppleShare servers. Among them are Server Manager and the suite of Server Tools that Santorini is publishing itself. Santorini is also publishing Server Tracker, a must-have application if you want to know what's really going on inside your file servers.

Now that we have the prerequisite marketing bullcrap out of the way, let's focus on using Server Sleuth to search the servers and come up with a listing of folders on the server by the size, label, and access privileges. This information will then be exported and used to create a listing of all folders that should be marked Essential, Hot, or In Progress. You will use this information when creating your restoration strategy and also when deciding which folders need to be backed up to near-line storage during critical periods.

Launching Server Sleuth

There's not much to Server Sleuth, other than the ability to figure out who owns what, the size of that data, the labels of the folders, and when it was last backed up. Not much, but a whole lot more than most administrators know without a tool like this.

The application shows the familiar **ST** of the Server Tools package. It also shows the label menu. When you double click on the icon, before Server Sleuth can actually open up and diagnose the server, type in the server's administrator key.

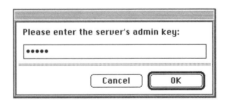

Entering the Server's Admin Key

The password is entered as bullet characters while you type. After you enter the password correctly, Server Sleuth's main window opens, and all volumes on the computer appear as hard drives.

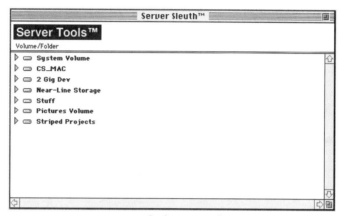

Server Sleuth's Main Window

Server Sleuth Views

Server Sleuth's views are the best AppleShare views I've seen. They are much better than the ones provided by Apple's AppleShare Administrator or even the Finder, because they are more in-depth. Here is how to take advantage of them.

Server Sleuth's Show Menu

This is the basic menu you use to gather the information you need from the server. There are six different views you can set, either individually or in combination. We'll go through each one individually, explaining its usefulness as we go.

Server Sleuth's Show Menu

The first three items in the list pertain to basic AppleShare privileges. Every folder on an AppleShare file server has these set of privileges associated with it. Let's look at the privileges for the folder in which I keep this book. Every folder has an **Owner**, a **User/Group**, and **Everyone** privileges. Whether these privileges are set or not, they still exist. (If you need to know more about these privileges, see one of our other books, *Managing AppleShare & Workgroup Servers,* also published by AP PROFESSIONAL, 1995.)

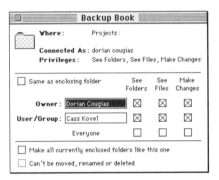

Privileges for a Typical Folder

Along with **Owner**, **User/Group**, and **Everyone**, there are certain access privileges that can be assigned to the folders. Users have the privilege of being able to see files within a folder, see other folders within the folder, and make changes to the folder (meaning removing, renaming, or deleting files).

Owner Privileges

Selecting **Owner Privileges** in the **Show** menu displays each folder's owner and the owner's associated access privileges. The **See Folders** privilege is depicted by a small folder icon. The **See Files** privilege is associated with a small page icon. The **Make Changes** privilege is shown by a small pencil icon. The absence of any of these icons means that the particular privilege is not assigned to the owner.

A word of advice: Make sure that the owner of important folders is anyone *but* the "Administrator." The Administrator account is set up as a default by the Apple-Share Admin software and doesn't pertain to a real person. The Administrator is assigned as the owner of all folders that don't otherwise have an assigned owner (even folders that aren't shared). It is okay to have the Administrator account own the top-level folder on a file server, but you don't want the Administrator account to own the other folders. You want *real* people who should be held *really account-able* for the well-being and administration of the information in those folders. Again, if you need to gain more of an understanding about this process, see *Managing AppleShare & Workgroup Servers.*

Talk to the top-level owners of the folders on the servers. They will be able to help you identify what information is more important than other information.

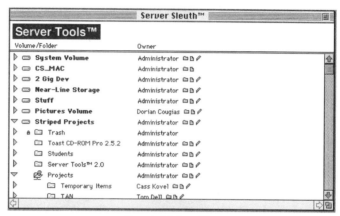

Owner's Privileges View

If no one has been manually assigned ownership of a folder, the ownership defaults to the server's administrator. This is one of your cues as a network administrator. Select a user on the network to own the folder. By doing so, you can work with the user to ensure that the information is identified and managed. You don't have time to manage all the data on your network. The data is better managed by the people who use it than by the administrator.

User/Group Privileges

Selecting **User/Group Privileges** from the **Show** menu displays each folder's User or Group and the User's or Group's associated access privileges. The **See Folders** privilege is depicted by a small folder icon. The **See Files** privilege is associated with a small page icon. The **Make Changes** privilege is shown by a small pencil icon. The absence of any of these icons means that the particular privilege is not assigned to the User or Group.

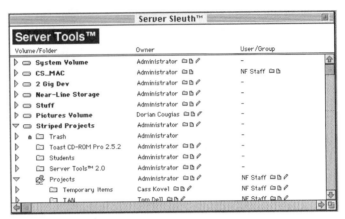

User/Group Privileges View

The absence of a User/Group name—folders with a "-" by User/Group—means that those folders do not have a specific user or group assigned to them. Therefore, those folders have no inherent user or group access privileges. By default, no user or group is selected for a folder that is owned only by the Administrator user.

Everyone Privileges

Because the Everyone user is actually the "Guest," there aren't any actual users associated with that name. Instead, folders are simply given access privileges. When you conduct your data evaluation, check for how much Everyone access is available within the folders on your servers. What you will need to *immediately* eliminate any guest privileges for folders that have been marked by the owners of the folders as Essential. If the data is *that* important, it shouldn't be accessible to everyone within the company. Mr. Murphy will be just waiting for some new user to come by and accidentally trash the whole folder or write a new folder of the same name on top of that one, effectively eliminating the data inside the folder and replacing it with something you don't necessarily want.

The following window shows that not too many folders have given the Everyone user access privileges. This is good, in that it keeps unwanted eyes out of places they don't belong. Again, if you find that you have many folders with Everyone privileges, it may be time to rethink your server security policy.

Server Sleuth™

Server Tools™

Volume/Folder	Owner	User/Group	Everyone
▷ ▭ **System Volume**	Administrator ▭ ▯ ✎	–	–
▷ ▭ **CS_MAC**	Administrator ▭ ▯	NF Staff ▭ ▯	▭ ▯
▷ ▭ **2 Gig Dev**	Administrator ▭ ▯ ✎	–	–
▷ ▭ **Near-Line Storage**	Administrator ▭ ▯ ✎	–	–
▷ ▭ **Stuff**	Administrator ▭ ▯ ✎	–	–
▷ ▭ **Pictures Volume**	Dorian Cougias ▭ ▯ ✎	–	–
▽ ▭ **Striped Projects**	Administrator ▭ ▯ ✎	–	–
▷ 🔒 🗀 Trash	Administrator	–	–
▷ 🗀 Toast CD-ROM Pro 2.5.2	Administrator ▭ ▯ ✎	–	–
▷ 🗀 Students	Administrator ▭ ▯ ✎	–	▭ ▯
▷ 🗀 Server Tools™ 2.0	Administrator ▭ ▯ ✎	–	–
▽ 🗀 Projects	Administrator ▭ ▯ ✎	NF Staff ▭ ▯ ✎	▭
▷ 🗀 Temporary Items	Cass Kovel ▭ ▯ ✎	NF Staff ▭ ▯ ✎	▭
▷ 🗀 TAN	Tom Dell ▭ ▯ ✎	NF Staff ▭ ▯ ✎	▭
▷ 🗀 QuickMail Course	Tom Dell ▭ ▯ ✎	NF Staff ▭ ▯ ✎	

Everyone Privileges View

Folder Label   Selecting **Folder Label** in the **Show** menu displays each of the folder's labels.

Server Sleuth™

Server Tools™

Volume/Folder	Owner	Label
▷ ▭ **System Volume**	Administrator ▭ ▯ ✎	None
▷ ▭ **CS_MAC**	Administrator ▭ ▯	None
▷ ▭ **2 Gig Dev**	Administrator ▭ ▯ ✎	None
▷ ▭ **Near-Line Storage**	Administrator ▭ ▯ ✎	None
▷ ▭ **Stuff**	Administrator ▭ ▯ ✎	None
▷ ▭ **Pictures Volume**	Dorian Cougias ▭ ▯ ✎	None
▽ ▭ **Striped Projects**	Administrator ▭ ▯ ✎	None
▷ 🔒 🗀 Trash	Administrator	None
▷ 🗀 Toast CD-ROM Pro 2.5.2	Administrator ▭ ▯ ✎	None
▷ 🗀 Students	Administrator ▭ ▯ ✎	None
▷ 🗀 Server Tools™ 2.0	Administrator ▭ ▯ ✎	None
▽ 🗀 Projects	Administrator ▭ ▯ ✎	None
▷ 🗀 Temporary Items	Cass Kovel ▭ ▯ ✎	None
▷ 🗀 TAN	Tom Dell ▭ ▯ ✎	Essential
▷ 🗀 QuickMail Course	Tom Dell ▭ ▯ ✎	Cool
▷ 🗀 Privacy Book	Cass Kovel ▭ ▯ ✎	Cool

Folder Label View

It also places a **Label** menu in the menu bar. This **Label** menu uses labels set on the computer from which you are running Server Sleuth—the file server, in other words. You can change any folder's label by selecting the folder and then selecting the appropriate label from the **Label** menu in Server Sleuth's menu bar.

Folder Size   **Folder Size** in the **Show** menu calculates each folder's size in megabytes and the number of files and folders within the folder.

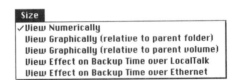

Folder Size View, Shown Numerically

As with the **Folder Label**, selecting **Folder Size** adds another menu to the Server Sleuth menu bar. This is the **Size** menu. The default for the **Size** menu is to show the numeric information for the folder; that is, the size of the folder in megabytes and the number of folders and files within the folder.

Size Menu

The first two graphical views show the size relative to other information in other folders or the volume on which the information is located. These views are great for getting a basic handle on folder sizes. I am confused about the first graph, and therefore have chosen not to show it. I do like the volume reference graph though. The other two views are backup specific. They show the time it takes to back up the information in each folder.

- **View Graphically Relative to Parent Volume**: This shows how large each of the subvolumes are as a percentage of the hard drive on which they are found.

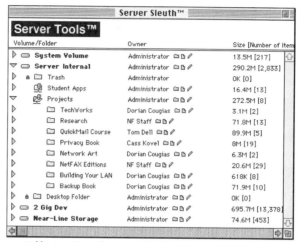

Folder Size View, Shown Graphically Relative to Parent Volume

- **View Effect on Backup Time over LocalTalk:** This shows how long it will take to back up each folder across a LocalTalk network. The time is based on 1 MB per minute transfer speeds. Notice that it isn't very fast.

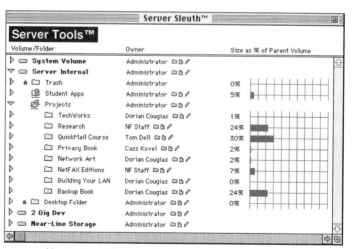

Folder Size View, Shown Graphically Relative to LocalTalk Backup Time

- **View Effect on Backup Time over Ethernet**: This shows how long it will take to back up each folder across an Ethernet network. The time is based on 4 MB per minute transfer speeds.

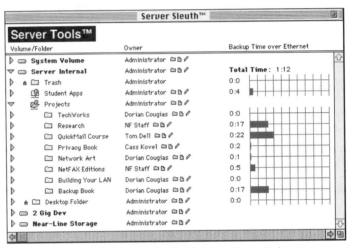

Folder Size View, Shown Graphically Relative to Ethernet Backup Time

Folder Dates **Folder Dates** shows three key dates for the folders: the folder's creation date, modification date, and backup date.

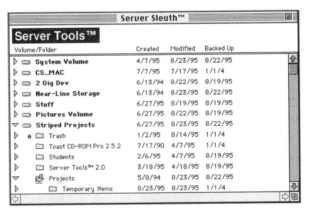

Folder Dates View

- **Creation Date**: This is obvious. It is the date the folder was originally created.

- **Modified Date:** This is the date the folder was last modified. Notice that most of the folders were modified on 5/8/94 and others on 5/9/94. This is going to be important in a minute.

- **Backup Date:** This is the date the folder was last backed up. Notice that many folders in the list have backup dates for 1/1/4. That is the default date for anything on a Macintosh that has a date field but doesn't know what to do with it. If all your folders have this date, this means that you forgot to set Retrospect's option to update the backup date of folders after you have backed them up. If some of the folders have backup dates of 1/1/4, this means that the backups are happening but not correctly. The date of 1/1/4 means that the folder has never been backed up. Look into it.

Tying It All Together

Server Sleuth Window Showing the Most Important Information

Now that you have learned most of the windows and views, I want to show you the view on which I base most of my decisions about what is labeled and what receives extraspecial attention during restores and backups. The preceding view is what I call my basic view, the one that I immediately configure. It shows me the folder's owner, label, and backup times over either LocalTalk or Ethernet. This one shows Ethernet.

The reason I start here is that I want to know who owns the folders. I really don't care so much about the users and groups, unless the owner of the folder is the administrator. Then I care. That is when I find out who belongs to the group and who in the group should be the person in charge of the folder's contents.

Next, I am interested in the size of the folder. I want to know how long it is going to take to back up this folder and presumably restore the folder, if necessary. I know that there are those of you out there who are saying to yourselves, "Restoring is *much faster* than backing up." Yes, it is much faster, *when it is in the process of restoration*. What that doesn't take into account is time to research and set up the restore. Therefore, the times reported here are, at best, optimistic.

Finally, I want to know how the folder is labeled, if it is labeled at all. This will give me a base knowledge of how much important information is on this server volume, and whether or not people are labeling the folders at all or labeling *every-thing* Essential. If the folders aren't labeled, I usually check with the owner. If the folders are overlabeled, I usually have a chat with the owner.

Exporting the Information

Whatever information you have showing in the window can be exported to a tab-delimited text file. That's the good news. The bad news is that you can't print it. The next picture shows a copy of the table Server Sleuth created for a view that basically showed everything about the servers. Notice that only the folders I had opened were exported. Also, what does not export is the graph information; instead, you see the straight numeric information.

Volume/Folder	Owner	Owner Privileges	User/Group	User/Group Privileges	Everyone Privileges	Label	Size [# of Items]	Creation Date	Mod Date	Backup Date
System Volume	Administrator	YYY	-	NNN	NNN	None	12.5M [203]	5/8/94	5/9/94	1/1/4
2 Gig Dev	Administrator	YYY	-	NNN	NNN	None	593M [12,833]	1/26/94	5/9/94	5/9/94
Server Internal	Administrator	YYY	-	NNN	YNN	None	226.8M [1,909]	5/8/94	5/9/94	5/8/94
Trash	Administrator	NNN	-	NNN	NNN	None	0K [0]	5/8/94	5/9/94	1/1/4
Projects	Administrator	YYY	-	NNN	YNN	None	225.7M [8]	5/8/94	5/8/94	1/1/4
TechWorks	Dorian Cougias	YYY	Consulting	YYY	NNN	In Progress	3.1M [2]	4/7/94	5/8/94	5/6/94
Research	NF Staff	YYY	-	NNN	YYN	None	67.7M [12]	3/28/94	5/8/94	1/1/4
QuickMail Course	Tom Dell	YYY	Consulting	YYY	NNN	Hot	89.9M [5]	12/4/92	5/8/94	5/6/94
Privacy Book	Cass Kovel	YYY	NF Staff	YYY	NNN	Essential	7.9M [19]	9/12/93	5/8/94	5/6/94
Network Art	Dorian Cougias	YYY	-	NNN	YYN	None	6.3M [2]	3/22/94	5/8/94	1/1/4
NetFAX Editions	NF Staff	YYY	NF Staff	YYY	NNN	Hot	19.8M [29]	3/10/93	5/8/94	5/6/94
Building Your LAN	Dorian Cougias	YYY	NF Staff	YYY	NNN	Essential	618K [8]	3/26/94	5/8/94	1/1/4
Backup Book	Dorian Cougias	YYY	Cass Kovel	YYY	NNN	Essential	29.9M [5]	4/24/94	5/9/94	5/9/94
Desktop Folder	Administrator	YYY	-	NNN	YNN	None	130K [1]	5/8/94	5/8/94	1/1/4
Near-Line Storage	Administrator	YYY	-	NNN	YNN	None	15.6M [157]	5/8/94	5/9/94	1/1/4

Server Sleuth Report

PUTTING THE LIST TOGETHER

Finished? Found everything? Good. You should now have a listing of all the computers and other devices on your network that you think need protecting. Here's a listing of our piddling systems at Network Frontiers that need to be protected. We have put this here so that you have a decent idea of what kind of information you should be bringing to the table to discuss your backup and restoration needs. You should have a listing of devices that need to be backed up and then a second listing of the information within the critical servers that needs to be restored.

Device Type	Network Name	Location	Downtime
File Server	Main Server	Training Room 1	Essential
Mail Server	Mail Server	Training Room 1	Essential
Contact Mgmt Server	Lynn's CPU	Ste 200	Hot
Printer	LWPro 630	Ste 200	Hot
Firewall	RISC Router #1	Training Room 1	Essential
Internet Gateway	900i	Training Room 1	In Progress
AR/AP	Cass's CPU	Ste 200	In Progress
Main Hub	Farallon Hub	Training Room 1	Essential
Backup Server	Back-It-Up	Training Room 1	Hot

Devices to Protect

If the preceding table shows you devices you need to protect, the next table shows you the information you need to protect within the devices you are protecting. Huh? In other words, once you have the computers up and running, how quickly will you need to restore the information? These must fit together. You can't have a computer listed as being In Progress, meaning that it can be restored in a couple of days, and then have the information listed in it as being Essential, meaning that the information has to be restored within a couple of hours. It wouldn't make sense to need to restore information without first ensuring that there's a computer to put the information on, now would it? Here's our table of information we need to restore at Network Frontiers.

Folder/File	Device Name	Location	Downtime
95 Contacts File	Lynn's CPU	Ste 200	Hot
Projects *f*	Main Server	Training Room 1	Essential
Projects Art *f*	Main Server	Training Room 1	Essential
Clients *f*	Main Server	Training Room 1	In Progress
E-Mail *f*	Mail Server	Training Room 1	Hot
Router Config Files	Main Server	Training Room 1	Hot
AR/AP Files	Cass's CPU	Ste 200	In Progress
E-Mail Gateways	Mail Server	Training Room 1	Hot
Marathon	Various	Training Room 1	Hot

Folders and Files to Protect

DETERMINING THE RISKS

Once you have your list and you've checked it twice (that's how Santa does it, according to the song), you have reached the "what can hurt these things" stage. There are two types of risk planning. The first type looks at all of the potential risks to the devices and information and then creates a plan stating, "This device can be hurt by this method and has this percentage of being hurt by that method." Then there's the type that *we* use that says, "This device can be hurt in the following ways, and it either will or won't be hurt, but we are going to plan like it will be." Why do we throw out the percentage factor? Because Mr. Murphy can't do fractions and percentages. He either comes to visit, or he doesn't come to visit. I'd rather be planning for him than *not* be planning for him. That's just me. You plan your percentages if you want to. I'm not into ciphering.

When planning, you have to determine whether it will cost you more to protect the device from the threat than it would cost you to physically replace the device or restore the information or both. Sometimes it is much cheaper to ignore the threat until it happens and then simply replace the device and restore the information. So, without further ado, here are your risks.

Physical Theft

I put this one first because the first time a company hired Network Frontiers to test its security plan, we sent in our guy who picked up one of the hard drives off the server and then carried it out the door. That's a fact. Nobody stopped him. It was great going in to the meeting to tell the company about its security breaches and then showing the drive outside the company's window! Anyway, you have to plan for physical theft as a threat.

Stupid User Tricks

Remember the original "horror stories" in the introduction to this book? Well, stupid user tricks are often more to blame for problems and disasters in the company than anything besides theft. If theft is the biggie to prevent, then stupid user tricks is the biggie you can't really prevent very much. You can't prevent a user from turning off the file server. You can warn users with placards and sticky notes and whatnot, but everyone will still be stupid at some point or another.

Device Failure

Drives break. Cables break. That's all there is to it. They never break when you can afford it, either. At a speech during MacWorld Boston, one of our staff members brought her PowerBook up to the stage and dropped it on the table. It broke. 60 seconds before my speech—with the demo I needed on it. Ouch.

Electrical

When I was trying to make my clients buy into disaster recovery planning in Chicago, I had only one taker. People would say to me, "What are we going to have, a flood?" Well, if you remember from the introduction, one day Chicago did flood. The water didn't rush up to the 30th floor and ruin a computer. However, it did rush into the basement where the electrical lines were and ruined those, which then shot electricity up the buildings, which in turn ruined a bunch of computers on the 30th floor. Therefore, one of the biggest things to watch for is electrical problems. Try to prevent them as much as possible.

One thing to plan for that you can't really prevent is when the electricity for your building goes out completely. That happened in the middle of a network management course once in San Francisco. We ended up taking the class to lunch at a local restaurant that still had power. That was fun: expensive, but fun.

Earthquakes, Fires, Floods, Tornadoes, and Bombs

These are all the things that will probably ruin your building if they hit you. There is not much you can do except bolt down your computers, put antibounce pads under them, and hope that they ride out whatever is hitting the building at the time. Even further, you will have to hope that whatever hits the building doesn't cause the building to fall on them. There is not much you can do with a computer that is under four tons of rubble.

Other Stuff

Okay, you make it up here. If you think of something to watch out for that you can also plan to do something about (your kid hitting the computer with a peanut butter sandwich doesn't count, John), link or fax us with your risk and your preventive methods, and we'll do something cool for you: maybe a date with Elvis or something.

FAX: (415) 896-1573

E-mail: Dorian Cougias   dorian_cougias@netfrontiers.com

           Tom Dell   tom_dell@netfrontiers.com

PART THREE: RISK PREVENTION

Risk prevention is applying the knowledge acquired during the risk analysis stage—what needs to be protected and the associated potential risks—to develop a plan and a budget for minimizing or totally eradicating those risks.

To tell you the truth, I don't take stock in anyone's ability to completely eradicate any given risk or set of risks. Anything in the world is possible and anything in the world can go wrong. Remember, Chicago never thought it could have a flood. I never thought I'd get married. Accidents happen. (That's a joke, sweetheart.) Ergo, this chapter is about the risks we discussed in the previous section, along with associated preventive measures and the costs associated with those measures.

Don't Bore Me with the Details . . .

- You can't eradicate all your risks.

- Make sure that the prevention of the risk costs less than the damage the risk could cause.

- You can't stop stupidity; look at how long we've had Congress.

- Buy a UPS. You are stupid if you don't. If that pisses you off, tough.

- RAID drives don't stop users from trashing folders and files. Trashed folders and files on a primary drive are also trashed on a mirrored drive.

- Many pieces of equipment can be bolted down. You can't bolt down hard drives, network connectors, keyboards, or mice.

- PowerBooks can't be bolted down while traveling but *can* be bolted down while in the office.

- Cables can be cut.

CHAPTER 3:
PHYSICAL SECURITY

My father's theory is that *anything* can be bolted down with 13-penny nails and 50-mile-an-hour tape. Heck, he thinks you can *fix* anything with that combination, too. So, if you want to cut this chapter short, call him (he's retired) and he'll make your computer equipment so secure that even *he* couldn't pry it up. Of course, if you don't want to deal with my father, you'll have to read this chapter and figure out what you can and can't secure and how much it will cost you.

PHYSICAL SECURITY OF WIRING GEAR AND CONNECTION DEVICES

It's not often that I hear about wiring racks, hubs, repeaters, switches, or routers being stolen. That is probably because they are usually locked away in wiring closets or in free-standing closets inside someone's computer room.

Locks on doors are good, and cheap. If putting something in a locked room is all the physical security you need, you will more than likely get the okay for the risk prevention system . . . unless, of course, the room also needs a special air conditioner or something.

Racks and Devices on Racks

Racks themselves can be bolted to the floor and the wall. That tends to make them somewhat difficult to steal. The equipment on the rack, such as hubs, routers, bridges, or switches, are in turn bolted to the rack itself. That makes them fairly secure as well. This is good, since this gear is normally pretty darned central to keeping the day-to-day networking operations going.

Free-Floating Gear

This is the stuff that is more difficult to secure. Minihubs put in a room for a temporary network, along with other temporary networking gear, sometimes will walk away. When we teach our networking courses, we occasionally lose gear somewhere along the line. Connecting devices, like transceivers, especially infrared transceivers, also disappear from the network. How much will this affect the security of the critical devices you are networking? I don't know. Do you normally put your critical devices on a temporary network with network connection devices sitting out on a table or something? Probably not.

PHYSICAL SECURITY OF COMPUTERS AND PRINTERS

These devices are more difficult to secure than routers bolted to a wiring rack locked in a wiring closet in a corner of the office. The easiest way to deal with the security of computers and printers is to remember that the larger the part, the more difficult it is to steal. The smaller the part, the easier it is to steal and the easier to fit in a briefcase.

CPUs and Monitors

Macintoshes and their monitors all have security cable attachments on them. Using these attachments, you can run security cables through them and then bolt them down to the table. If you are concerned with the physical security of your CPUs and monitors, bolt them down. This doesn't cost much and is easy to do. We think that Kensington makes the best products for this purpose, and special thanks go to Leslie Purmal at Kensington for sending over the following two illustrations. The picture on the left is the overall setup for a Macintosh and a monitor that can be bolted down to any desk. It is called the **Apple Security Kit**. The picture on the right is the special cable you would need for your PowerBook. Kensington also has a separate product for your desk, in case you don't want to or can't chain it around a leg as shown.

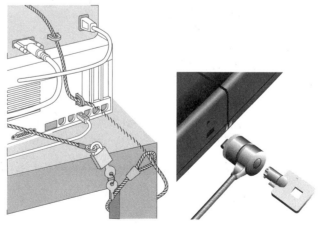

Apple Security Kit for CPUs and Monitors (left); PowerBook Version of Apple Security Kit (right)

Vendor Contact

Fortunately for us, Kensington security products can be found in most Macintosh product-related catalogs, superstores, and dealers. Otherwise, you can contact them directly at:

Kensington Microware, Ltd.
2855 Campus Drive
San Mateo, CA 94403

Phone: (800) 535-4242 or (415) 572-2700

FAX: (415) 572-9675

Hard Drives and Keyboards

Hard drives and keyboards are difficult, if not impossible, to secure. An exception to this is the RAIDbank5 from MicroNet; that son-of-a-gun weighs about 60 pounds. If someone is going to take *that* thing, it is going to cost some sweat. Anyway, since you really can't count on securing your hard drives and keyboards, plan on replacing them if necessary. You need to plan to have an extra drive or two and an extra keyboard and mouse or two on hand when one goes bye-bye.

Other Peripherals

One of our clients has a system that relies on a scanner for input. This is a MARS data input and retrieval system. It is important for the server to be up because of the amount of data to be continually input. Then one day the scanner was gone. Whoops! Nobody planned for that. Nobody had secured it. Nobody ever thought that it would be stolen. The client waited a week for the new scanner to come in from the dealer. That's a long time. Things as large as a scanner can often be locked in place with a security cable. If you are worried about the physical security of your peripherals, one of the features that you should look for when purchasing the peripheral is the ability to bolt it down somehow.

CHAPTER 4:
STUPID USER TRICKS

Stupid user tricks sometimes can be prevented but usually cannot be prevented. The basic rule is to do what you can and then do a lot of praying.

So, it's time to tell a tale about us. While working on our AppleShare book, we had borrowed some hard drives and associated gear from MicroNet and other vendors. Upon receiving the gear, I decided it would be a great idea to use the hard drive on MicroNet's tape backup assembly to stripe one of the drives on our own server. We could then see what it would be like and see whether we would gain any improvement from doing this. Of course, the files I put on the drive were the ones that I knew we would be using during the writing of the book project itself.

Well, one day when we were about finished and were beginning to send back equipment, I received a call from our office staff. For some reason, they couldn't find our Projects folder with the book information in it. I found out they had taken down the server, pulled off the MicroNet tape backup unit, and shipped it back to MicroNet. Of course, the general response from all involved seemed to be, "Since I didn't set up the server, I didn't know the drive was striped." As the drive was a borrowed drive, nobody had taken the time to check the servers to see whether there were any new drives on it that needed backing up.

In short, our books hadn't been backed up for about a month, one half of the striped drive was at our office and the other half was at MicroNet in Irvine. If not for some frantic calls, this book *and* the AppleShare book would have been a tad more past deadline than normal.

"Stupidity Prevention" for Wiring Gear and Connection Devices

There is no need for us to break this section down into "rackable" and "nonrackable" devices. The prevention plans for these types of devices instead fall into a couple of categories: power and precarious hazards.

Garanimals for Power Supplies

Don't laugh. We have garanimaled our entire training room so that all Compatible Systems routers using a certain power supply and the power supply itself are numbered "1." The reason for doing this isn't so obvious to someone who has never blown up a hub or switch by plugging in the wrong power supply . . . not that I've ever done that myself (yeah, right).

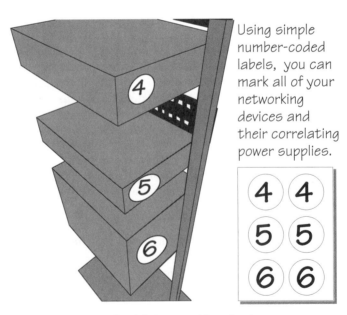

Using simple number-coded labels, you can mark all of your networking devices and their correlating power supplies.

Number-Code Devices and Power Supplies

Stupidity Prevention for Cables and Connectors

Stupidity prevention for both cables and connectors comes in a simple package from a company called Rip-Tie in San Francisco. Actually, it is right down the street from our office. How many of you have what is shown in the following picture happening in your office? How many of you are lying and say that you don't? By the way, that means pretty much everyone out there who has a computer in the office.

Typical Cable Snarl Under and Between Desks

Well, you needn't fear any longer. Rip-Tie's product keeps your cables out from under the desk where a user could trip on them and get hurt (right, Bill?). A user who trips also pulls the network cables out of the back of the computer, usually ruining the AAUI connector (which isn't the strongest, anyway) that holds the Ethernet cable in place. There are a couple of versions of Rip-Tie's product. One version comes with a sticky backing so you can hold your cables up above the ground, as in against the wall. The other version comes with a tie strap so you can secure it to the cabling in back of your computer and then tie all of them together at once. They use velcro fasteners so you can untie the cables quickly and easily if you need to add more to the bunch or if you need to rearrange them.

Since I was writing this portion of the chapter, I decided to take a walk over to Rip-Tie and talk with the owner, Michael Fennell. Nice guy. He explained that the product shown on the left in the following sets of pictures, the Rip-Tie Cable-Wrap, is used by connecting to one of the cables on the back of the computer (using the tie-down) and then wrapping all the cables together using the velcro portion of the wrap. I show one of these holding the computer cables together in the following picture on the right.

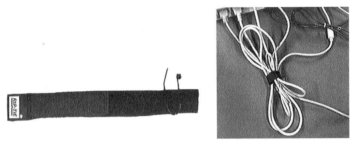

Rip-Tie CableWraps

The other product, called the Rip-Tie CableCatch, is used to keep cables up and out of the way, like on a wall or the back of a table. In the following picture, we show the Rip-Tie CableCatch holding some data cables.

Rip-Tie CableCatch

The products are fairly inexpensive, around $2.75 each. In our opinion, for around $6.00 a computer (less, if you buy in bulk), you can't go wrong. For ordering information, contact Rip-Tie at the following:

The Rip-Tie Company
PO Box 77394
San Francisco, CA 94107

Phone: (800) 348-7000 or (415) 543-0170

FAX: (415) 777-9868

"Stupidity Prevention" for Computers and Printers

User mishaps at the computer level come from more than just tripping over cables and ripping up the system. This is where, realistically, most of the problems occur. Can you prevent them? Not all of them, but you can give it a good try. We have broken this section down into the following parts: "Anything that Uses Power," "CPUs and Monitors," "Drives and Peripherals," "Keyboards," "Floppy Drives," and "Viruses."

Anything that Uses Power

I lump these all together because you need to do only one thing—put up a poster by every outlet servicing a computing device and have it say the following:

> ## Do not unplug the computer.
>
> ## Do not plug in the vacuum cleaner.

Power Poster for Receptacles

Also, make sure that you post this notice in whatever languages the cleaning people speak. This *is* a politically correct statement. I put up one of these signs only to watch the cleaning guy unplug my UPS so he could plug in his vacuum. When I asked him if he read the sign, he said, "Que?" Make a whole bunch of these signs (PIP or Insta-Print can print them with adhesive backing) and post them everywhere they are needed. We have translations for Spanish, German, French, Italian, Korean, Greek, and Chinese. Call us if you need these translations, or if you have translations for languages we don't have.

CPUs and Monitors

Stupidity prevention at the computer and monitor level is easy and involves a couple of pieces of equipment and a strong company policy about being dumb.

Although you can't fire dumb people for being dumb, you can fire them for doing dumb things, like putting a latte (very strong coffee to you folks who don't know) on top of the monitor to "keep it warm longer," only to have it dump into the monitor when they go to grab it. Monitors don't like coffee. Here are a few preventive measures you can take against dumb situations.

CPU Stands Companies like Kensington Microware, Ltd. (see page 82), make products to hold some of the older and larger computers (like the MacII line) up on their sides. I have seen too many of these MacIIs with cracked cases caused by having been knocked over by the computer users. The stands aren't that expensive and should be seriously considered if the computer is on its side.

Smokeless Ashtrays I don't want to sound like I'm schlepping some weird stuff here, but hey, they work. How many times have network administrators lifted the cover off a computer that is being used by a person who smokes? Even if there is a no-smoking policy in the building or company, many of these users will work in the evenings and weekends and will still smoke. For all users I can't break of the smoking-in-front-of-their-computer habit, I buy one of those smokeless ashtrays with the little fans in them. Cheesy and weird, but they work. I think that they are available through any fine "chatchka catalog."

No Teddy Bears Don't laugh. I found a monitor completely fried once because some user (don't ask who, Terry) had put her teddy bear collection all over the monitor, thus not allowing any heat to escape. It caused the monitor to fry, and once it did, because she thought it was on fire, she threw her soda at it. Of course, the soda hit the computer instead. Thus, the company should enact some kind of policy saying that objects should not be placed on the computers or their monitors.

Drives and Peripherals

This could be called the "screwing-in-the-screws" portion. Most of the problems I have encountered with drives and peripherals are because they aren't connected the right way. They also don't screw in the SCSI cables all the way (or at all). They then move something while the server is running and whammo, one of the drives is no longer in service because it isn't plugged in all the way.

While we are at it, let's talk turkey about terminators and SCSI cables. The general rule is that if the peripheral device came with a terminator, it should have the terminator attached to it at the end of the SCSI chain. If not, the device is probably internally terminated. If you forgot what terminators look like, APS has provided us with a real nice picture of three of them side by side. Take a good look at them because the absence of them on your SCSI chain can cause as much damage or as many problems as not having the cable screwed in properly.

SCSI Cable Terminators

While I'm at it, I might as well talk about the SCSI cables themselves. Good SCSI cables are like a pound of prevention. Just ask any tech-support guy at Dantz Development, the folks who make Retrospect. JoAnne, Dantz's Goddess of Tech Support, says bad SCSI cables are the problem in about 5–7% of all calls they receive. In the following pictures, we show two SCSI cables; the one on the left is a "bad" SCSI cable, and the one on the right is APS's SCSI cable.

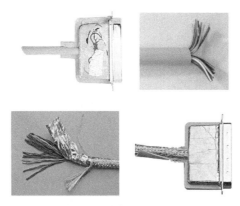

"Other SCSI" (left); APS SCSI (right)

Keyboards

Keyboard Condoms is what I call the funny-looking plastic things that fit over standard keyboards (not my keyboard, which is one of those Carpal Tunnel jobbies that bends sideways so I don't get wrist cramps while writing). Why do you need these? Ever seen what soda and candy bar pieces do to a keyboard? Ever try to stop your users from eating at their desks? Ever try to make users put one of those plastic things on their keyboards? Probably not. They actually do feel funny. Thus, the only people who use them are those who have ruined a keyboard once and are therefore forced to use keyboard covers upon life-threatening sentences.

Tip: Here's a step-by-step way to clean out spills on keyboards. Thanks to Daniel Knight of Ada, Michigan for this great tip!

1. Shut down your computer ASAP.

2. Disconnect your keyboard and mop up the spill.

3. Drain your keyboard and bring it to a large sink (or bathtub, for home users).

4. Rinse your keyboard with tap water for several minutes.

5. Drain your keyboard.

6. Set your keyboard on edge and let it dry overnight.

Odds are, if you follow these steps immediately after a spill, your keyboard will be as good as new.

Floppy Drives

Keep the floppies out of the drive. There, I've said it. It made me happy. Also, find yourself a can of compressed air (or hire a politician to come through every so often) so you can blow the gunk out of your floppy drives.

Viruses

Somebody recently asked whether to check their files for viruses before or after they were backed up. There supposedly aren't any dumb questions, but this must come pretty close. Yes, please use virus protection on a daily basis, and keep your antivirus software up to date. If a file is infected with a virus before it is backed up, it will be infected when it is retrieved, and there is the additional possibility that the entire backup could be contaminated.

Yeah, go ahead and backup without virus protection!

CHAPTER 5:
DEVICE FAILURE

Stuff breaks. Fact of life. You can't stop it. Therefore, the planning should focus on the fact that it is going to happen, and you need to plan for the occurrence rather planning to prevent it. This failure rate even has a name. It's called MTBF, or Mean Time Between Failure. This is how long your devices are supposed to go before they break, and yes, some day they will break. Just like cars rust in Chicago, devices break—unless, of course, it's the one computer in the office that nobody wants and you'd just *love* it to break so you can buy a better replacement. But, such is life—it just doesn't happen that way.

This chapter is devoted to helping you plan a prevention strategy for what happens when your key devices fail. Some of the main questions are: How long can you wait if your main router goes down? If you are Internet dependent, how long can you wait until your Internet access is back up? How long can you wait until your other WAN connection to the mainframe for your bookkeeping comes back up on line? These are things you have to think about when a key device goes down.

The term you need to become *very* familiar with is *cross-shipping*. Cross-shipping is when you buy something, it breaks, and as you are shipping your broken device back to the company, it is sending you a new one so you have it at the first FedEx or UPS delivery the following day. Without cross-shipping, you are at the two-day mark *at best* before you have your device back up and running—or, more realistically, before you have a *new* device in and running.

DEALING WITH FAILURE OF WIRING GEAR AND CONNECTION DEVICES

The failure of wiring gear and connection devices is both more difficult and easier to handle than computer device failure. It is easier to handle if you have a spare somewhere and have the configuration files ready to download to the device. The failure of these devices is more difficult to handle if you don't.

Racks and Devices on Racks

Remember those routers, hubs, bridges, and switches you were supposed to be listing as key gear? Remember the maximum allowance for downtime? If any one of these devices can't be down 1–24 hours, make alternative plans to have a device ready to go in order to bring your network back up. With these devices, either they work or they don't. Even the power supplies and power supply connectors are ones that nobody has ever heard of before or that you can't obtain easily.

If you have cross-shipping with your vendor, you can have a new one in the morning (if yours breaks before FedEx makes its last pickup). If you don't have cross-shipping, you are up to three days out of luck. If you can't afford to have a new router sitting on the shelf ready to go, see if a local computer dealer will "shelf" one for you for a certain amount of money. Many dealers will do this, but it depends on the relationship between the client and the dealership. This translates into what kind of money your company has to spend per year to have the dealer do this in lieu of losing you as a client.

Free-Floating Gear

Free-floating gear doesn't have to be protected from failure as much as other gear, so you can probably leave it out of this protection plan. If it is free-floating gear, you can even think of it as your backup protection for when the main devices fail. I know we do. We have gear we use strictly for teaching. Our disaster recovery plan stipulates that if some key networking device fails, steal one from the training room until the original is fixed or replaced. If training is happening at the same time, we are generally out of luck. A decision must be made about whether to deprive the office or deprive the students.

DEALING WITH FAILURE OF COMPUTERS AND STORAGE DEVICES

Failure of devices like computers holding important data is more complex than dealing with a failed router. When dealing with computer and storage device failure, plan for how quickly you need the *data* on the computers. This is sort of a backward planning project. First, figure out your total allowance of time, then find out how long it takes to restore the data; whatever time remains is for the restoration or replacement of the hardware itself. In the following table, I show data markings in the far-right-hand column for information that is **Essential** (4 hours), **Hot** (24–48 hours), and **In Progress** (72 hours). Working back from there, we figure out how much data can be restored within those settings and then how much time you have left to restore or replace the CPU itself. Notice that you can easily double each of the settings as you progress from Essential to In Progress.

CPU "Restore" Time	Size in Gigabytes	Total Number of Sessions	Time in Hours to Restore Data	Need Within This Many Hours
2.22	2	low	1.78	4
1.16	2	medium	2.84	4
20.44	4	low	3.56	24
18.31	4	medium	5.69	24
40.89	8	low	7.11	48
36.62	8	medium	11.38	48
57.78	16	low	14.22	72
49.24	16	medium	22.76	72

Restoration Times and Equipment Replacement Times

It shouldn't take a math major to figure out that if your server goes down with data that needs to be restored in four hours, you won't be able to obtain a new one in time. Therefore, plan an alternative method for computers in the four-hour range.

Also notice that one of the columns is entitled "Total Number of Sessions." Why is that there? Glad you asked. It is now time to learn a little about how backing up to tape works and how the way you plan your backups affects how long it is going to take to restore your data. We are going to look at how backups are accomplished using the most common of backup storage devices, the DAT tape. I think that once you understand this, the preceding table will be even clearer.

Backup Operations

There are different types of backup operations. One is the *full backup.* This involves always backing up everything to a given tape. The first time you back up, you are asked to name your tape and also to name the catalog for the tape. If you ever use the same tape for another full backup, the information about the tape and the catalog is erased. A second type of backup is called a *changed-file backup,* or a *normal backup.* This entails everything being backed up once; then only files that have changed are backed up during each subsequent operation.

Full Backups

The most effective method of backing up is to back up each and every volume in its entirety every day. This gives you the best ability to restore your server easily when something happens. However, this approach uses the most capacity and takes the longest time. As a rule of thumb, you should at least:

- Back up all data completely to at least three different tape systems on a rotating weekly basis (see the following section on generational backups) and keep at least one set of backup files off site in case of a calamity.

- Perform milestone full backups before and after dangerous or important events, such as office moves or power outages.

Changed-File, or Normal Backups

A changed-file backup strategy stipulates that the network administrator make a full backup once and then back up only the files that have changed since the last backup. Retrospect calls this a "normal" backup, and I use the same terminology throughout the remainder of this book. One of the problems with normal backups that restorations take longer, as the most current files usually end up on different tapes. Let's look at a typical volume—my hard drive, for instance—and examine how it would be backed up on a changed-file system and where the files would be stored on the tape. I've displayed the contents of my hard drive in the following window and have sorted it by folder and modification date. The folders modified longest ago are on the bottom, with the most recently modified on top.

Dorian's Drive	
Name	Last Modified
▷ ☐ Applications	Thu, Apr 28, 1994, 1:53 PM
☐ New S/W Serial Numbers	Thu, Apr 28, 1994, 1:49 PM
▷ ☐ System Folder	Thu, Apr 28, 1994, 1:03 PM
▽ ☐ In-Progress	Mon, Apr 25, 1994, 2:53 AM
▷ ☐ Backup Book	Wed, Apr 27, 1994, 12:21 PM
▷ ☐ TechWorks	Mon, Apr 25, 1994, 3:28 AM
▷ ☐ NetFAX	Mon, Apr 25, 1994, 12:27 AM
▷ ☐ Personal E-Mail Guide	Sun, Apr 24, 1994, 6:17 PM

My Hard Drive

If I backed up every day (of course I do—you don't think I'd write this book and not follow my own rules, do you?), starting with the 24th of April and ending on the 28th of April, I would have a total of five backup sessions on my tape: one for each day.

Let's assume that I started with a full backup. All information on the drive pictured in the previous screen shot would be stored in the first session. From there, a new session would be created each day after that. The backup software looks at my hard drive's directory and backs up only the information that changes. The information that changed after the first full backup would be recorded in the second session. From there, each day a new session would run, and any files that changed would be backed up, with each new session being appended where the last files left off. The next series of diagrams shows the tape being divided into five different sessions and also shows where each of the files is located on the linear tape.

Let's go through the process of backing up a single drive for the week, and I think what happens will become more clear. Keep something in mind as we progress— the more sessions you have, the more distributed the files are on the tape. The more distributed the files are on the tape, the longer it will take Retrospect to figure out where they are and to restore them.

The first time a full backup process happens on the tape, all information from the computers is copied to the tape in linear order. Some of the backup software companies will perform full backups even though their software calls it a "normal" backup and they later make the distinction between "full" and "normal," or "incremental." But you can rest assured that if nothing has previously been backed up to the tape, *everything* is backed up the first time.

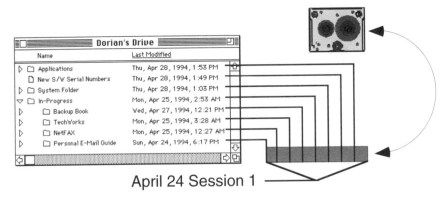

April 24 Session 1

Tape Backup with Session 1

All files have pointers to Session 1. This is because Session 1 was a full backup and backed up everything on the drive. If you needed to restore your drive after a full backup, the time it would take your backup software to find the files would be greatly diminished, as they are all in linear order on the tape. From here, only the files that change are backed up in the subsequent sessions, as shown in the following diagram. Session 2 now has a couple of files that Session 1 also contained.

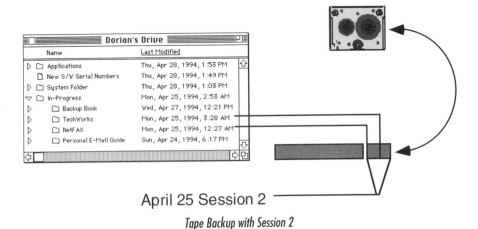

April 25 Session 2

Tape Backup with Session 2

Session 3, shown in the next diagram, has absolutely no information in it. That's because nothing changed on that day (I was playing hooky that day). In reality, most backup software won't even record the session if nothing is there.

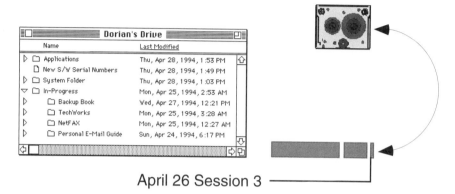

Tape Backup with Session 3

Sessions 4 and 5 (in the following diagram) both show files because on each day, I had worked on and altered some files. Now there are several updated files.

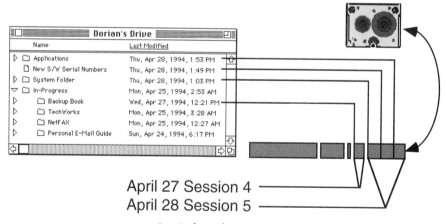

Tape Backup with Sessions 4 and 5

What this means for you, the administrator, is that files can be located in multiple sessions on a tape backup. The *New S/W Serial Numbers* file, for instance, is located in the first session (because of the full backup) and is also located in the last session, as it was altered on that day.

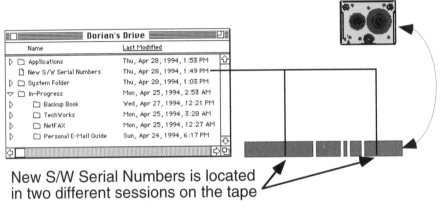

New S/W Serial Numbers is located in two different sessions on the tape

A Single File in Multiple Sessions

Because of this, you must take care when restoring your files. If you restore your files without paying attention, you might restore an older version of a file instead of the most recent version. Good backup software will protect you from that problem, though. The other, and more important reason to note this is that the more sessions you have, the longer it will take your backup machine to figure out how to restore the files you need. Think of this:

• A session equals a single volume being backed up.

• If you have 100 computers, you will have a minimum of 100 sessions per day (given that *something* is being backed up on each of them each day).

• Let's add 50 extra drives spread across the network. That brings us up to 150 sessions for each day.

• You create a backup script that backs up each computer every day and doesn't wipe out the catalog until the beginning of the new week, and you back up five days a week.

• That makes 5 days × 150 sessions (volumes) per day = 750 sessions per week.

Get the point? I hope so, because there are some folks out there who haven't created a full backup or wiped out the catalog in some way ever. I looked over a client's backup plans once and read the server's catalog to show that there were 13,500 current sessions within the catalog. Yup. Forever is about how long it would take to restore something from that backup server.

Bottom Line

The conclusion you should be drawing from this is that a small number of sessions—say, under 100—won't cause you many problems. However, a large number of sessions—anything over 750—takes massive amounts of time. With fewer sessions, you can plan for your restores to run at around 0.9 GB per hour. With a moderate number of sessions—around 500—plan for about 0.5 GB per hour to be restored. With a large number of sessions, it really depends on the calculation speeds of your Macintosh, and they can be *quite* slow.

Lead Time on Computers and Drives

So, I call the local Mac-only dealership, supposedly the best and the biggest in the Bay Area, with around seven stores. I say I need an 8150 *today*. When the salespeople stop laughing, they say they can get me one *tomorrow*, but it has only a 1-GB drive, and I need a 2-GB drive. They say they sold the single extra 1-GB drive in stock but can get one for me in two days. So, I call APS, which can have one shipped to me so that it arrives here at the same time as my server—around 10:30 the next day. There goes restoring anything in the Essential or Hot 24-hour categories if I need a new server to which to restore the information. What is there to do? A couple of things. Both of these things imply that you have either a standby server (here's your chance to put that honking computer on your desk because you can claim you need it for the standby server. Of course, you also need lots of RAM so it's ready to go, right?) or standby storage capabilities or both. The way to deal with the lag time is to set up special on-line storage or to set up near-line storage or both.

On-Line Redundant Storage and When to Use It

Many people don't need to use on-line redundant storage of information. On-line storage means that you are either mirroring the contents of your storage media or "shadowing" the contents of the storage media. There is a fine difference between the two. Mirroring means writing the information to your primary storage media while simultaneously writing the same information to a secondary source. Shadowing means writing the information to the secondary source a split second after writing it to the primary source, which is just enough time to verify that the data wasn't corrupted before writing to the secondary source.

When I wrote the first version of this book, I thought the only time you would want to mirror your systems is when you are protecting something, like an electronic mail server that needs to be accessible 24 hours a day, 7 days a week, 365 days a year. I targeted e-mail systems only in corporations with a network design document stating that the mail server must never go down and that if it does, it should be replaced, up and running, within an hour. The only way to do this is to have the data mirrored so if the primary drive becomes corrupted, the secondary drive can immediately take over. This would then allow the administrator to replace the primary drive. The primary drive would then become the secondary drive because the computer is now running on what used to be the secondary drive.

I've changed my mind, though. I know many other types of corporations that need on-line redundant storage systems. Corporations like catalog houses and other production facilities need such systems, and although they need on-line redundant storage, they need near-line storage as well.

Near-Line Storage and When to Use It

Most of us who think we need on-line storage actually need near-line storage. Near-line storage occurs when essential information is copied in native filing format to a secondary storage device so that if the primary device fails, the secondary device can activate quickly and easily while the first is being repaired. So, what's the difference between near-line and on-line storage? Near-line storage doesn't happen simultaneously or near-simultaneously, and it doesn't usually happen to all information on a given drive. Normally, several subvolumes are identified and set to be copied in native format to a secondary drive within a given time period. For example, in the following diagram I marked two folders as being Essential on my hard drive. I then set up a near-line backup system to copy the contents of these folders to a different drive every two hours. The first time the copy occurred, it would have to copy everything in the folders. Thereafter, only those items that had changed or were newly created would need to be copied over. This is the same as Retrospect's normal backup operations.

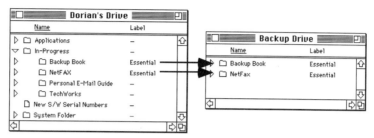

Near-Line Copy of My Hard Drive Contents

One good thing about the near-line copies is that they are normally stored in Finder format. This means that if anything happens to my hard drive, all I need to do is grab the information from the secondary drive and begin working. The best thing about near-line backups is that the copies are at timed intervals. This means that if I'm working on the folder and the entire folder is accidentally deleted or I screw up a file, it isn't automatically screwed up or deleted on my mirrored drive. Where mirrored drives are used to keep a computer up and running constantly, near-line backups are used to keep essential data secure from screwups and corruption. That's a big difference.

Off-Line Storage

Off-line storage is just what you think it is. It is information stored in such a way that it is not readily accessible to users. When you perform backups to tape or archives to tape, you are storing the information in an off-line format. And that, folks, is what the majority of this book is about. So, since there is a lot to cover, we'll just leave off here by reiterating that you need to do your backups, including the data that is also being backed up, to an on-line redundant or near-line system.

CHAPTER 6:
ELECTRICAL PREVENTION
(WHY YOU SHOULD USE A UPS)

This chapter deals with teaching you how to prevent electricity. Okay, maybe it doesn't. It *does* teach you that a $8.00 K-Mart power strip just ain't enough power protection for your $10,000 server. Know what I mean, Jed? I should note here that much of the section on UPSs in this second edition was revised and researched by Brando Rogers, Network Frontiers's UPS Goddess.

Electricity is as erratic as a wild animal. Foolish administrators tend to believe that their networks are immune or that they can change an electric current's state of being just by harnessing its power. The rest of us take the animal for what it is—unstable, unpredictable, and therefore completely unreliable. The likelihood of your experiencing power problems is a question of *when,* not *if.* A study by IBM reported that the average computer experiences 20 power-related problems every month. You can liken a network's relationship to a UPS to a diabetic's relationship to insulin. The electrical condition must be regulated carefully to ensure the well-being of your system. In an imperfect world, electric currents, like blood sugar levels, can dip, drop, cl skyrocket. Homeostasis is achi

Two Patriot UPSs

through the introduction of an energy equalizer. What will happen and when is not something that can always be predicted. You can, however, expect the unexpected and arm yourself accordingly. With regard to electricity protection, if you feel the old excuses creeping up—"I don't have the money," "I don't have the time," "I know how to take care of my network."—remember, ignoring good advice now will surely come back to haunt you later. Don't wake up to this reality: Your data is lost, your equipment is totaled, your time and money have been wasted, and all your denials are turned to regrets.

So buy a UPS, okay?

Ultimate Server Defense Plan

DON'T BORE ME WITH THE DETAILS . . .

- Buy a UPS. Buy a good UPS.

- AC power problems happen continually. You have to be prepared for them.

- The best UPSs are on-line regenerative inverters, which are also called double conversion UPSs. Hybrids are a close second, but they still come in second. Off-line UPSs run a dead third.

- Plan for a load balance of about 1.25 times what you think you'll need today. Like an eight-year-old's new suit, you'll grow into it.

- Once you know the load you need the UPS to carry, plan for 133% more than you'll require, given that UPSs can be trusted to provide well for only about 75% of the rated load, and 100% of your load is worth protecting.

Just a Story Our office is in downtown San Francisco. Great city. Our office is on the waterfront along a street called the Embarcadero. Great area. While we were writing the first edition of this book, the city decided it was going to put in a really cool trolley system last year, right in front of our building. *Right* in front. Of course, the trolley system is electrically powered, with really cool old-fashioned street lights and everything. To put this stuff in, work crews had to tear the heck out of the roadway in front of our building, and they had to perform a lot of electrical work. Guess whose building lost its power four times in a single week? "The power was only out for a second," said the building manager. "Well," said I, "it only takes a second to drop a file server." Even though our file server didn't drop, because it was on a UPS, all the workstations and modems that weren't on UPSs dropped like flies at a flyswatter convention. Ouch. This same problem recurred for a period of about four weeks. Not fun. So, take it from a guy who really knows—buy a UPS that matches your needs. Here's what you need to know about power and how to figure out your UPS needs.

WHAT YOU NEED TO KNOW ABOUT POWER

The Macintoshes, printers, scanners, monitors, and other devices we use require only 5–12 volts of direct current (DC). Wall outlets supply 120 volts of alternating current (AC) of power in the United States and Canada, 220 or 240 volts in Europe, and either 120 or 220 everywhere else. Direct current (DC) travels in the same direction continuously. Alternating current (AC) reverses its direction 60 times per second in 120-volt systems and 50 times per second in the 220-volt systems. Because of these differences, each Macintosh and other computing device contains power supplies that convert the AC power to DC power at the voltage levels needed, while filtering small fluctuations in the original current. Small fluctuations in current? Yep, that's what I said. All electrical currents aren't direct flat currents. They fluctuate. Currents flow in sine waves. If you want to know exactly what they are, call your old science teacher. You should have been awake during high school. The voltage value of the sine wave current is called the root-mean-square, or in other words, the average value of the peaks and valleys of the wave of the electrical current:

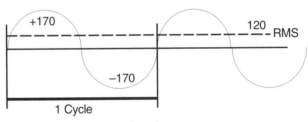

Traditional Sine Wave

Computers use what is called a non-linear load, or square sine wave, which approximates the normal sine waveform. The current is normally more than double the linear root-mean-square current. The ratio between the non-linear current and the linear value is called the crest factor ratio. Computers are designed to draw their full load power (all drives running, everything happening at once) at the peak of each of these non-linear waves.

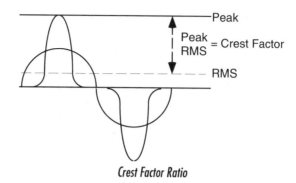

Crest Factor Ratio

As computers are designed to draw power at the peak of each wave, they are built so they dispense up to 20 milliseconds of current provided by their charge storage capacitors (the things that fry your hair if you aren't grounded and open your Mac to add RAM). So, in essence, your Mac is probably resilient . . . to a point. There are some nasties out there that will definitely ruin your day.

Blackouts   This is a complete loss of power. No lights. No cameras. No action. This is worse than unplugging your computer in that when the power comes back on, it might cause a spike (see following). A significant drop in voltage (below 80 volts) can be considered a blackout as well, as most equipment will not operate below this level.

Brownouts   A brownout is when voltage levels fall below 102 volts. Brownouts can be caused by too many users pulling power from the system. For example, when everyone decides to turn on the air conditioner in the summer, a brownout can occur. Brownouts last anywhere from a fraction of a second to hours on end.

Sags   A sag is just like a brownout, but the power falls between 105 to 102 volts. Both sags and brownouts can be caused by utility companies attempting to negotiate peak load times and by the operation of heavy equipment, such as elevators, compressors, and shop tools.

Surges and Spikes   A sudden and extreme increase in voltage is a surge or a spike. Lightning striking and going through the system can cause a spike (over 1,000 volts). When a building's or electrical company's generator must produce an enormous amount of voltage to turn back on everything that turned off during a blackout, a surge (under 1,000 volts) generally occurs. Also, switching off high-powered appliances, like air conditioners, can cause a burst in voltage levels, a surge lasting less than a second. Surges and spikes turn perfectly useful computers into door stops. Theoretically, all Macintoshes are designed to withstand surges of up to 5,000 volts. Yeah, right, and the IRS admits accounting mistakes (only to you, Andy).

Noise   Noise is the general term for flaws in the electrical system that affect the quality of the power moving through the copper wires. Electromagnetic frequencies (EMFs) coming from elevator motors, HVACs in the ceiling, and other large apparatuses are the usual culprits.

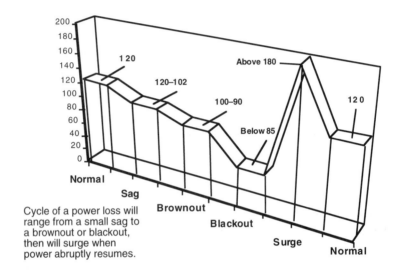

Cycle of a power loss will range from a small sag to a brownout or blackout, then will surge when power abruptly resumes.

Typical Blackout Cycle

To avoid all these problems, make sure that a good, solid electrical firewall is placed between your essential computers and the power coming out of the wall. You'll be looking to UPSs for this protection.

So, What's a UPS?

An uninterruptible power supply (UPS) is a device placed between the power from the outlet and your computer to act as a wall of protection against electrical problems. What can a UPS do for you? According to a FAQ document on uninterruptible power supplies, a UPS's functions should include "absorbing relatively small power surges, smoothing out noisy power sources, continuing to provide power to equipment during line sags and for some time after a blackout has occurred." (UPS FAQ maintained by Nick Christenson. E-mail address: npc@ minotaurljpl.nasa.gov.)

There are five typical components of a UPS, and in the following list I profile each one. (The following information was adapted from one of the best books ever to come out about disaster recovery: John William Toigo's *Disaster Recovery Planning: Managing Risk and Catastrophe in Information Systems*, Englewood Cliffs, New Jersey: Prentice-Hall, Inc., 1989.)

Rectifier and Battery Charger This converts the power supplied from the wall outlet into DC current. The DC current is used to charge the UPS's storage batteries, as well to supply power to the UPS's inverter.

Inverter The inverter converts the DC power into clean, regulated AC power, which is then sent to the computer equipment attached to the UPS.

Storage Batteries Storage batteries are lead acid or nickel cadmium cells that remain charged, and with off-line UPSs remain in reserve, until a power outage or brownout. With on-line UPSs the batteries themselves are a feed-through for the conditioned power sent to the computing devices.

The batteries are the most important part of the UPS system. It will be the batteries that ultimately keep the computers up and running during times of power outages—and more commonly, brownouts, sags, and surges. The amount of "power time" remaining on the batteries depends on how often the batteries have to be used in the course of a given day. Remember that it takes longer to recharge the batteries than it does to run them dry. So, if you purchased a UPS that you think will keep your systems up for a half hour due to the battery power, think again. A typical outage cycle doesn't come abruptly. It comes after several sags, surges, brownouts, surges, and then blackouts. The number of times the UPS's batteries had to kick in *before* the total outage will ultimately determine how long the UPS can last during a *total* blackout.

Also, batteries eventually die. Everyone with a PowerBook knows that. One day the batteries in the UPS are going to die. Know *when* that is going to happen and be prepared to change them. If this is the type of system that is always drawing power directly from the batteries, it must also allow you to change the batteries without first shutting down the computer—unless, of course, you don't mind bringing the file server down to replace the batteries.

Bypass Switch and Control Logic

The bypass switch is normally on for off-line UPSs so the wall outlet power can be sent directly to the computer systems. For these systems, the control logic system is the device that "decides" to switch from direct AC power to battery power. For on-line systems, the control logic detects when the incoming power supply has failed and alerts the device of trouble. No power switching is necessary, because the power to the computers is continually drawn from the battery system.

RS232 Interface and Alarms

Your UPS should alert you when it detects power problems. Bells, whistles, or flashing lights are all good ways of doing this. An LCD display that tells you what kind of power problems were encountered is better than simple alarms. An RS232 interface—a serial cable that can be run to the back of the Macintosh—is even better, as long as you can obtain the information you need without having to jump through too many hoops. There are some software products on the market designed to work with these RS232 ports that will even start the shutdown procedures for the server. Be aware, though, that some server software requires a person to physically click an **OK** button or two before the server can shut down. Of all the software on the market that "watch" UPSs, we like APC's PowerChute the best. While the Macintosh version is good, the PC version is terrific. We cover PowerChute in depth in our book, *Managing AppleTalk Networks*.

TYPES OF UPSs

Off-Line UPS

Off-line UPSs, also known as UPSs with a standby power supply (SPS), are bad news. During normal operation, an off-line UPS sends the incoming AC power (coming out of the power plug in the wall) directly to the computer. During normal operations, the UPS also trickle-charges the battery system. However, when the incoming voltage drops below 102 VAC (enough to qualify as a "brownout") a circuit in the UPS detects the fluctuation and switches the power source from the incoming wall outlet to the battery. The super short (5–20 milliseconds) loss of power the computer experiences is called a glitch. That glitch will really screw up some of the computer systems, will drop the phone lines on a modem, and will cause other "annoying" problems. Additionally, off-line UPSs provide very little protection from frequency variations, line noise, spikes, and brownouts. In other words, off-line UPSs provide absolutely 0% line-conditioning. So, what's good about them? They are cheap. Whoopee-doopee, if you ask me.

On-Line Regenerative Inverter UPS

On-line UPSs always provide power directly from the battery system to the computers, which means that when the power goes, there isn't any switching and thus no switch-over time. The reason the real McCoys are called regenerative inverters (or double-conversion UPSs) is that they are continuously filtering the AC power to DC. Then, through a process that involves inverting AC power to DC power, they regenerate *clean* AC power for complete protection. This power is usually in a perfect sine waveform, meaning that the voltage is perfectly regulated and the frequency is stable. These UPSs offer the greatest degree of insurance against problems associated with power lines. Some disadvantages of on-line UPSs include their increased heat production, power consumption, and ticket price. Despite the fact that the inverter in a "true" UPS is always operating, their reliability is typically unaffected. Further, off-line UPSs that suffer failure most frequently do so in part because of the lousy quality of their inverters.

Here is a listing of all appropriate on-line regenerative UPSs for networking:

Manufacturers of On-Line Regenerative UPSs		
Deltec Electronics Corp.	220–18,000 VA	(800) 854-2658
Clary Corporation	500–5,500 VA	(818) 359-4486
Exide Electronics Corp.	800–1,500 VA	(800) 554-3448
IntelliPower, Inc.	650–1,500 VA	(714) 587-0155
Liebert Corporation	1,000–18,000 VA	(800) 877-9222
Minuteman Software	500–1,000 VA	(800) 238-7272
EPE/TOPAZ (Square D Co.)	900–10,000 VA	(800) 344-0570
Toshiba International Corp.	600–18,000 VA	(800) 321-1412
TRIPP LITE	450–2,000 VA	(312) 329-1601

Hybrid UPS

Between off-line systems and on-line systems are a whole bunch of on-line wan-nabes. Look for terms like "line interactive," "single conversion," "load sharing," "triport," or "ferroresonant transformers." The addition of interactive design and the use of ferroresonant conditioning cause an off-line UPS system to use a "ride-through" approach when converting the load transition from AC power to the inverter-supplied power. Sometimes this ride-through approach doesn't work, and the UPS will misinterpret a brownout as a blackout, thus kicking in the battery-supplied power. This can cause problems down the line if it happens a few times before a brownout. The batteries kicking in might dwindle their reserves to a point where they can no longer hold a sustained charge large enough to power the computer systems during the upcoming blackout.

If you are wondering, the "ferroresonant conditioning" isn't so much a surge suppressor like some manufacturers and distributors claim. Double-conversion UPSs provide true surge protection because the power is always flowing through the battery. Ferroresonant designs incorporate huge reactance through the use of a magnetic coil, but all this does is smooth out the electrical anomalies; it doesn't provide insurance against surge protection. That must be left to the auxiliary surge protection circuits provided by the product.

Manufacturers of Line Interactive UPSs		
Acme Electric Corp.	1,000–2,000 VA	(800) 833-1373
Alpha Technologies, Inc.	600–15,000 VA	(800) 322-5742
APC	200–2,000 VA	(800) 800-4APC
Best Power Technology, Inc.	500–18,000 VA	(800) 356-5794
Controlled Power Co.	400–25,000 VA	(800) 521-4792
Deltec Electronics Corp.	220–2,200 VA	(800) 854-2658
Emerson Electric Co.	750–2,100 VA	(800) BACKUPS
Liebert Corp.	600–2,000 VA	(800) 877-9222
Minuteman Software	500–2,000 VA	(800) 238-7272
Oneac Corp.	400–1,800 VA	(800) 327-8801
EPE/TOPAZ (Square D Co.)	600–2,000 VA	(800) 344-0570
TRIPP LITE	250–2,000 VA	(312) 329-1601

LUXURY ITEMS

Although certain functions are absolutely essential to the operation of a UPS, there are also several luxury options available that further secure data and property. Some of these include short-circuit protection, automated shutdown and restart after long power outages, monitoring and logging of power usage, and a display of the voltage/current on the line and of the draw of specific pieces of equipment. Some of the more advanced UPSs can work directly with monitoring and logging software components via SNMP and a network connection. Assuming that your network is on a UPS, troubleshooting can be controlled automatically or from a remote location.

Here are a few clues to determining the quality of a UPS:

- Remember, the best condition for your network is to have a UPS that produces a pure sinusoidal output. The nearer the AC output approximates a sine wave, the less conversion work for your equipment, and thus your system will last longer and reach optimum levels of efficiency.

- Find out if and how the UPS vendor or manufacturer supports its equipment. Does it offer a special operation warranty, maintenance contract, and direct telephone support? Beware if none of these apply. The performance of the UPS is probably reflected in the lack of support for it.

- Make sure that the UPS has a manual bypass device. If, God forbid, your UPS breaks down, you must have the ability to pass power through it to the rest of your system. The inability to access power equals additional downtime.

Recommendation: We recommend the APC UPSs right now. They seemed to be the only company willing to let us test their UPSs to the fullest. PowerChute informs the computer to which it is attached that there is a problem with the UPS. You can then Apple-Script a response to the problem, as in e-mailing you about the problem. Other companies have sent us their marketing bru-ha-ha to read, but none stepped up to the plate for testing like APC. We'll keep you posted in our quarterly CD about the specifics of their products. We will also give you an in-depth review of a UPS, taking it apart and showing you what's going on inside. It's easier to do in a multimedia CD than it is to do in a book.

How Much UPS Is Enough?

UPSs are rated in *volt-amps*. A UPS should provide enough power so the attached systems can make it through a typical outage cycle without the batteries of the UPS being completely drained. The typical duration of a power outage, power regain with surge, and a return to normal power is about 15 minutes. What? Yessiree, Bob. Those first moments usually kill most appliances, copiers, computers, and air conditioners in *all* the offices in the building. Then the building's electrical system has to overcompensate to bring all that power back on line at once. You didn't think it would all settle down in a minute or two, did you?

Load Requirements

Basically, a load requirement means how many *devices that draw power* you want to hook up to the UPS. If you are hooking this up to your file server, this means the file server (CPU) itself, the monitor, the external hard drives, and the tape drive if it is external. If this is an ARA server, it also means the modems. Get the picture? Don't forget to add those hard drives you are going to be buying in the next few months. Here is the UPS load requirement for one of our servers:

Quadra 800

External 3-GB Drive

Two Global Village Modems (for ARA)

NuBus card for ARA 2.0

External Tape Drive

Black-and-White Monitor

Device Power Requirements

How much power each of these devices needs will be listed in the user's manual under *watts* (the *power* draw) or *amps* (the *current* draw). Since UPSs are specified in terms of watts and volt-amps, you will have to do some converting. The VA rating for this load is produced by multiplying volts and amps. Total the requirements for amps and then multiply that number by 120 volts. If you know the wattage load for the components of the system, you can convert the watts to VA by multiplying the watts by 1.4. Since watts are easiest to find, I've figured ours in watts converted to VA. The UPS you select should be *comfortably larger* than the VA rating you come up with. Remember, UPSs test well running systems that are less than or equal to 75% of their VA rating. Therefore, once all the other numbers are in you should multiply the total by 133% for that extra cushion.

Device	Watts (* 1.4)	VA
Quadra 800	303.00	424.20
External 3-GB Drive	59.70	83.60
ARA NuBus Card	13.30	18.60
Two Global Village Modems (for ARA)	20.00	28.00
External Tape Drive	9.50	13.30
Black-and-White Monitor	30.00	42.00
	Total	**609.70**
	× 133%	810.90

Since most UPSs come in ranges of 360, 460, 660, 950, 1,300, 1,800, and up, we decided that a 950 was in line with what we wanted today but that a 1,300 would probably be the best for us, allowing for expansion within the next year.

QUESTIONS YOU SHOULD ASK

- Does the product support all critical network devices? If you have the confidence to pull the plug, you know your devices are safe.

- Can you test the UPS hardware on the network from a remote location? Is the UPS software network capable? If so, does it support more than one UPS across the network? If so, how?

- Is an automatic log of significant power events available? The more information garnered from the UPS itself regarding its operation, the better.

- Is there indication of load level, battery capacity, input volts, AC loss, low battery, overload, temperature problems, or squirrels chewing the cable?

- If plugged into the server, can you change the UPS's batteries without rebooting the file server? In other words, do you have to shut down your computer before changing the UPS's batteries?

- Can the file server be shut down *automatically by the UPS,* in an orderly way, in case of a prolonged power failure? Is this function included, or will you need to add the appropriate software?

CHAPTER 7:
EARTHQUAKES, FIRES, FLOODS, TORNADOES, BOMBS, AND DISGRUNTLED POSTAL WORKERS

California has a new state song, *Slip slidin' away.* Just kidding. Folks, since I've been in the business, I've seen Chicago flood and most of the Midwest float away. One of my clients had a tape stuck in the server that it put on top of the roof in the flood. Another client had just finished its backup plan when the earthquake hit in California. Thankfully, the company lost only a couple of keyboards. I have a client in the Midwest, right smack in the middle of Tornado Alley, who says, "Disaster recovery plans are very low on my list. Nothing has ever happened here." He is a fool, and you know what they say about fools and their money. . .

So, I'm going to talk about how to prevent these things, right? Ha, ha, ha, ha, ha. Don't think so. I will discuss how to make the damage less devastating, because in the end, that's about all you can do.

LESSENING THE DAMAGE TO WIRING GEAR AND CONNECTION DEVICES

Notice that I didn't say anything about *stopping* the damage, now did I? That's because you can't. You *can*, however, try to prevent the damage as much as possible when your gear gets thrown around the room like a pigskin at a football player's reunion. The bouncing and falling and dropping and cracking hurts the computers almost as much as walls falling on them. I can't stop the walls, but I can help with the rest.

Lessening the Damage to Racks and Devices on Racks

There is actually a wiring specification for how racks should be bolted down, published by Global Engineering. The standard is the EIA/TIA 607. The standard states that you should be bolting your racks to plywood on the walls. This is called bonding. It also says that you should be grounding the racks, but I'll leave all the specifics for our network design book, *Designing AppleTalk Networks* (also published by AP PROFESSIONAL). You should buy it. It's good reading and your purchasing it will  make my publisher very happy. He's not always a happy guy. He seems to like yelling at me a lot for typing in sentences like these that, while they make the book interesting, cause it to have "too many pages." Heck with him, let's you and me have a good time, eh? Getting back to those wiring racks, the picture here shows one of my client's wiring racks, or the top of it, anyway. This shows the proper way to bolt it down at the top. The reason you can't see the plywood to which it is bonded is that the entire wall was plywood and for some reason, the client thought it would look better painted. Oh, yeah, that really looked great. The client even matched it to the color scheme of the wiring spindles—**not**.

Lessening the Damage to CPUs, Hard Drives, Monitors, and Keyboards

I've lumped all of these together because they can all be protected the same way: with Michael Fennell's magic velcro straps. Remember Michael? If you don't you can go back and read about him. We showed his products back on page 85. He's made some great straps for CPUs, monitors, and keyboards. There was a second

approach I mentioned, which my father uses frequently. It has to do with 13-penny nails and 50-mile-an-hour tape. I promised, though, that I wouldn't show any of those pictures here—very ugly. My father is not ugly, mind you, just what he does with the nails and tape. . . fixed a whole car like that once, you know.

Also, put what another of my clients calls "antibounce" material under your computers and monitors. It's made from the same stuff as mouse pads. The only idea here is to keep your computer or keyboard from bouncing off your desk during something like an earthquake, bomb, or your employees playing Nerf football. You folks in St. Louis shouldn't be laughing; you sit on a big fault line as well.

Lessening the Damage to Data

Ah, now we get to the heart of the matter: How do you lessen the damage to data? First, back up to something you can take off site, like DAT tapes. Second, guess what? **YOU TAKE THEM OFF SITE!** Neat how that concept works, isn't it? You can ensure that the data is secured off site by conducting what are known as generational backups.

Generational backups are used when you have grandfathers, fathers, and their sons working together. I'm kidding. Generational backups are so called because they involve rotating tapes on site and off site in sets. The first set is called the Grandfather, the second is called the Father, and the third is called the Son. Yes, some male came up with that terminology. To do a generational backup, you should start a log book with columns for tapes labeled A, B, and C. I begin our backups on a Friday so a full backup can be performed over the weekend. During the first week, take a new tape, label it A, and complete a full backup. This tape is used throughout the week to store incremental backups. Log each of the dates in column A.

During the next week, take a new tape, label it B, make a full backup, and log the date in column B. Once the full backup has been performed, you can take tape A off site for security, while using tape B to perform incremental backups the rest of the week.

When week 3 rolls around, you again use a new tape, label it C, and perform a full backup. After the full backup has been performed, take tape B off site and bring tape A on site again so it is ready at the end of the week to replace tape C. You then perform incremental backups the rest of that week using tape C. The following chart shows this process.

	Friday	**Monday**	**Tuesday**	**Wednesday**	**Thursday**
Set A	2/1/94 Full Backup	2/2/94 Incremental	2/3/94 Incremental	2/4/94 Incremental	2/5/94 Incremental
Set B	2/6/94 Full Backup	2/9/94 Incremental	2/10/94 Incremental	2/11/94 Incremental	2/12/94 Incremental
Set C	2/13/94 Full Backup	2/16/94 Incremental	2/17/94 Incremental	2/18/94 Incremental	2/19/94 Incremental

Your Backup Schedule

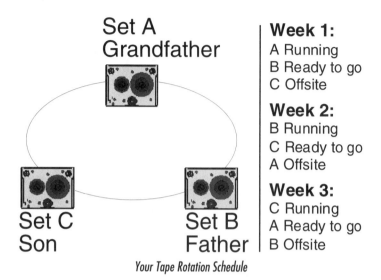

Set A
Grandfather

Set C
Son

Set B
Father

Week 1:
A Running
B Ready to go
C Offsite

Week 2:
B Running
C Ready to go
A Offsite

Week 3:
C Running
A Ready to go
B Offsite

Your Tape Rotation Schedule

Rotate the A, B, and C tapes each week, so if something happens and the tape becomes corrupted, you lose only one week's worth of files. Remember to keep one of the copies off site at all times.

Rule of Thumb from Tom Beardmore "Never, ever leave your DATs in the drives when the drive is not doing the backup." Now, here's Dorian's addendum, "Yeah, right." Since you probably aren't going to follow Tom's advice, at least clean your drives once a week, preferably right before your full backup.

Where do you keep your tapes when they are not off site? APS Technologies sells what it calls a media vault. It is a safe designed specifically to protect data media from building fires. I've seen one of these boxes and, in my opinion, they might even be strong enough to withstand most things falling on them. According to the company that makes them, they are guaranteed not to exceed 110°F, which is below the temperature that data tapes begin to fade out (somewhere around 125°F). Tom Beardmore made a great point in the original book as well: Most of the damage during a fire is from smoke, humidity, and the fireman's hose.

Don't confuse a media vault with a fire safe. Fire safes, unless certified for use with magnetic media, are typically rated to protect their contents from reaching the char point of paper, about 450°F. Although the labels on media stored in such a fire safe will probably be readable after a building fire, the media itself will look like the LaBrea Tar Pits at the bottom of the safe, and that ain't Black Gold or

Texas Tea, Jed. High-quality media safes are available from a variety of manufacturers.

Planning Your Off-Site Storage

First of all, a big thanks goes to Keir Lieberman, who is sitting right next to me as I write this. He's from DataSafe, the folks I mentioned in the first book. When planning your off-site storage, you need to know a few things. Here they are.

- What kind of media do you have? DataSafe needs to know by the millimeter, as in 4mm or 8mm tapes, and whether it's microfiche, linear tape, or magnetic tape. You need to know more than just the tape brand name.

- Why do you want to store it there? Do you need just archival storage, or do you need tape rotation? How many tapes do you have, and how often do you want to rotate them?

Pricing and Structure

Let's walk through a small site proposal.

Transportation Transportation to and from the site, once a week, rotating your tapes in and out is one cost. Network Frontiers's cost is $105.00 per month. Many times this can be avoided by dropping off and picking up the cartridge yourself. You'll still be hit with a handling fee, but that is usually about a fifth of the total cost.

Container Usage and Storage They give you nifty metal containers with nice bar codes on them to use while with their service. This fee is for that cool container (no, you can't provide your mother's cookie jar) and also for the storage of the container. Network Frontiers' cost is $40.00 per month for up to four containers. Essentially, they are $10.00 each, and the size of the container doesn't affect the cost. Each holds 20 tapes.

Library Maintenance This is for a separate archival can and covers DataSafe's moving your archival tapes out of the transportation containers and putting them in the archival containers. Network Frontiers's cost is $10.00 per month, for up to four containers.

Insurance Insurance is separate. There's a plan to fit every need (even if you didn't know you had the need).

Cost of Emergencies

DataSafe has a 120-minute response time between 3:30 P.M. and 7:30 A.M. The cost for retrieval is $70.00, plus a $2.00 fee per container. Between 7:30 A.M. and 3:30 P.M., the service is a bit cheaper, at $50.00 for transportation and the same $2.00 fee per container. It still takes the same amount of time. If you aren't in a hurry and can wait four hours, the call and delivery costs around $30.00 plus the $2.00 handling charge.

So, if you are like me and wondering how the hell you are going to remember which set of tapes to ask for, don't fret. They have a handy-dandy little piece of paper, called a *transmittal list,* that goes with each container. This transmittal list has the container number and a field for your information describing the tapes contents, such as "Set A," "Recipes," or "Important Client Stuff."

DataSafe Container

Recommendation: Okay, if you are reading this and live in Ogunquit, Maine, and are wondering whether there's a DataSafe around the corner, think again. Move to Boston. Just kidding. The folks at DataSafe are a member of ACRC (American Commercial Records Centers) and can make cross-recommendations for those of you in different cities across the country. DataSafe can be contacted at:

DataSafe
PO Box 7794
San Francisco, CA 94120

Phone: (415) 875-3800

FAX: (415) 875-7495

Chapter 8:
Da Budget for da Risks and da Implementation Plan

Why did I write the chapter heading that way? Because I had a client who would always say, "Is da budget for preventin' da problem cheaper dan da breakdown?" He was from Chicago—from Winnetka, actually. I called him "Big Noise from Winnetka." I'm very far away, so I can say this. Anyway, another thing to consider when you are thinking of the potential risks and how to protect the computers and devices from those risks is what it costs for that protection. What does it mean if the cost of the protection is more than the cost of replacement after the problem hits? Remembering that the business of business is business, any time one decision costs more than another, you can figure that the bosses and bean counters will want to go with the cheaper one. Anything that costs more to protect than it is worth probably won't be protected. On the other hand, if you show that the worth of something is massive and that the cost to secure it is minimal, the product will definitely receive funding for protection.

This chapter is presented in narrative form. I'm using this as a test to see whether you like this kind of writing. It grew out of a discussion with a theologian friend (here's to you, PW) who is into "narratives with pockets." Narratives are nothing new; the pockets he is talking about are cross-references. So, let's take a walk through a small site (based on a real one) and examine what it takes to put together a budget and implementation plan for our network in question.

INTRODUCTION TO OUR SAMPLE NETWORK

Welcome to Acme Rubber Chickens, Inc. This narrative will walk you through the process that the network administrator at this small company would have to take to create his backup plan. It will include everything except writing the scripts themselves. Those scripts will then be written in either ARCserve or Retrospect, depending on whatever software you choose. However, before the scripts can be written, the backup and prevention plan has to be created, and the bud-

Acme *Rubber Chickens, Inc.*

get has to be presented and approved. Therefore, we will walk through the entire process that should take place. This should give you a good tie-in to everything else we've written. Where appropriate, we will refer you to the rest of the book so that you can go back and review the in-depth processes (and whys and whatfors) if necessary.

The reason that the network administrator is conducting the risk analysis is that it is a part of his job ("The Backup Plan Coordinator will develop the company policy for the protection of information assets for [whatever your department is called]. The coordinator shall set a yearly budget which is approved by [whoever has the final say on budgets in your company or department]." on page 477). He has assembled a team of players within the company for the job, including himself, the budget director, and key members of each work team in the company. The reason for the budget director is obvious. The reason for the key team members is that the network administrator will need to check with them on an ongoing basis during the risk analysis, and get their input into how long they think that they can do without some of the critical network services in case of an emergency. Their input will help him create the implementation plan.

Risk Analysis for Acme Chicken, Inc.

Remember the earlier section, "Finding What You Have (and Where It's At)" on page 22, about how to find the computers on the network? The first thing our fearless network administrator did was to create a network map using LANsurveyor. That map is shown on the right. It shows that there are three routers, two of which are Compatible Systems MicroRouter 1000Rs, capable of 128K Frame Relay, which is what he is using in network 1. Network 2–3 and network 6–7 are both regular Ethernet networks. Notice that the Acme

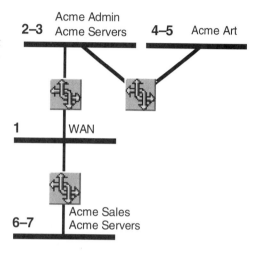

Servers zone appears in both of them. If you don't know why, see our books about network management and network design, *Managing AppleTalk Networks* and *Designing AppleTalk Networks*. The reason network 4–5 exists is that they wanted a separate, secure network from the rest of them. That is the art network. Users from the other zones cannot see the servers in the Acme Art zone. This is accomplished using the Compatible Systems RiscRouter 3000. Again, if you need to know more about that, too, see our network design and management books.

Once he had his network map, he then used SaberLAN to create a networking table of all workstations and the networks to which they were assigned (see "Install Information-Gathering Software" on 43). He ended up with the following:

- Information about each storage device on the computers in both offices, including the amount of total storage space and free space, and an estimation of the percent of information change that happens daily on each computer.

- The type of network connection for each computer, whether LocalTalk or Ethernet, for the throughput planning portion of the backup analysis.

- Other network information to help find the computer when looking to back it up remotely, such as the computer's name and home zone.

The next step, once armed with this information, is to walk the network and find out where the computers are located physically, rather than logically, within the network setting.

Walking the Network

This is the physical layout of both of Acme Chicken's offices, located in San Francisco about 10 miles from each other. The Townsend Street office is the office that holds most of the administrative people and designers, and the Geary Street office is mainly the sales office (it takes a special kind of person to sell rubber chickens, you know).

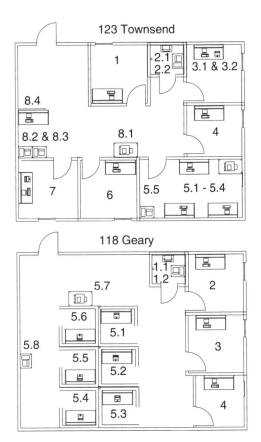

The network administrator marked each of the rooms on the floor plan with a number. This would make it easier to physically locate the computers in case something were to go wrong with the backup or a computer needed restoration. As the rooms are numbered in a clockwise fashion, so are each of the computers within the rooms. Again, this is to facilitate locating the devices later.

Creating the Backup Capacity Plan

While walking the network, the administrator gathered enough information about each of the workstations and servers he encountered to create the backup plan capacity chart. We originally told how to create and fill in this chart in the section "Information You Need to Know" on page 38. Here is a sample of the first and last page of the chart the administrator created while walking the network:

Capacity & Throughput Planning Chart

Computer Name	AppleTalk Connection	Zone	Volume Name	Vol. Cap	Free Space	% Change	Daily Backup	Volume Backup Date	Type	Physical Location
Joe's Mac	EtherTalk 2.0	Acme Admin	Joe's Drive	120	20	0.05	6.00		Standard Fixed Disk	1, Townsend Bldg
Townsend Main	EtherTalk 2.0	Acme Servers	Striped Projects	2000	975	0.05	100.00		Striped	2, Townsend Bldg
	EtherTalk 2.0	Acme Servers	System Volume	128	64	0.05	6.40		Mirrored	2, Townsend Bldg
	EtherTalk 2.0	Acme Servers	2 Gig Dev.	2000	600	0.05	100.00		Large Format	2, Townsend Bldg
Sam's PowerMac	EtherTalk 2.0	Acme Admin	Internal HD	280	100	0.05	14.00		Standard Fixed Disk	3, Townsend Bldg
Sam's PowerBook	LocalTalk (printer port)	Acme Admin	Internal HD	120	84	0.10	12.00		Standard Fixed Disk	3, Townsend Bldg
Sandy's Computer	EtherTalk 2.0	Acme Admin	Inthernal HD	500	100	0.05	25.00		Standard Fixed Disk	4, Townsend Bldg
Jack's Cool Computer	EtherTalk 2.0	Acme Art	Macitosh HD	2000	120	0.05	100.00		Large Format	5, Townsend Bldg
Tommy Boy	EtherTalk 2.0	Acme Art	Macintosh HD	2000	500	0.05	100.00		Large Format	5, Townsend Bldg
	EtherTalk 2.0	Acme Art	CD-R	2000	650	0.25	500.00		Large Format	5, Townsend Bldg
	EtherTalk 2.0	Acme Art	Various	128	100	0.50	64.00		Removeable	5, Townsend Bldg
Fred the Bear	EtherTalk 2.0	Acme Art	TheDrive	2000	848	0.10	200.00		Large Format	5, Townsend Bldg
DPI & Production Server	EtherTalk 2.0	Acme Art	System Volume	128	40	0.05	6.40		Standard Fixed Disk	5, Townsend Bldg
	EtherTalk 2.0	Acme Art	Internal Drive	872	600	0.05	43.60		Standard Fixed Disk	5, Townsend Bldg
	EtherTalk 2.0	Acme Art	R51	4032	2000	0.05	201.60		RAID5	5, Townsend Bldg
	EtherTalk 2.0	Acme Art	R52	4032	1000	0.05	201.60		RAID5	5, Townsend Bldg

Capacity & Throughput Planning Chart

Notes:

Add the total of all **LocalTalk** server capacities (Size in Meg column) and enter that figure into the Capacity in Mbytes cell to the right. **200**

Multiply the Capacity in Mbytes cell by 1.16 to allow for verification (we highly recommend that you use verification). **232**

Divide the Total Transmission amount by the 51 Mbytes per hour throughput rate to obtain the estimated transmission time. **4.55**

Add the total of all **Ethernet** server capacities (Size in Meg column) and enter that figure into the Capacity in Mbytes cell to the right. **26098**

Multiply the Capacity in Mbytes cell by 1.16 to allow for verification (we highly recommend that you use verification). **30273.68**

Divide the Total Transmission amount by the 326 Mbytes per hour throughput rate to obtain the estimated transmission time. **92.86**

Add the Total **LocalTalk** backup transmission time (along with the LocalTalk to Ethernet Router additional time), and the **Ethernet** transmission time (along with the Backbone Router additional time) for a total backup time estimate. **97.41**

This calculation will be done for you by adding the change rate for each computer together, calculating both the Ethernet and LocalTalk transmission times, and then creating a summary in this field. **6.64**

Add the total **LocalTalk** and **Ethernet** capacity figures together, along with teh daily backup cacualtions, then divide that number by 6.4 (DAT Compressed tapes offer 6.4 Gig of storage per tape) Gigabytes to obtain the number of tapes you'll need to backup this info. **All fractions should be rounded up to the next highest integer.** **6**

Front and Back Pages of the Backup Capacity Planning Chart

Completing the Risk and Prevention Analysis

As the network administrator walked the site to determine the backup needs of the computers, he also walked the site to determine other potentially vital equipment (see "Define Critical Network Operations" on page 51) and other potentially vital operations (see how to "Define Critical Company Functions" on page 57). From there, a full table of equipment was put together, listing all high-risk equipment in the office. The administrator listed *all* the equipment in the office so that someone other than the administrator could point to a piece of gear and say, "That is really important, too." Even though the workstations and Power-Books were listed as generic "desktop or mobile devices," this at least causes the reviewer to question the item and to maybe suggest adding it to the special priority list.

From this walk-through and "talk-through" with the users at each site, he generated a table of equipment that is vitally important to the company's well-being and normal functioning. Once the equipment was identified, the five basic prevention categories ("Physical Security of Wiring Gear and Connection Devices" on page 80, "Physical Security of Computers and Printers" on page 81, "Stupid User Tricks" on page 83, "Dealing with Failure of Wiring Gear and Connection Devices" on page 94, "Electrical Prevention (Why You Should Use a UPS)" on page 105, and "Earthquakes, Fires, Floods, Tornadoes, Bombs, and Disgruntled Postal Workers" on page 121) were covered, along with the one-time and yearly costs associated with each category.

Note: To help you with this, we have created a very simple three-part form that you can print and fill out manually, or you can use Informed Designer, which is what we use when working with the form. This table, which represents the budget as well, is what should be presented for approval. The first page lists all the equipment, equipment locations, and how long it can be down (relative to our earlier chart; see "Cost of Downtime" on page 9). The second page shows three types of risk prevention, all carrying one-time price tags. The third page shows two more types of risk prevention, but these carry yearly price tags. This is effective when planning a budget or presenting to a committee. It is compact, precise, and comprehensive.

So, with printed tables in hand and a really wonderful book from Network Frontiers called *The Complete Guide to Macintosh Backup Management, Second Edition,* to be used as *the* reference guide (nice plug, huh, Chuck?), the administrator went into his meeting, spent 20 minutes there, and had the budget approved so he could move on to the procedures development stage. (Hey, it *could* happen!)

Critical Network Operations Risk Analysis & Prevention

Intial Device Analysis

FileServer 8150	Townsend Main	2, Townsend	Essential	
Cannon Fiery RIP	Color1	5, Townsend	Hot	
File Server 8150	OPI & Production Server	5, Townsend	Essential	
File Server 8150	DB & Art	8, Townsend	Hot	
Quadra 700	Main Mail	8, Townsend	Hot	
MicroRouter 1000R	Townsend WAN	2, Townsend	Hot	config files are stored in townsend main
MicroRouter 1000R	Geary WAN	1, Geary	Hot	config files are stored in geary main
File Server 6150	Sales DB & Mail	5, Geary	Essential	
File Server 8150	Geary Main	2, Geary	Essential	
LW 16/600	Geary LW	5, Geary	Hot	
Wiring Rack	RACK at Townsend	2, Townsend		
Wiring Rack	RACK at Geary	1, Geary		
9 Desktop CPUs	Various on desk	at Townsend	In-Progress	
2 mobile CPUs	Various mobile	at Townsend	In-Progress	
3 Desktop CPUs	Various on desk	at Geary	In-Progress	
6 mobile CPUs	Various mobile	at Geary	In-Progress	

Critical Network Operations Risk Analysis & Prevention

Planning info, page 2

Townsend Main	Security Kit	$15	RIP-TIE bundle	$7	950 VA UPS	$800
Color1	Security Kit	$15	RIP-TIE bundle	$7	300 VA UPS	$179
OPI & Production Server	Security Kit	$15	RIP-TIE bundle	$7	950 VA UPS	$800
DB & Art	Security Kit	$15	RIP-TIE bundle	$7	660 VA UPS	$600
Main Mail	Security Kit	$15	RIP-TIE bundle	$7	660 VA UPS	$600
Townsend WAN					See RACK at Townsend	
Geary WAN					See RACK at Geary	
Sales DB & Mail	Security Kit	$15	RIP-TIE bundle	$7	950 VA UPS	$800
Geary Main	Security Kit	$15	RIP-TIE bundle	$7	950 VA UPS	$800
Geary LW	Security Kit	$15	RIP-TIE bundle	$7		
RACK at Townsend					1300 VA UPS	$1,000
RACK at Geary					1300 VA UPS	$1,000
Various on desk	Security Kit	$15	RIP-TIE bundle	$7		
Various mobile						
Various on desk	Security Kit	$15	RIP-TIE bundle	$7		
Various mobile						

Critical Network Operations Risk Analysis & Prevention

Planning info, page 3

Townsend Main	Will shift CPU to MainMail, Mirrored HD, reg backup	$75	Offsite Storage per year	$1,860
Color1	Same Day, Onsite Service Contract - yearly	$350		
OPI & Production Server	Will shift CPU to MainMail, RAID5, Dup portions	$75	See Townsend Main	
DB & Art	Will shift CPU to MainMail, Mirrored HD, reg backup	$75	See Townsend Main	
Main Mail	Will shift CPU to DB & Art - Extra HD offline, backup	$1,750	See Townsend Main	
Townsend WAN	Cross-ship Swap okayed with Compatible			
Geary WAN	Cross-ship Swap okayed with Compatible			
Sales DB & Mail	Will shift CPU to Geary Main, Mirrored, reg backup	$1,750	Offsite Storage per year	$1,860
Geary Main	Will shift CPU to Sales DB & Mail, reg backup	$75	See Sales DB & Main	
Geary LW	Same Day, Onsite Service Contract - yearly	$150		
RACK at Townsend	No extra protection - all gear readily available			
RACK at Geary	No extra protection - all gear readily available			
Various on desk	Regular Backups	$675		
Various mobile	"catch as catch can" backups	$150		
Various on desk	Regular Backups	$225		
Various mobile	"catch as catch can" backups	$450		

Three-Part Risk Analysis, Prevention, and Budget Form

PART FOUR: ON-LINE REDUNDANT STORAGE PROCEDURES

I'm not going into a lot of detail here about how great and wonderful RAID systems are. Yes, they are great. However, listen to me, and listen to me good:

Although RAID is great for added protection, do not use it instead of a formal backup strategy!

Are we all on the same sheet of music here? Good. Let's get down to business then. There are three types of RAID that we recommend: RAID 0, RAID 1, and RAID 5. If you don't know what they are, read this section. You will learn not only what they are but also which is most appropriate for your needs. Just know this: If you are going to use RAID 5, then:

Use the MicroNet RAIDbank for RAID 5.

We think it's awesome. It will not truly increase speed (it isn't supposed to), but it will give you the level of protection you need.

Don't Bore Me with the Details . . .

- Use mirroring if you want a fast way to bring your computer's data back up if the drive crashes.

- Use RAID 5 if you don't want the drive to go down. There is a big difference between the two.

- Mirror drives must be a "pair," because excess data on the larger of the two drives can't be used for much.

- Expect a small (around 1.5–2%) reduction in speed when mirroring. If using MicroNet's RAIDbank, there is almost no reduction in speed.

- Apple's RAID software and MicroNet's RAIDbank don't offer any notification when a drive fails, such as a page or e-mail. You have to monitor this yourself. This is a major flaw in both systems, and both companies should feel your wrath over it.

CHAPTER 9:
INTRODUCTION TO RAID

This chapter was co-written by Lynn Heiberger, our Managing Partner.

RAID: Apple's manual for their implementation of the technology says that it stands for Redundant Array of Independent Disks. Go figure why the U.C. Berkeley research group that coined the acronym thought of that name; the last thing this application does is make multiple disks independent. RAID makes them interdependent, as they are dependent on one another for either mirroring or striping (as we are about to show you).

RAID is also said to mean Redundant Array of Inexpensive Devices, which is more appropriate, although the *Apple RAID Software Administrator's Guide* says something different. Even with this goofy name, however, Apple RAID is a manageable tool with some good features and is sufficient for the needs of most networks.

Now, if you go all-out, biggest-boy-on-the-block crazy, you will want to consider a third-party solution from the MicroNet folks: the RAIDbank. We nearly broke our backs just dragging one into the office, so we figure something that heavy must be good! In fact, it is, and we'll talk about setting it up, too.

Why Set up RAID?

You may want to set up RAID for two simple reasons. First, you can use RAID to write the same data on two different disks at all times, a process called mirroring. If a server's hard disk crashes while mirroring information, it is only a brief inconvenience instead of an expensive and perhaps economically fatal loss in productivity for your network users. The second reason to use RAID is to improve data access performance through a process called striping. This lets your users spend less time waiting for the server to deliver up their data.

RAID is governed by a few international standards that correspond to the level of performance they offer. We'll talk about three here:

Level 0 This provides larger volume formats through striping, a technique that spreads parts of files across more than one disk. The designation "0" is unintentionally appropriate, because that is how much protection against data loss it provides. This level has no redundancy. It is only used to create a larger volume from a set of smaller volume drives.

Level 1 This provides data redundancy through mirroring, a technique that puts duplicate data on more than one disk. It does not provide a boost in performance.

Apple RAID software supports RAID Levels 0 and 1.

Level 5 This provides both data redundancy through mirroring and larger volume sizes through striping and simultaneous input/output. RAID Level 5 is the best-of-both-worlds option.

The MicroNet RAIDbank supports Level 5, as well Levels 0 and 1.

So, let's start RAIDing!

SETTING UP APPLE RAID SOFTWARE

If you can walk and chew gum at the same time, you can use Apple RAID. It is an easy application to implement, use, and understand . . . as long as you don't use the manual! You must be using a Workgroup Server 6150, 8150, or 9150 with the System 7.1.2 or later. RAID does not work on older servers. It has to work with PowerMac computers. You can't use it with an 680X0 computer. In addition, the drives used with RAID must be 200 MB or larger. You can have between two and four of them. As far as basic settings go, you just need to have virtual memory turned off.

There are three possible formats for an Apple RAID volume: striped, mirrored, and standard. Striped (RAID Level 0) and mirrored (RAID Level 1) volumes we have already discussed. Standard volumes are just like regular volumes. Yawn.

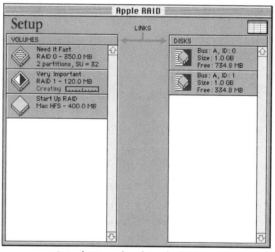

Striped, Mirrored, and Standard Volumes

Volumes can encompass one or more disks. Think of them as "virtual" hard drives. Disks are what they are, individual hard drives: nothing virtual about them. Disks can be divided into partitions. Partitions reside in the same unit of space but appear separately. One disk can have multiple partitions and through striping, one volume can span several disks.

There is a way to utilize this information to efficiently set up and use RAID and, lucky you, it is accomplished in eight easy steps.

Step 1: Back up All Your Drives

The warning in the next dialog box is no joke. As you proceed with the creation of your RAID volumes, you will see it for yourself.

⚠ Initializing a disk for Apple RAID deletes any data stored on the disk. Is it OK to proceed and delete existing data?

Cancel   OK

Bleep, Bleep, Danger, Will Robinson!

Back up all the data you don't want to permanently go bye-bye before proceeding. This should include your System Folder, which you will need to reinstall.

Then shut down the server.

Step 2: Restart from the CD

RAID comes on the WorkGroup Server software CD along with the system installers. Place the CD in the CD-ROM drive and restart the server while holding down the C key. This ensures that the Macintosh boots and runs from the CD.

Step 3: Launch RAID

RAID Icon

With the RAID CD as the startup disk, launch the RAID application. The Apple RAID main window appears.

Step 4: Initialize Drives

To initialize drives, select the hard drives you will be using with RAID on the right (Disks) side of the Apple RAID main window . . .

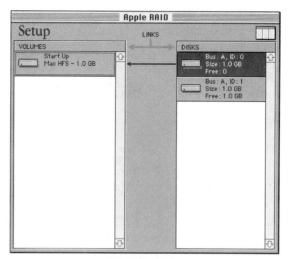

Uninitialized Drives

... then choose **Initialize** from the **Disk** menu. Next, take out your knitting. This process takes a while. When you are finished, you will see the newly initialized disks represented by new Apple RAID icons.

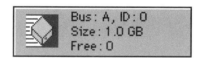

Icon of Disk Initialized with Apple RAID

Step 5: Create a Startup Volume

Choose the server's usual startup disk on the right side of the window, then select **New** from the **Volume** menu. The Create New Volume window appears.

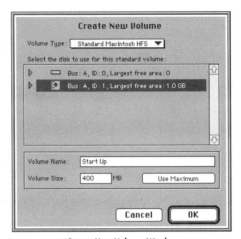

Create New Volume Window

We encourage a mirrored startup volume, like the one we will create here, but you can create a standard volume as well. A mirrored startup volume is useful in that if the startup drive fails, your System Folder with all the extensions and control panels configured the way you set them will still be available on the secondary volume. Choose this in the **Volume Type** field.

Volume Type Pop-Up

In the **Volume Size** field, type in a large enough size for the data you expect to install on your startup volume. This will be a percentage of the amount of free space that already appears in the **Volume Size** field, or it can be the whole thing, if you prefer.

Enter an appropriate name for the drive in the **Volume Name** field. *Drive of Death* is not a suitable name, unless, of course, you are the local mortician or coroner.

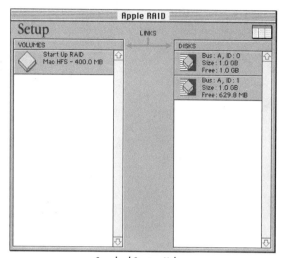

Standard Startup Volume

Step 6: Restore System Folder to Startup Volume

Restore the System Folder from your backup to the new startup volume. If you are starting from scratch, you can use one of the appropriate installer aliases on the CD to install a fresh system.

Step 7: Install Apple RAID on Startup Volume

Launch Install Apple RAID on the CD alias to have this software added to the System Folder on your new startup volume.

RAID CD

Remember, at this point the Macintosh is still running from the RAID CD. You now need to change over to your startup volume from the RAID CD for actual startup using the Startup Disk control panel.

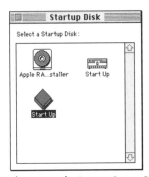

Switching to Regular Drive as Startup Disk

Step 8: Restart!

Finally, restart and reboot Apple RAID for further volume creation. You will find that it has been moved to the Apple Menu Items folder within the System Folder.

Before you get cranking on striping and mirroring, go buy a couple of new magazines at Fred's Wirehead Emporium. Volume creation takes 2–5 minutes, depending on your configuration, and, as you have already noticed, initialization can take more than 15 minutes per drive. I know I could have told you sooner, but then you never would have started.

RAID volume creation can be a lengthy process.

SPREADSHEET CITY

Golly gee whiz, we just wouldn't be network administrators if we didn't have another gosh darn spreadsheet, now would we? The spreadsheet in the next couple of illustrations helps to organize your volumes. Apple has included it with its Apple Workgroup Server bundle. We have made an electronic version of it for you that can be found on the CD that ships with this book. We think ours is better.

Selecting Volume Types and Sizes

First, list your volumes in the **Volume name** fields. Next, decide whether easy access to large volumes is a priority. If the answer is yes, stripe them. If something is vitally important, the volume should be mirrored.

Just a little hint: The CEO will be delighted if she can read her information easier, but she will fire you if she cannot access her volume and the backup tape is in the bank vault. The bottom line is safety before glory. If something is neither needed quickly nor of an essential nature, it should be made a standard volume. File this form along with your backup planner form so that if you need to restore a server that has been RAIDed, you'll know how to reformat the hard drives.

Select Volume Types and Sizes			
Volume name	Volume type and size		
	Mirrored	Striped	Standard
Start Up			400 MB
Very Important	100 MB		
Need it Right Away		720 MB	
The Boss's Stuff	200 MB		
George's Humongous File		1.2 GB	
Staff Files			1 GB
Subtotal		x2	
TOTAL **(Minimum required disk capacity)**	600 MB	1.92 GB	1.4 GB

Spreadsheet for Generating Striped, Mirrored, or Standard Volumes

After the size is entered, the minimum required volume capacity should be computed. In this example, 3.92 GB, or 3,920 MB, is the total. We are in luck. We have two internal 1-GB drives and two external 2-GB drives.

Assigning Partitions for RAID Volumes

Now, assign your partitions for the volumes. In the next table, first enter the capacity of each drive under the disk's SCSI bus ID. Then enter the partition sizes needed. This is carried over from the first table on the top half of the thin line within the fields (this is a dotted line in Apple's chart). The number below the thin line is the balance of space left on the drive after that.

There is method to my madness. I kept the two striped volumes on their own drives to maximize speed. In addition, I kept the data moving along two data paths by using an external drive and an internal drive.

| Assigning Partitions for Apple RAID Volumes | | | | | | | | | | | | | |
| Internal SCSI bus ID (with disk capacity in MB) | | | | | | | External SCSI bus ID (w/ disk capacity in MB) | | | | | | |
0	1	2*	3*	4	5	6	0	1	2*	3*	4	5	6
1000	1000						2000	2000					
400													
600													
100								100					
500								1900					
	360						360						
	640						1640						
200								200					
300								1700					
	600						600						
	40						1040						
								1000					
								700					

Spreadsheet for Assigning Partitions

The main reason for striping *George's Humongous File* (first table) was to give him easy access to the file, without having to split the file. I was also able to give him speed by not bogging down the drive with standard or mirrored volumes. This leaves the buffers more readily available for fast reads and writes.

My internal drive on SCSI bus ID number 0 is faster than my drive on external SCSI bus ID number 1. For the startup drive (the natives get restless if I can't restart the server quickly) and all the mirrored volumes, I chose the faster drive as my primary drive. I put the standard volume, named *Staff Files* (first table), on the slower drive, as this volume is used the least.

Now that you have set up your standard RAID volumes and filled out your spreadsheets, it's time to set up those volumes you have decided to stripe or mirror.

PROCEDURE FOR STRIPING, OR RAID LEVEL 0

To create a striped volume, simply select **New** from the **Volume** menu and choose **Striped - RAID 0** from the **Volume Type** pop-up menu. You may choose 2–4 RAID-initialized drives to hold your striped volume.

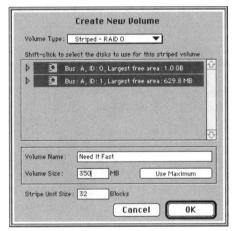

Creating a Striped Volume

A striped partition can be as small as 10 MB, but the total volume size cannot exceed 2 GB for CPUs with System 6 or 7 and 4 GB for CPUs with System 7.5 or later. Enter the total volume size and the name and click **OK**. You have created a striped volume.

If you want an up-close and personal look at your partitions, click the spreadsheet icon in the right-hand corner. Is this fun or what?!

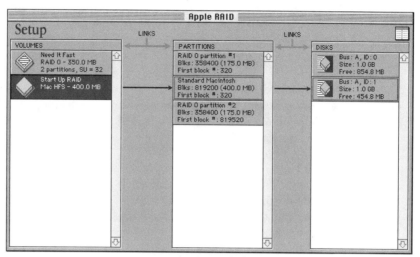

A Striped and a Standard Volume

There is one reason to stripe if you have only internal drives: to spread a large volume over multiple drives while maintaining the illusion of having its data contained on one volume. Where one drive would not suffice, you can now use RAID to keep your large volumes appearing intact, instead of chopping them up and placing the subdocuments (anyone seen the new version of Word? Arrrrgghghh!) on different drives. RAID sets up the pointers so it appears that you are working on one volume.

PROCEDURE FOR MIRRORING, OR RAID LEVEL 1

Since you are making a copy of a volume when you mirror, you need to select a volume with enough room on it to hold the "reflection." Begin by selecting a disk in the right of the Setup window and choosing **New** from the **Volume** menu, as we did earlier.

In the Create New Volume window, select the faster of two drives as your primary disk, since that is the drive from which you will be reading. Next, shift-click to include the disk intended for the mirror, or nonprimary drive. Give your volume a name and a size as we did in the startup drive setup section. Click **OK** to complete the creation of your mirrored volume.

In addition to creating your mirrored volume from scratch, you can create a mirrored volume from a standard volume if it has been initialized by the RAID application. Simply select the standard volume in the left side of the Setup window and choose **Create Mirrored Volume** from the **Volume** menu. The Select Mirror Disk window appears. Select a destination for the mirrored volume with the necessary space available.

Selecting a Mirror Drive

There is also a parameter option for mirroring that appears when you click **OK**. If you are doing many other processes, decrease the **I/O Rate** and **I/O Size** settings in the Mirror Create Parameters window. If you are doing the nocturnal thing and nobody else is around, you can blast through with larger I/O hits.

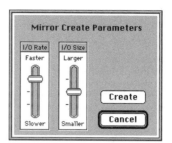

Mirror Creation Parameters

Mirroring has two major perks. It is easy to restore (no DAT tape to mess around with), and the information on the volume is as old as the last write, not the last backup. Mirrored data should be your crucial data. Although backing up on DAT tapes is cheap, using hard drive space as a storage mechanism is not. I will let you do the math on this one.

Speedy RAID

Making your read/write functions faster has great appeal. Just imagine: "Hey baby, want your drives to bust a move?" We would all save lots of time if we could cut our read/write time in half. It would mean a new breakthrough in faster processors and software that would increase the capabilities of drive heads.

But is RAID really faster? The answer is: RAID is faster only if your network is faster. If you are running LocalTalk, have less than Category Five cabling, or never dust your SCSI bus, a FAST SCSI card should not be your next purchase. However, if you are successfully running fast Ethernet (100 Mbps), you can reduce your read/write times by more than half with the implementation of RAID Level 0. You will garner the best performance by using identical drives identically configured and by running off separate SCSI buses with FAST SCSI cards. It all boils down to money versus time.

In conclusion, I can give you the same answer I give to students when they ask me about moving to fiber: When you have your network perfected and everything is running at 100 Mbps, then come to me about increasing your network speed with fiber as opposed to twisted-pair. Take our class or buy our book *Designing Apple-Talk Networks* to figure out that analogy.

A Few Rules

Remember, rules are made because you just have to draw the line somewhere. We can't have you wild and wacky network administrator types up in the night making 4-GB mirrored volumes, now can we? Here are a few guidelines to follow when thinking about using RAID:

- RAID volumes cannot be larger than 2 GB for CPUs running System 6 or 7 or 4 GB for CPUs running System 7.5 or later.

- There can be no more than 10 Apple RAID volumes per server.

- There can be no more than eight partitions per disk.

- The default for stripe unit size is 32 blocks. Increasing or decreasing this may improve performance, but the default is acceptable in most cases. Remember your file sizes!

- Keep your striped volumes on one set of disks and your mirrored volumes on another set of disks.

- Put more primary mirrored volumes on the faster drive, but balance the load so that not all volumes are being read from the same drive. In other words, if drive A is two times faster than drive B, put 2/3 of your primary volumes on drive A and 1/3 of your primary volumes on drive B.

- There is no hard-and-fast rule for striping configurations, but there are some guidelines. If your network is greased lightening, take advantage of as many drives as are available for striping. The more buffers available on drives, the more space you have for writing.

RAID Recovery Procedures

OR
Life May Be Like a Box of Chocolates But Not Always a Bowl of Cherries

There are downsides to RAID Level 1 and RAID Level 0. For Level 1, mirroring slightly degrades performance during the write phase. However, the degree to which mirroring degrades performance is the same degree to which striping improves it. Don't sweat the minimal degradation if your data is important.

With regards to RAID Level 0, the biggest downside is the increased possibility of corruption, since there are two or more disks being used for striped volumes. Also, we did not see any great improvement in speed when striping to the internal drives on the Server 9150. Unless you are dealing with large volumes that need to be spread out over several drives, I would wait a few versions before striping on the internal drives of a 9150. The speed factor does not affect performance improvement enough to warrant running the risk of having to restore an entire volume if just a section on one disk is corrupted.

Life After RAID

What if you don't like having RAID drives? Tough. No, really, although RAID does not have a feature that allows you to un-RAID drives, many third-party applications or the application that came with your external drives can be used to restore your drives back to their original format. In case you forgot, this is what the RAID main window should look like when your drives are un-RAIDed and the system has been reinstalled.

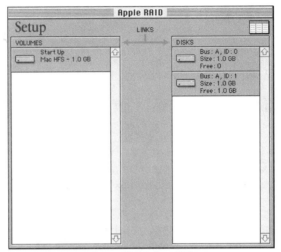

Server 9150 Before RAID

If you do un-RAID your drives, make a copy of the volumes on a non-RAID drive for retrieval, or you can simply do a restore from your backup. Dantz's Retrospect and Cheyenne's ARCserve account for restoring to either a RAID configuration or a normal configuration.

Recovering from a Crisis

Here are some potential crisis situations that could occur while using RAID, as well as some possible solutions.

Restoring RAID

My entire system went down and I need to restore. When I do a restore with Retrospect or ARCserve, will my volumes be rebuilt in the same form—striped and mirrored—as that in which I created them? Will they be distributed to the correct drives?

No. In this case, you are out of luck. When restoring volumes that have been backed up with Retrospect Remote or other software, the volumes are restored but not their RAID configuration. The Preferences folder for RAID is not saved, and thus there is no way to know what went where. Bottom line: Make a screen shot of the Apple RAID Setup window each time you change your setup, and keep a hard copy in a safe place.

If you need to restore, first reconfigure the drives exactly as they were configured before the crash, naming all the volumes as they were named, with all the drives being used in the same configuration. You can not just pop in the DAT tape and the volumes will be restored as RAID Levels 0 and 1 on the appropriate drives. In short, you need to start from scratch.

No Drive Available

I see the drive, but RAID doesn't. What's wrong?

Is it plugged in? Is it turned on? Are all the SCSI cables, buses, cards, and drives in working order? Is there a terminator in the last SCSI bus of the chain? If yes, then check for duplicate SCSI bus ID numbers.

Also, don't forget that SCSI bus ID number 2 is reserved for DAT drives and SCSI bus ID number 3 is reserved for CD-ROM drives (internal for 9150, external for 8150, and the 6150 has only one bus). SCSI ID number 0 is reserved for the internal drive on the 6150 and the 8150. The 9150 reserves SCSI ID numbers 0 and 1 for the two internal drives. Once you have rectified the problem, restart the server and relaunch RAID.

Can't Create New Volumes

RAID is rejecting my choices for creating a new volume. Why?

One more time. You must select two or more RAIDed drives with enough space available to create either a mirrored or a striped volume. RAID does not default to drives. You must select and configure them. Reread "Spreadsheet City" on page 147, if you've forgotten how to do this.

Also, you cannot make a mirror of a shared volume while it is in use. This is the case for AppleShare or Macintosh file sharing. The manual didn't mention anything about striped volume creation from a shared volume, but it would be unwise to create any RAID volume while the files of the volume are in use elsewhere. That is why network administrators are nocturnal. We must work while the rest of the world sleeps.

Rebuilding Fails

Why isn't my rebuild working?

You need to rebuild to a working drive. RAID does not fix drives. It only tells you that there is a problem. Also, don't try to write a mirrored volume to the primary drive. This kind of defeats the purpose of having backup information on another drive, doesn't it?

If One Drive in the Mirror Fails . . .

The RAID icon is flashing and everything is plugged in and working—gulp. You launch RAID. Phew, it is not a bad striped partition that is missing, but one of the drives designated for mirrored volumes has gone bad. All that hard work has paid off. You now have to recover your mirrored volumes.

For a **Failed** error, first rebuild your drive using the RAID application that created them. An **Out of Sync** error means that someone did something silly, like shutting down the server improperly (see Server Etiquette—just kidding) or an Act of God occurred, like a power outage. In this case, you need only to rebuild the ailing volumes. Their icons will be flashing in the RAID application window.

To rebuild a mirrored volume, select the flashing volume and choose **Rebuild** from the Volume menu. If the disk is **Out of Sync**, RAID will know what disk to select. Otherwise, you need to select the disk you want for the reflection of your mirror. Once again, you can reset the parameters for small or large I/O size, depending on how quickly you want to rebuild.

PROCEDURES FOR **RAID 5**

If you need access to your information no matter what (unless, of course, the building is burning or is under about four tons of rubble), you need RAID 5. RAID 5 allows for drives to die midstream and repairs the information on the fly. RAID 5 drive makers state that if a drive dies, there is enough parity information in the other drives to rebuild the files as the users request them. Is this for real? I'll tell you—I tested it. I set up MicroNet's RAIDbank for RAID 5, striped across four drives. I then wrote a 6 7-MB QuickTime movie to the drives—the original Apple commercial. I started playing it across the network to my computer, and then I removed one of the drives . . . midstream. Guess what? The movie played. It was a bit rougher, but it played. I couldn't believe it. So, I got some beers, invited over some geek friends, and we kept pulling the drive out and running the test for an hour. Fascinating.

Recommendations

If you are going to set up a RAID 5 system and are wondering which of the file servers to put it on, follow our recommendation and use an 8150 with a RAID-bank system from MicroNet. If Apple ships a server version of the 9500 before this book is outdated, then move to that. It's the 604 processor version of the 8150 (601) processor, with more features, but the same basic build.

8150 with MicroNet RAIDbank

This is our favorite setup for building a solid, well-protected server. The server also comes with a really fast DDS-2 DAT tape drive that can be used to back up the RAIDbank's hard drives. Also, make sure that you buy an extra drive for the RAIDbank, in case one of them fails.

Setting up MicroNet RAIDbank Software

Apple's implementation of RAID Levels 0 and 1 is probably as far into the technology as most organizations need to go. If, however, you want all the power and performance your Apple Workgroup Server can muster, MicroNet Technology, Inc., offers an impress-me-to-death option that supports RAID 5 in the form of the RAIDbank Disk Array.

The RAIDbank's 44-pound tower contains up to six hard drives and two power supplies. You can buy rack-mount and desktop configurations, but we think the desktop one looks cooler, being about the same size as the Apple Workgroup Server 9150. These drives, ranging in capacities from 510 MB to 2.04 GB each, are stacked against a dual or single I/O SCSI backplane that permits them to be "hot-swapped." If a drive goes down, you just yank it out and pop in another one from the shelf. The dual power supplies are redundant, support voltages from all over the world, and can do load sharing. Finally, you can lock the darn thing.

The RAIDbank we'll talk about here is attached to the Apple Workgroup Server 8150 or 9150 through a FAST and WIDE (16-bit) SCSI-2 NuBus accelerator card made by ATTO Technology, Inc. This actively terminated SiliconExpress IV card is said to outperform the Macintosh's built-in SCSI port by 1,400% with transfer rates as high as 20 MB per second. AppleShare can use the NuBus card's parallel processing capabilities to feed data to the disks and the network simultaneously. In addition, the SiliconExpress card's use of busmastering lets it shoot data straight into RAM without any pit stops at the CPU.

Other SCSI accelerators that work include:

- ATTO SiliconExpress II

- BusLogic BT-848

- FWB Jackhammer

- 68000 RAID Warrior

There may be others that will work, as well. In the future, MicroNet will be releasing plug-ins to its RAIDbank software that will support accelerator cards. Of course, the RAIDbank also works with the Macintosh's built-in SCSI port and dual SCSI ports supported by SCSI Manager 4.3. Remember, though, if you are using the native SCSI interface off an 8150 server as opposed to the ATTO card, you can only utilize four addtitional SCSI ports as two of them are in use by the server's DAT drive and CD-ROM drive.

Hooking up your SiliconExpress and RAIDbank is best left to the manufacturer's manuals, as it will depend on the options you purchased. Be sure and back up your server before you touch a thing, just in case. Both products also come with software, too. We will discuss what you should do with this software in the following sections.

Using SiliconExpress Utilities

Drag the SiliconExpress control panel from the utilities diskette into the Control Panels folder of the System Folder. Next, restart the Macintosh.

When the server comes back up, select **SiliconExpress** from Control Panels in the **Apple** menu. You'll see a window similar to that of SCSIProbe, except that this control panel can see more than one SCSI chain. Click **Slot** to see the devices hanging off the Macintosh's internal SCSI bus (A), external SCSI bus (B), or devices accessed through the NuBus cards.

Server's Internal Bus Seen from SiliconExpress Control Panel

There are numerous checkboxes in the control panel window listed by SCSI ID. To enable any of these choices for the drives hanging off the NuBus card, you need only select the checkboxes that correspond to the ATTO card itself (SCSI ID 7). This automatically selects the checkboxes for the card's associated drives.

For use with the RAIDbank, select the **Allow Disconnect** and **Always Install Driver** checkboxes for each of its drives. You might as well select **Always Install Driver** for all SCSI IDs. This ensures that the SiliconExpress card has no trouble communicating with any SCSI device you might hook up or move later.

Properly Configured NuBus SCSI Chain Seen from SiliconExpress Control Panel

Don't select **Asynchronous SCSI**. It will degrade performance. If you didn't buy your SiliconExpress card along with your RAIDbank, make sure that the one you have has ROMs of version 1.3 or later installed.

Using RAIDbank Manager

You must install two files from the RAIDbank Manager diskette onto the server in order to use your RAIDbank. These are RAIDbank Manager itself, an application that can be placed anywhere on the hard drive, and RAIDbank Manager extension, which goes in the Extensions folder of the System Folder.

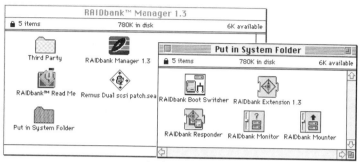

RAIDbank Manager Diskette

We recommend that you throw in the other extensions found on the diskette as well, but you won't need these for setting up the RAIDbank. Next, restart the server. When it comes back up, you are ready to harness this big boy! Using the same principles as when working with Apple RAID, here is a way to do this.

Step 1: Launch RAIDbank Manager and Add Drive

Boot up the RAIDbank Manager application. In the RAIDbank Manager window, all the RAIDbanks in the server's zone are listed under **Partition List**. Click the **Set-up** button in the upper-right-hand corner of the window to continue. In the Array set-up field that appears, click the **Add** button.

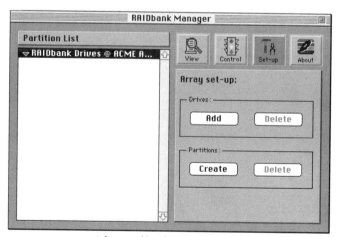

Selecting Add in the Array Set-up Field

163

This generates the **Add Drive** field, in which you will see the SCSI accelerator card and the drives of the RAIDbank attached through it. Select these and click **Add** to move them to the **Partition List** field.

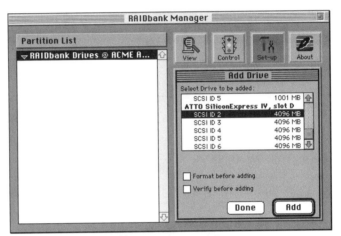

Adding Drives to Partition List

Step 2: Create Partition

Once all the RAIDbank's drives appear in the Partition List window, click **Done** to return to the Array set-up field. Next, click **Create**.

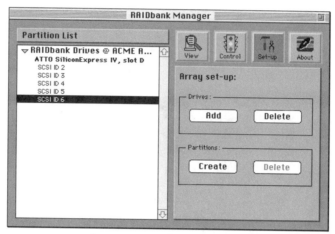

Choosing Create in the Array Set-up Field

In the **Create Partition** field that is generated, give the soon-to-be server volume a name in the **Partition name** field. For all intents and purposes, you can think of these partitions as volumes. That is how they will appear to users.

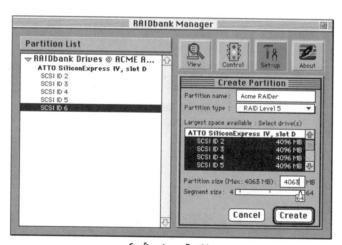

Configuring a Partition

Under **Partition type**, choose **RAID Level 5** in the pop-up menu.

Selecting RAID 5 as Partition Type

Shift-click to select all the drives in the **Largest space available** field, then type in a number for **Partition size**. RAIDbank Manager will plug in the highest possible division automatically by default. This provides balance, so we will accept the default for this example. MicroNet considers a **Segment size** of 64K to be optimal for RAID 5 partitions created from three RAIDbank drive modules. When using more than three drive modules, however, smaller segment sizes are better. On a Power Macintosh with dual SCSI ports, try 16K. Again, though, this should be based upon the file sizes. You don't want to put a bunch of 3K files in a drive with 64K block sizes. Each file will take up an additional 61K of space, and that's a lot of waste.

Creating the partition takes time. When it's finished, the window with the **Array set-up** field appears, and you see the new volume in the **Partition List**.

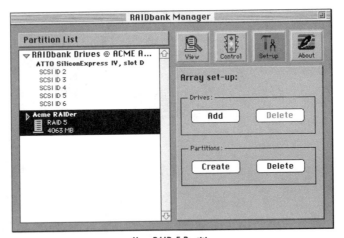

New RAID 5 Partition

Step 3: Repeat Step 2

Repeat this process until all the space on the RAIDbank's available drive modules is dedicated.

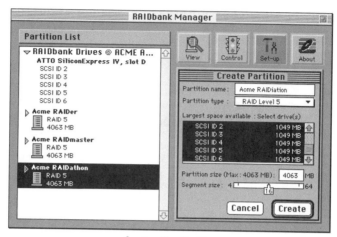

Creating More Partitions

You are finished! Years from now, when you look back with nostalgia and want to show your grandchildren just where the old network volume they have grown to love came from, you can boot up RAIDbank Manager, click **View**, and select a partition to show them its constituent SCSI IDs. Gosh, won't that impress them!

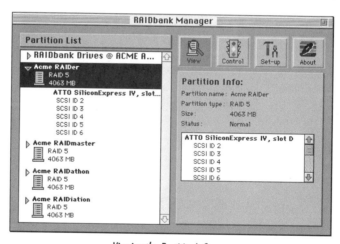

Viewing the Partition's Source

Things to Watch out For

Be aware of these things when using your new we-buried-the-Joneses RAIDbank:

- MicroNet continually updates its drivers. Know about the newest software available by regularly contacting tech support. You can find the contact numbers by clicking **About MicroNet** in the RAIDbank Manager window.

- RAIDbank really blasts the SCSI chain. When using SCSI accelerator cards, use active termination. In fact, MicroNet recommends active termination even for slower drives attached through the Macintosh's built-in SCSI port.

- Don't use the Startup Disk control panel to select a RAIDbank partition as the startup volume. It won't work, as the partitions may be spread over more than one drive. Instead, use **Set Boot Partition** in RAIDbank Manager. This will ensure that the Macintosh boots from the correct modules.

- Install the RAIDbank Manager extension, whether or not you are booting from a RAIDbank partition. RAIDbank Manager won't run without it.

PART FIVE:
NEAR-LINE REDUNDANT
STORAGE PROCEDURES

This section is about creating near-line backups to a single source by using Retrospect 3.0's new **Duplicate** feature. Retrospect is the software application from Dantz Development Corporation currently shipping with every Workgroup Server that has a tape drive. It also ships with most third-party tape drives on the market. This is neither a software manual for Retrospect nor a definitive instructional guide, but we do want to give you an overview of the information necessary to quickly and effectively create near-line backups of your essential folders.

Near-line backups should be run *from* the file server, backing up very important information *to a different drive* than the one from which you are backing up the information. The goal of near-line backups is to make a copy of any files or folders you can't afford to lose *and* that have to be restored in under four hours. How is this different from a mirrored drive or RAID 5? The big difference is that with a mirrored or RAIDed system, whatever files a user trashes on the primary drive are immediately trashed on the secondary drives as well. So, in essence, near-line backups are a form of user-action prevention. If you are less PC about the whole thing, you could say that near-line backups are a form of stupidity prevention.

Don't Bore Me with the Details . . .

- If you have essential information on your network, do near-line backups.

- Communicate with your staff about the definition of a folder labeled Essential, and work with them to protect their data. It isn't that difficult.

- You need to manually create and test your near-line backup. Once you are satisfied that the information is being backed up correctly, you can back it up automatically.

- If you need to restore, do it manually. Running the backup from a server ensures that the Users & Groups data is preserved.

- Check the reports regularly to ensure that you are backing up what you think you are backing up.

CHAPTER 10:
CREATING NEAR-LINE
BACKUPS

Dantz Development Corporation's Retrospect (version 3 and later) can be used to back up the hard drive contents of individual workstations or AppleShare servers to floppy diskettes, attached removable hard and optical drives, or other hard drives. It is particularly useful in making near-line backups, as it allows for full and selective backups, stores the backups in Finder format, and has several scheduling features. This chapter, appropriately, deals with how to create near-line backups of information labeled Essential. If you recall from earlier in this book ("Four-Hour Mark" on page 11), Essential information has the following characteristics:

Essential data must be able to be restored by the four-hour mark. That means that realistically, you have three hours to restore, considering that the first hour is usually lost to figuring out that the drive isn't going to come back and that Norton should have remained a character on an old sitcom. Accounts receivable, key documents, the company's client database, and a project due yesterday with the client coming in six hours from now are all Essential data. Essential data also could be dictated to you by legal liabilities with your clients. Not being able to replace this data within a four-hour time frame, or at all, will cost the company dearly. Reconstructing or "catching up" on this data could either bankrupt the company or cause it to lose a major account. You will probably be fired if the data isn't restored within the appropriate time frame, especially if the client or project is worth twice your salary.

Remember, when creating near-line backups, we are working only with folders marked Essential. The object of near-line backups is to maintain a copy of the files and folders that must be restored immediately. Your objective in this case isn't really to protect the entire server from disaster; it is to protect the files on which you are working from mishap. Mishaps can come from hard drives dying. They can come from servers going out due to electrical problems, and when the server dies while the files are open, they will become corrupted. Mostly, they occur when users trash entire folders on which others are still working. They also occur when a user accidentally corrupts a file or makes changes to a file and saves the changes, only to realize that he or she didn't like or want the changes. To be able to restore files immediately, it makes sense to know which files to protect.

The folders I am going to use for my examples are shown in the picture to the right. This is the server "Projects" in my office. On one of the drives of the Projects server, there are eight folders, all of which contain "live" information for projects already under way. As projects come close to the finishing point, we make sure that we identify the folders in which they are found and then go

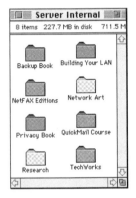

about providing extra protection for those folders. Notice that we've labeled three of the folders Essential, using the **Label** menu in the Finder.

You can use Server Sleuth, enclosed with this book, to show you which folders have already been marked Essential by the folders' owners. A typical Server Sleuth window is shown in the following diagram, with a single folder marked Essential.

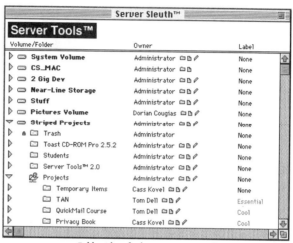

Folder Identified as Being Essential

I'll walk you through the steps taken to identify the folders, and from this process, you will be able to duplicate the effect on your network.

Step 1: Communicate with the Staff

The first thing we do when a project goes "live" is to obtain the project's deadline from our Project Manager, Lynn. Lynn has all sorts of charts and graphs that tell her when she should begin the "Get-It-Done" nag. We always know when a project should move up in the In Progress, Hot, and Essential hierarchy, because the deadline reminders from Lynn become more frequent. We also communicate with one another. At the staff meetings, our administrator receives a list of all Essential projects. After that meeting, he walks over to the server and runs Server Sleuth to check and make sure that the projects are labeled correctly. This is accomplished by opening Server Sleuth on the server and expanding the folder hierarchy until the folders in question are located. Server Sleuth has an option to open all folders at once, but this doesn't work well on large file servers. On small ones, it might be faster, but on large ones, with tens of thousands of folders, it's probably not a good idea. The following screen shot shows the chart Server Sleuth exported for the view the administrator set. Notice that three of the folders were marked Essential. It's now time to ensure that these folders are protected.

Volume/Folder	Owner	Owner Privs	User/Group	User/Group Privs	Everyone Privs	Label
System Volume	Administrator	YYY	-	NNN	NNN	None
2 Gig Dev	Administrator	YYY	-	NNN	NNN	None
Server Internal	Administrator	YYY	-	NNN	YNN	None
Trash	Administrator	NNN	-	NNN	NNN	None
Projects	Administrator	YYY	-	NNN	YNN	None
TechWorks	Dorian Cougias	YYY	Consulting	YYY	NNN	In Progress
Research	NF Staff	YYY	-	NNN	YYN	None
QuickMail Course	Tom Dell	YYY	Consulting	YYY	NNN	Hot
Privacy Book	Cass Kovel	YYY	NF Staff	YYY	NNN	Essential
Network Art	Dorian Cougias	YYY	-	NNN	YYN	None
NetFAX Editions	NF Staff	YYY	NF Staff	YYY	NNN	Hot
Building Your LAN	Dorian Cougias	YYY	NF Staff	YYY	NNN	Essential
Backup Book	Dorian Cougias	YYY	Cass Kovel	YYY	NNN	Essential
Desktop Folder	Administrator	YYY	-	NNN	YNN	None
Near-Line Storage	Administrator	YYY	-	NNN	YNN	None

Server Sleuth Table

Step 2: Choosing the Near-Line Storage Location

The **Duplicate** function of Retrospect produces an exact copy of the files from one disk to another, destination disk. The duplicate keeps files and folders in their original hierarchical order and can therefore serve as an instant replacement to an original disk that has crashed. This is much like the hardware-based mirroring process. Remember, though, that the destination for the near-line backup should have an equal or greater volume size than the source files and folders that you are backing up.

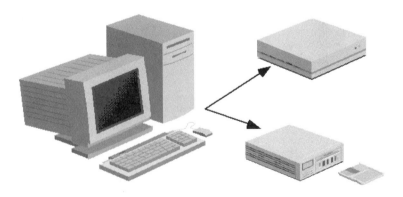

Duplicate Backup Location Possibilities

We suggest that you add another hard drive to the file server or that you use something like a SyQuest or Magneto Optical drive for storage. Although SyQuest drives are faster, MO drives are more durable. The reason we like removable drives is that they can also be used for other things. Retrospect will back up to *whichever* disk is in the removable drive, though, so you need to remember *not* to leave a disk in the drive that you don't want overwritten during the backup times. It makes sense, but some people forget . . . like me.

Step 3: Selecting the Source Volume with Retrospect

You are now ready to launch Retrospect and begin the near-line backup process. When you launch the application, you see the window shown in the next picture.

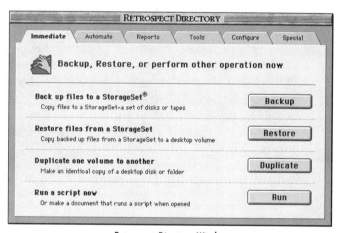

Retrospect Directory Window

Move to the second tab in the window, the **Automate** tab, as we are creating a script that will automatically run the duplication process at regular intervals. Once in the Automate portion of the window, click **Scripts** to create a new script.

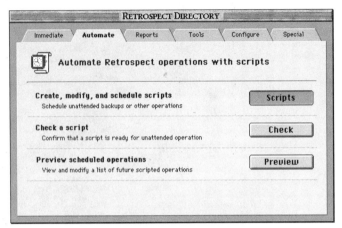

Automating a Script by Using Retrospect

When you click the **Scripts** button, a window appears that is really the database of all the scripts you have written. If this is the first time you are writing a script in Retrospect, the window should appear empty. Once you have created and saved a script, it appears in this window.

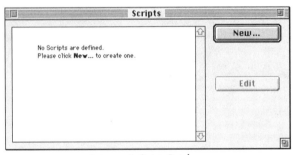

Retrospect's Scripts Database

Clicking **New** brings up a dialog box asking what type of script you would like to perform. For now, you are going to select the **Duplicate** script.

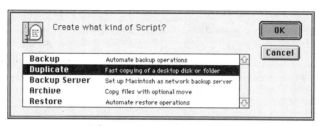

Selecting to Create a Duplicate Script

Select your script type and click **OK** to bring up a dialog box in which you enter the script's name. Make sure to name it something descriptive, in case someone else needs to run it while you are away. Click **New** to create the new script. A blank script window appears. It has buttons for each step you need to take to create your backup script. For now, click the **Source** button to choose the appropriate source.

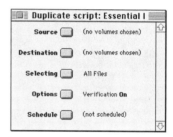

After you click **Source** in the empty script window, a dialog box appears showing all the currently available volumes that can be backed up. Retrospect 3 has a new concept called the **Local Desktop**. If you select the **Local Desktop**, Retrospect automatically selects all volumes that are locally mounted at the time of backup. It will, however, exclude any floppies, mounted servers, or locked removable volumes, such as CD-ROMs.

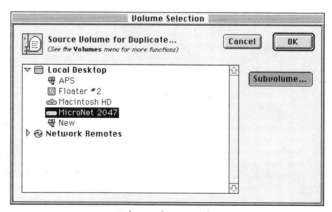

Volume Selection Window

Since that's *not* what we want to do, select the volume in which the data to be backed up resides. Since we don't want *all* the information inside the volume, click **Subvolume…** so we can identify an individual enclosing folder (a folder and all the contents within the folder) to be the source of the backup. Clicking **Define** selects the folder.

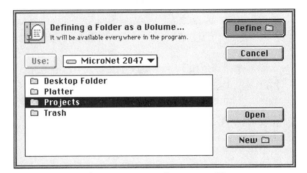

Selecting Projects as the Source Folder

Once you have defined a folder as a subvolume, the volumes list changes to reflect the fact that the folder exists and has been selected.

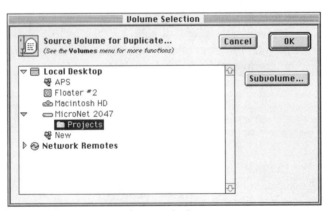

The New Subvolume

The script window's **Source** location is also updated with the new information.

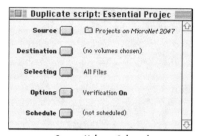

Source Volume Selected

Step 4: Selecting the Destination Volume

It is now time to select the destination volume for your near-line backup. Because you aren't duplicating the entire contents of a hard drive, you don't want to wipe out the entire contents of the destination drive when duplicating. Simple rule: If the source is a subvolume, the destination should be one as well. Hence, the next step in the process is to select a destination subvolume into which Retrospect will put the information being duplicated. To begin the process, click the **Destination** button in the script window.

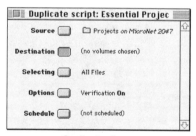

Destination Button

Retrospect will then open the window that shows all the available destination options for the duplication process. Remember, this time, you are *not* supposed to select the same volume you selected before. This time, select a destination subvolume in which to place your duplicate copies. In the following window, we chose the 128 MO removable named *Floater #2* and clicked the **Subvolume...** button.

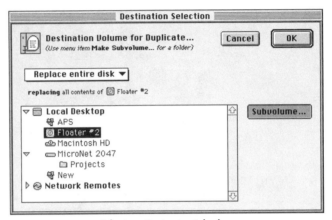

Selecting a Destination Subvolume

After you click the button, a window appears asking you which folders you would like to define as the appropriate subvolume. Since this is a blank disk, I made a folder called *Projects Duplicates.* The reason you need to make or select a folder to back up to is that you might be making duplicates of several folders. Without a container folder, they will all appear on the root directory of the volume to which you are backing up.

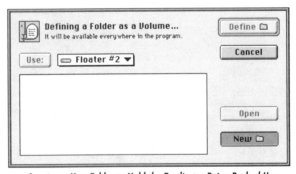

Creating a New Folder to Hold the Duplicates Being Backed Up

After creating the folder, click **Define** to select it as the destination volume. In the previous picture, the **Define** button is grayed out because there are no subfolders within the volume. Once you have created at least one folder, the **Define** button becomes accessible, and you can select a folder you created. Once the folder is defined, you are returned to the volumes window where the new folder is selected.

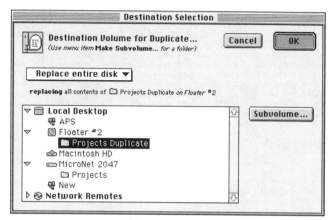

New Folder Selected as Destination

There are two options at this point. The first option is for you to select the small pop-up that says **Replace entire disk** of the destination folder with the contents of the folders being duplicated. The second option is to select **Replace any corresponding files** of the destination folder with new or updated files being duplicated. Replacing the entire contents means that whatever files are being backed up are the files that will be in the destination folder. Replacing the contents merely updates older versions of the files in the folder with newer ones. It does not delete any files that the user might have renamed or removed. I'm not advocating one way or the other. I personally don't care which you choose. However, if you are doing this to mitigate the "stupidity" factor in the office, you might want to replace the corresponding files. This ensures that you have everything. Once a file is copied into the duplicated folder, it is left there. It is updated only if a new file matching the same creator, type, and creation date exists with the only difference being the modification date. Be aware, though, that if you have a lot of files that change, you will really need to monitor the size of this folder. Once a change has been made, the file is there and the folder's size will begin to balloon.

When finished selecting the destination folder, Retrospect shows the new destination in the script window, as shown in the next screen shot.

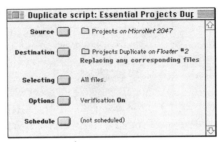

Duplicate Script Destination

Step 5: Setting the Selectors

When you first begin your duplication scripting process, the option for selecting the folders and files to be backed up is set to **All files**, meaning that everything within the source folder will be duplicated. Since all you really care about are the folders (and files within the folders) marked Essential, set a selector that tells Retrospect that all you want to back up are the appropriately marked files and folders. To do this, click the **Selecting** button in the script window.

When you first click **Selecting**, you are presented with a window that has a few options in it but not the ones you want. So to reach the right options (yes, you can get here from there), click **More Choices**, and a window like the one in the next picture is displayed. The window has two options: one for including files and folders and one for excluding files and folders. You will be working with the pop-up arrow that lets you *include* files and folders.

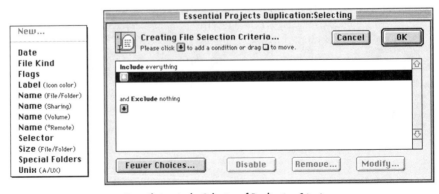

More Choices in the Selection of Duplication Criteria

When you click and hold the top (or the bottom) arrow, the dialog box shown on the left of the window in the preceding picture appears. It has all sorts of wonderful and special options for choosing folders and files to be backed up. Dantz has made it easy for us to find what we are looking for by creating a selector for file and folder labels. If you don't believe me, look. It's the fourth from the top. Once you select it, you see . . . yes, one more window. This window allows you to select the specific label for your folder or file that you want to be backed up. Don't worry if the user has changed the label's name or color on his or her computer. This selector is set by position, and whatever the position is that applies on the computer being backed up is the label Retrospect will match and then back up.

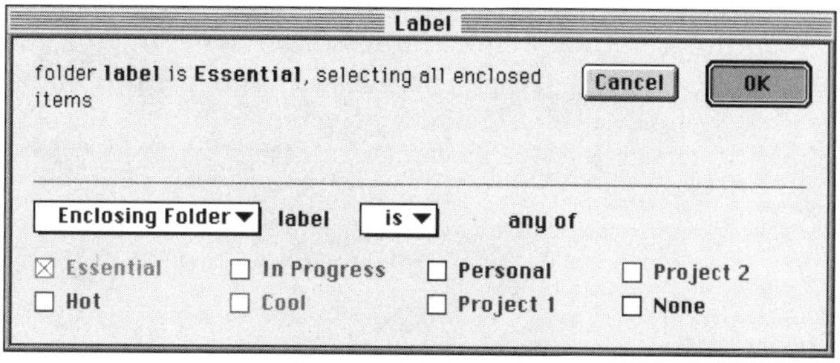

Retrospect's Label Criteria

Again, ensure that you select **Enclosing Folder** instead of a folder or file. **Files** will back up only appropriately labeled files. **Folders** will back up appropriately labeled items inside a folder at the first level. If a folder contains *other* folders, they won't be backed up (or any of the information within them).

When you are finished clicking **OK** buttons, you finally return to the script window. Retrospect displays the new selection criteria for you, showing you what will be included in the duplication process.

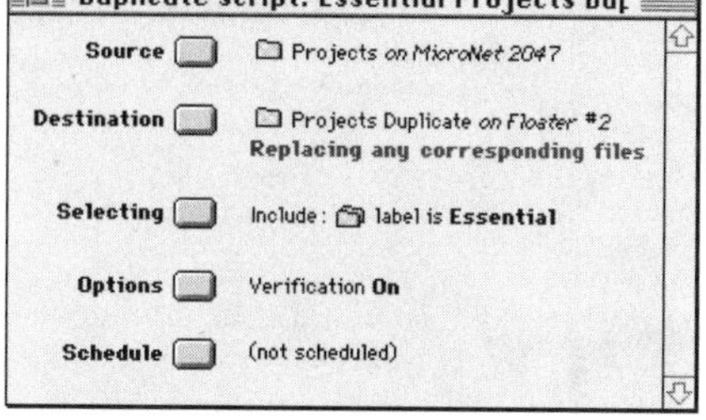

Selecting All Enclosing Folders Marked Essential

Step 6: Creating the Schedule

I just love Retrospect's new and improved scheduling capabilities. The old ones were a bit of a pain in the butt. To finish off the duplicating process, schedule when this duplication should occur. We've found that the best times for day-in and day-out processes are 10:00 A.M., 2:00 P.M., and 6:00 P.M. duplications. Setting the schedule for 10:00 A.M. grabs files after users have made their first morning changes or picks up anything that someone did late at night. Setting the schedule for 2:00 P.M. picks up files after lunch with the changes people made during the morning. Scheduling for 6:00 P.M. ensures that you have whatever changes people made before they went home for the night (he says while writing this at 9:36 P.M. on a Sunday). So, it's time to humor me again and follow *my* schedule. Click the **Schedule** button to get this under way.

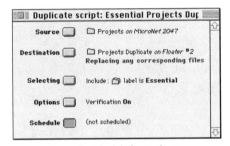

Create the Schedule for Duplicating

Since you haven't created any schedules yet, you will have a blank schedule window in your script's schedule database. Click **Add** to create the new schedule.

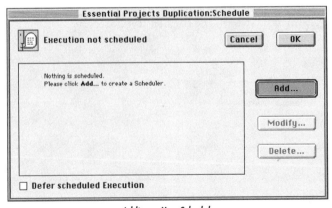

Adding a New Schedule

Once you have clicked the **Add** button, there are three choices: **Day of Week**, **Repeating Interval**, or **Single Date**. Choose **Day of Week** for what you are attempting in this situation. Leave **Repeating Interval** and **Single Date** for other things. Remember this choice, because you are going to come back to it two more times during the creation of this script.

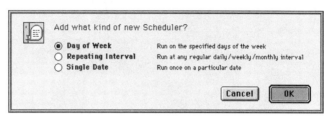

Three Scheduling Choices

Let's assume we are working with a semi-normal company (unlike Network Frontiers, where we all work like dogs, seven days a week . . . Here's a riddle for you: What do you get when you work your fingers to the bones? Bony fingers. It's something my dad used to say, and I think it means work smart instead of work hard. He always worked hard, though, so I don't really get it. Anybody care to e-mail me and explain it?). Click Monday through Friday. Don't worry about the number of weeks field, as you want it to repeat every week. Thus, the **1** is acceptable. Set the time for 10:00 A.M. and click **OK** to add the schedule to the script.

```
┌───────────────────────────────────────────────────────────┐
│         Essential Projects Duplication:Day of Week          │
│  Do Duplicate Every .MTWTF., starting 8/7/95 at 10:00 AM    │
│                                          ┌────────┐ ┌──────┐ │
│                                          │ Cancel │ │  OK  │ │
│                                          └────────┘ └──────┘ │
│                                                             │
│   Start:    8/ 7/1995 Mon        10:00  AM                  │
│                                                             │
│   Run on:  ☒ Monday      ☐ Saturday                        │
│            ☒ Tuesday     ☐ Sunday                          │
│            ☒ Wednesday                                      │
│            ☒ Thursday                                       │
│            ☒ Friday                                         │
│                                                             │
│   Weeks:   │1        │                                      │
│                                                             │
└───────────────────────────────────────────────────────────┘
```

Setting the Duplicate Schedule

Now add two more schedules. Both of them will be for the same days, Monday through Friday, and both of them repeat every week, so the **Weeks:** field says **1**.

However, the difference in the two new schedules will be that one of them is set for 2:00 P.M. and the other is set for 6:00 P.M. Once these are added, the schedule database is updated to reflect the three schedules:

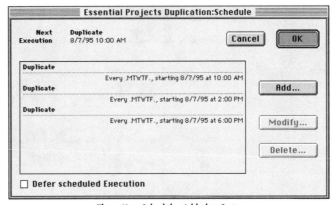

Three New Schedules Added to Script

Finally, clicking **OK** adds the schedules to the script and returns you to the basic script window.

Finished Script

You are now finished. Close and save the script. Your backup will run on time.

PART SIX:
SETTING UP THE
NETWORK BACKUP

When setting up the network backup, there are two words with which you had better be familiar: *capacity* and *throughput.* If you know how these two words affect what you back up, how long it will take, and how much storage space you will need, you are home free. If you don't know what these two words mean to your backup and restoration plan, you are playing naively with your network, and your little world is about to be shattered.

Put simply, capacity covers how much information that needs to be backed up there is on the drives. Throughput is how quickly your backup is going to go. Slower throughput affects backup capacity, as the slower the throughput, the more capacity the data needs on tape.

Now, while you are nodding your head to show that you understand this already and are wondering why in the world I'm making a big stink about this, let me tell you that since writing the first book, we have met many people with this grand plan to back up across their WAN.

NOT.

We have done some testing, and I want to show you some of the results of these tests. You'll be amazed at what you see.

DON'T BORE ME WITH THE DETAILS . . .

- Measure the amount of data you need to back up by analyzing how much total storage space you have, not by how much you are using right now. In other words, measure by how much each hard drive is able to hold, as opposed to how much you have in each drive today.

- Plan for storage capacity at least 1.5 times the total amount of data you plan to back up. This allows for the changes you will make during the week.

- Try to back up to Digital Audio Tape (DAT) or Digital Linear Tape (DLT).

- Use Magneto-Optical (MO) drives or a good hard drive to back up all essential files in near-line Finder format.

- Floppies are only for sneakernet and PowerBook users who need to back up a only few key files.

CHAPTER 11:
PLANNING FOR THROUGHPUT

Okay, there are a few things you need to know about throughput before you start planning for it. Here's one of my favorite blackboard exercises for both students and clients. Given a 10 Mbps Ethernet network, a 60 MHz client workstation with an attached drive that has a throughput of 4.3 MB per minute, and a backup computer running at 110 MHz, with a DDS-2 DAT tape with the speed ratio of 20.5 MB per minute, what is the throughput rate for data transfer from one computer to the other?

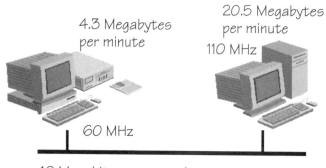

Throughput Question

By the way, I'm not going to give you the answer here. If you want it and can't figure it out, my e-mail is dorian_cougias@netfrontiers.com. E-mail me.

PLANNING FOR THROUGHPUT

You have to plan for throughput for the computers on your network. You have to plan for it because how quickly the computers can be backed up dictates how many computers can be backed up during a given period of time. To put it simply, if you are backing up your computers at night and you start your backups at 6:00 P.M. to be done by, say, 9:00 A.M., you have 15 total hours for backup procedures. Right about now you might be thinking that you could back up a whole lot of computers in 15 hours. Well, yes and no. Between writing the first and second versions of this book, we decided we would do a ton of throughput testing. We wanted to see how different network architectures affect the throughput of a backup. We also wanted to see what types of computers and drives affect the backup times. In this section, we present a synopsis of our findings.

First, we created a test network with all the "fixins" we could think of at the time. Undoubtedly, you will read this and come up with many more "fixins" than we did. The next picture shows a rough diagram of what our test network looked like, which I'll go through piece by piece.

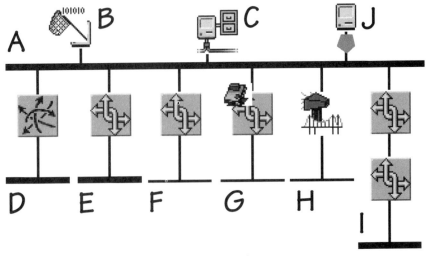

Network Design for Throughput Testing

A. This is the standard Ethernet network we used. It was a hubbed Ethernet network, using a Farallon 16-port Ethernet hub. The cabling was all Category Five except for the extra "cable extenders" we added in other tests. These "cable extenders" were eight Farallon EtherWaves for one test—four extending on one side for the backup machine and four on the other side for the machine being backed up—and then six Tut SilverStreak daisy chain connectors for a second test—all six being daisy-chained on one side of the hub going out to the backup machine.

B. This computer was running both Skyline and Satellite from AG Group. This is the software we chose to capture the network packet information that we used to create the throughput charts shown in a few pages.

C. This was the computer performing the backups. We used a 110 MHz Workgroup Server 8150 with an internal DDS-2 DAT drive.

D. For one of the tests, we used a Tribe EtherSwitch, which is an Ethernet-to-Ethernet 5-port switch.

E. For another test, we used the Compatible Systems RISCRouter 3000E, which is a 4-port RISC-based router. Of the four ports, two are for Ethernet, and two are for LocalTalk.

F. Connecting the users down to LocalTalk, we used the Farallon StarRouter, which is a combination Ethernet-to-LocalTalk router and a 24-port LocalTalk hub (multiport repeater).

G. We wanted to see how well computers could be backed up if the network was running on "air." Thus, we attached the computer being backed up to a Photonics infrared cooperative connector and attached that to the Ethernet network via the Apple Internet Router running on a Power Macintosh 6100/60.

H. While we were on the air kick, we decided to throw in the Digital Ocean Groupers, which are radio frequency network connectors. This was attached to the Ethernet network via their StarFish Ethernet-to-RF bridge.

I. For the long haul, we wanted to see how long it would take to back up a computer over a WAN connection. Thus, we hooked up a 128K frame relay network, using two Compatible Systems MicroRouter 1000Rs.

J. Finally, we wanted to see what would happen if we connected to Ethernet with the EtherWave serial transceiver from Farallon. This transceiver connects LocalTalk computers to Ethernet, using a specialized transceiver and a high-speed serial link to the computer.

The Results Are In . . .

Okay, here's what we found. First of all, it seems to us that if you are performing a backup on an Ethernet network, as long as the network is within design constraints, there aren't going to be any significant differences in backup times from a straight Ethernet network to a switched or routed backbone topology.

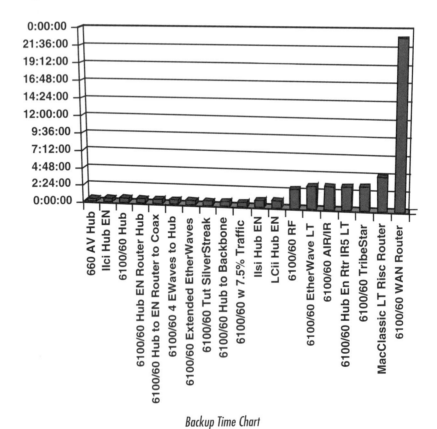

Backup Time Chart

The same thing can be said for LocalTalk, infrared, and radio frequency, or even using an EtherWave to attach to the Ethernet network. It seems to us that there isn't much you can do to an AppleTalk network design (again, within design specifications) that will change the backup times.

However, it was easily proved that backing up over your WAN, unless you are running something like a T1 (1.5 Mbps), will be just a tad slow. Yes, Al, that's an understatement. By the way, if you were wondering, the backup time over the 128K WAN link was 22 hours, 49 minutes, and 01seconds. It took so long for this test to conclude that we had to perform it over the weekend. The next chart makes this even clearer, showing the difference in a WAN backup from a normal backup of a 6100/60 over an Ethernet network.

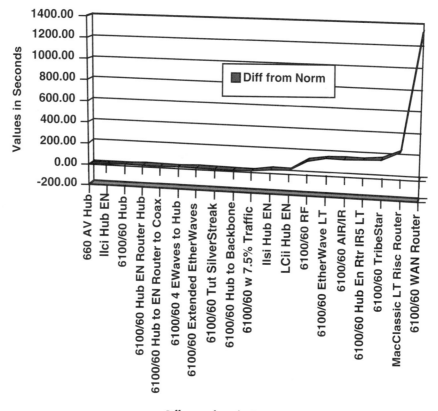

Differences from the Norm

Conclusions for Planning Purposes

The conclusions you can use for planning purposes are pretty simple. We have built these conclusions into the planning template we created for you and ship with this book. Use this information when planning how long it will take to back up the computers in your office.

- Figure newer (PowerPC and '040) Macs on Ethernet to back up at a general average of around 5.5 MB per minute. Some of them are faster, registering at 6 MB or more, but the overall is still 5.5 MB.

- Figure older ('020 and IIsi) Macs on Ethernet to back up at a general average of around 3 MB per minute.

- Figure alternative Ethernet (RF and serial EtherWave) to back up at around 1.1 MB per minute.

- Figure most anything on LocalTalk to back up at about 0.85 MB per minute.

- Figure on taking a long nap if you want to back up over the WAN.

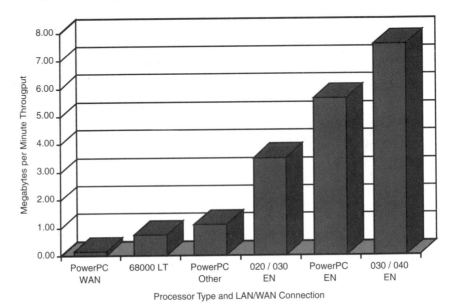

Overall Throughput

CHAPTER 12:
PLANNING FOR
CAPACITY

The most important issue when choosing a backup media is capacity. You'll need more capacity than the total actual capacity required in any single backup session. The greater the number of megabytes you have to back up, the more important it is to back it up in a single step. The more cumbersome a backup system is to use, the less likely you are to use it. Higher-capacity storage devices are more expensive, but they offset the extra cost of the drive by saving on the time you would spend baby-sitting the backup process.

In this chapter, we'll be going over the pros and cons of various media types and devices, using examples from vendors we trust, such as APS and MicroNet. For more specific information about their products, see the CD-ROM that came with this book. We'll also compare the price per megabyte of the various types of media, but remember, this is a volatile industry and prices change quickly. In some cases, such as with high-capacity tapes, you will find the per megabyte cost of backup media is so little as to be hardly worth figuring (these are listed as $0.01 per megabyte or less).

SOME BASICS

If you perform a full backup at the end of each week and a normal backup of modified files at the end of each day, it is more convenient to keep the normal backup on the same tape or disk with the full backup. That way, if you need to restore a file, you will have to look at only one tape or disk for the latest versions of all files. If you archive each generation of data files for any given project, you will find that a larger-capacity tape or disk means fewer volumes to search through when you need to refer back to the archived file. You should have sufficient capacity to back up without interfering with daily work. This probably means using enough capacity to perform an overnight backup in which you don't have to sit there and wait to change the backup media. However, some networks have many servers with drives that are much larger than any single backup system can handle with an individual disk or tape.

Virtually any backup software application will let you store a single backup session over multiple tapes or disks. This is called *tape-spanning capability.* Tape spanning prompts users to insert the next tape or disk in a series during backup and retrieval. A few systems today come equipped with tape autoloaders. These alleviate the need to baby-sit a multiple-tape backup process. Autoloaders holding 5–12 DAT cartridges are available. As an alternative to autoloaders, some software lets you to stack DAT drives and other storage devices, looking to the SCSI chain for the backup media it needs to continue operations or when one of the devices is full. This is called *cascading.*

Apple has shipped an unexpected amount of Workgroup Server 8150s and 9150s with DAT drives in them. If you are one of those organizations that has several servers with internal DATs around the company or anywhere else, then the DAT autoloader from MicroNet is for you. This is due to the nature of Retrospect 3.x's ability to support a dedicated backup server running different types of backups continually. We've found that having seven DATs simultaneously available (six in the autoloader and one in the server) gives you unparalleled backup capabilities. You can have your normal tape, secondary tape, archive tape, and three others loaded and ready to go at once. You could even have one backup server running an extensive archive tape system with three or four 8-GB DDS-2 tapes loaded and available—while you are still running your normal backups. So our new conclusion is: If you have multiple servers, your next choice should be a DAT autoloader (we like MicroNet's 48/6). If not, then you might want to look at distributing several single DAT drives across your network (we like APS's HyperDAT).

CAPACITY ISSUES

You need to plan for those times when you have more data to back up than you have media capacity.

Let's imagine you are backing up to SyQuest cartridges. SyQuests capacities are available in 44 MB, 88 MB, and 200 MB in the 5.25-inch format, and 105 MB and 270 MB in the 3.5-inch format. Bernoulli cartridges come in similar sizes. If you are backing up to optical disks, your capacity is limited to 650 MB per side. Digital Audio Tapes (DATs) start at around 1.3 GB of encompassed storage on a 60-meter DDS-1 tape, go up to 4 GB of compressed storage using 90-meter tape systems, and can reach 8 GB of compressed storage on 120-meter DDS-2 series tapes and drives. The way of the future, Digital Linear Tape (DLT) drives, can compress up to 20 GB on a DLT20 tape and 40 GB on a DLT40 tape. Keep these numbers in mind when you are planning for backup capacity. Again, you want to choose media that gives you more capacity than you have information to back up. As this isn't always feasible, at least ensure that you have backup media that is as large as possible. To give you an idea why, consider this: If you were to back up 2.5 GB of data, you would have to *change* media:

1,785	times if you use 1.4-MB floppy diskettes;
57	times if you use 44-MB removable cartridges;
28	times if you use 88-MB removable cartridges;
23	times if you use 105-MB removable cartridges;
19	times if you use 128-MB Magneto-Optical disks;
8	times if you use 270-MB removable cartridges;
3	times if you use 650-MB optical disks;
1	time if you use a noncompression DAT;
0	times if you use 8mm high-capacity tape, compressed 4mmDAT, or DLT.

If you have more information to back up than you have storage capacity, you are going to have to baby-sit the backup process. With any of the cited media types *except* the tape drives, you will have to stay on site during the backup process or leave and schedule your returns so that you are there relative to the time the software is asking for new media. With tape mechanisms, there will be probably a need for one media change, and after a few backups, you can calculate when you will have to return in order to finish the backup process. However, with tape mechanisms, you might not have the capacity you *think* you are supposed to have. There is a big difference between the technology used to write to tape mechanisms and the technology used to write to platter mechanisms. In the following sections, we have broken down backup storage media into two categories: *block-addressable* mechanisms and *streaming tape* mechanisms.

Remember the Golden Rule:

Simplicity is the key. If it is difficult, you won't stick with the plan. The simplest plans have the most followers.

I once visited a client out on the East Coast who scheduled an early-morning meeting at 6:30 A.M. Since it was a new client, I didn't ask why the meeting had to be so early. When I arrived there, the smell of McDonald's Egg McMuffins was wafting through the air. The entire network administrative staff was at the meeting, just having finished their breakfasts. It seems that the night before  *was when they began their large-capacity backups. They would all meet early the next day at the local McDonald's, get breakfast, and then come in to change their DAT tapes so the backups would be completed before the work day began. It was also a great time to have a meeting with the network staff, as they were all in the same place at the same time—with no user problems to interfere with the meeting!*

BLOCK-ADDRESSABLE TECHNOLOGY

I was talking to a student the other day who thought that all hard drives operated like record or CD players, wherein the "needle" passed over the drive's surface, gathering information written in "electronic spiraling grooves" on the drives. Close, but still wrong. Floppies, removable drives, and hard drives are all disk-based media that use what is called *block-addressable* systems. All disk-based media on the Macintosh is formatted in concentric circles called *tracks*. These tracks are then divided into *sectors,* or *blocks*. The tracks and blocks are set up by the formatting software that is either a part of the Macintosh operating system (for formatting Mac OS hard drives and floppies) or shipped with the drive itself. When a Macintosh writes to the drive or reads from the drive, it is writing the data or reading the data from these blocks on the disk. The following diagram is what a drive might look like with several blocks of data written to it.

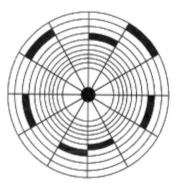

Drive with Various Blocks of Data

Note: The sectors on real drives are not aligned the way they are on the drive in the picture. I'm not a gifted enough artist to draw sectors the way they really look, so hit the "I believe" button for a minute or two here. If you want to know more in detail about drives, sectors, read-write heads, and the like, you should read an excellent book by Bob Brant called *Macintosh Hard Disk Management,* published by McGraw-Hill, 1992.

How Are Sectors Determined?

To start with, all drives reserve a certain percentage of their sectors for the drive's *directory*. That's why your 44-MB removable cartridges actually have around 42 MB of usable space. Each drive's directory contains pointers, or "flags," that identify the location of data written to the drive. When we users "trash" files, what we are really doing is deleting the directory entry for that file. The drive doesn't go to each sector and replace the contents with blank space. Instead, the next time a file is to be written to the disk, the drive's directories tell the computer that those previously used sectors are now open for new files. This is why if you "trash" a file and then want it restored, you shouldn't write anything to the drive in the interim. You need to use your recovery software before those blocks have been overwritten.

There is much more information the directories take care of, but this isn't the place to go into all that. If you want to know more about it, read Bob's book. It's a good book.

The *sectors* are set up according to the total amount of space on the drive. The larger the drive, the larger the sectors for the drive. This is because there can be only 65,536 total blocks per drive. Floppy diskettes are formatted with 512-byte (or 0.5K) sectors. Older hard drives start at around 80 MB, but the block sizes actually start at 64 MB. A drive formatted for 64 MB will have a 1K block size, giving it a total of exactly 65,536 blocks. Each additional 32 MB of drive space adds 0.5K to the block sizes. Thus, a more modern 1-GB drive will have block sizes of 16K, again giving it a total of exactly 65,536 blocks.

Drive Size	Block Size
< 64 Mbytes	1 Kbyte
64 - 96 Mbytes	1.5 Kbytes
128 Mbytes	2 Kbytes
180 Mbytes	3 Kbytes
256 Mbytes	4 Kbytes
512 Mbytes	8 Kbytes
1 Gigabyte	16 Kbytes
1.5 Gigabytes	24 Kbytes

Standard Drive Sizes and Allocation Blocks

Two benefits of block-addressable media are:

- Once the drive is formatted properly, you know exactly how much storage space it can hold. Tape mechanisms don't work the same way. Tape mechanisms also do not always produce consistent results. Drives do.

- Because block-addressable media stores the directory on the disk, there isn't a need to store a backup catalog in a separate location. Retrospect, for instance, will store a Macintosh *file* catalog as a part of the backup file itself. It won't store the Macintosh *disks* catalog with the backup file, because that file can span multiple disks. It maintains the catalog as a separate entity.

Now that you know how block-addressable drives work, let's look at the media with which they work.

Floppy Diskettes

Floppies are the least expensive backup media. Users always have floppy drives and are bound to have mass quantities of extra floppy disks around. To back up to floppies, a program must back up across several disks in a single setting. Backing up to a floppy can meet the needs of some low-end individual backups, but backing up to floppies cannot be used for server backups, because of their low capacity. We recommend that floppy backups be performed by mobile computing users only and then only for key files. They should make two copies of the floppies for security.

Price per Megabyte

800K **Double-Density Diskettes** (uncompressed) =	$0.85
1.44-MB **High-Density Diskettes** (uncompressed) =	$0.55

Removable Drives (SyQuest, Bernoulli, Magneto-Optical, WORM, and CD-R)

Another type of block-addressable media is the removable disk. Removable disks come in assorted varieties. There are *magnetic* removable disks, such as SyQuest and Bernoulli, and there are *optical* disks, such as WORM drives and Magneto-Optical drives.

Removable magnetic disks are very popular in large graphics networks and with prepress professionals, as graphics files can be too large to fit onto regular floppies. I have one client who creates pages so big that only two of them can fit onto a single 88-MB removable SyQuest cartridge.

Removable magnetic media is not well suited for backup procedures, because of its relatively low capacity. Standard SyQuest cartridges come in 44-MB, 88-MB, 105-MB, 200-MB, and 270-MB sizes. The SyQuest EZ135 uses 135-MB disks. Standard Bernoulli cartridges come in 35-MB, 65-MB, 90-MB, 105-MB, 150-MB, and 230-MB sizes. The Iomega Zip drive uses either 25-MB or 100-MB disks. An exception to the rule is the Iomega Jaz drive, which uses a 3.5-inch disk similar to that of the SyQuest but holds an impressive 1-GB of storage.

Removable optical disks are better suited in terms of capacity. Magneto Optical (MO) disks typically hold 128 MB, 230 MB, or 650 MB per disk. This provides a lot of capacity when used as storage space but not that much capacity for backup media when compared to tape. Also, access times for these drives are in the 150-plus millisecond range, compared to 18 or so milliseconds for standard magnetic media. This means that they are slow to respond to normal disk queries and disk reads or writes, which makes large backups take just shy of forever. However, because they use standard disk access technology (meaning that they can be mounted on the desktop like any other disk), they make great archival and near-line storage media. Files can be archived there and searched later, when needed.

WORM (Write Once, Read Many) optical drives hold about 650 MB per disk side, much like the MO drives. The trouble with these CD-like disks is that once written to, the disks cannot be overwritten. This makes them lousy standard backup drives but great archiving drives, especially if what is being archived has legal implications. Once files are written to the drive, they are locked and cannot be replaced, so there is a permanent record of the material on the drive.

CD-Recordable (CD-R) drives are very similar. Sometimes called "one-off machines," their advantage over WORM drives is that the CD-ROMs they produce can be read by regular CD-ROM drives. They are suitable for archiving and for software distribution. We produced the master for the CD-ROM that comes with this book on just such a drive: a MicroNet HD Master 2000 Pro.

Note: Here's a helpful hint from Ken Lien at Kodak, a guy who knows a lot about writing data to CDs. CD-ROMs aren't as indestructible as you might think. Although data you archive to CD-R won't be damaged by magnetism, you still have to worry about light, temperature, humidity, and scratching, some of which can cause the thin gold reflector to flake off on the cheaper disks. Kodak's disks use a special organic dye recording layer and a scratch-resistant overcoat to combat this problem, and Kodak claims that its disks will be good for 100 years or more. How much data can you archive on a writable CD? According to Kodak, about 240,000 pages of ASCII text, or the contents of 550 floppies!

Price per Megabyte

270-MB **SyQuest Cartridges** = $0.24

200-MB **SyQuest Cartridges** = $0.40

105-MB **SyQuest Cartridges** = $0.57

88-MB **SyQuest Cartridges** = $0.63

44-MB **SyQuest Cartridges** = $1.02

135-MB **SyQuest EZ135 Cartridges** = $0.15

APS SQ 5200 (200-MB) SyQuest Drive

230-MB **Bernoulli Cartridges** = $0.47

150-MB **Bernoulli Cartridges** = $0.66

90-MB **Bernoulli Cartridges** = $1.05

100-MB **Iomega Zip Cartridges** = $0.20

1-GB **Iomega Jaz Cartridges** = $0.12

APS 230-MB MO Drive

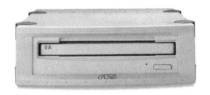

APS 1.3-GB MO Drive

1.3-GB **Magneto-Optical Disks** = $0.08

650-MB **Magneto-Optical Disks** = $0.11

230-MB **Magneto-Optical Disks** =	$0.17
128-MB **Magneto-Optical Disks** =	$0.22
650-MB **CD-Recordable Disks** =	$0.02

MicroNet HD Master 2000 Pro

Hard Drives

Generally, hard drives shouldn't be used for network backup storage systems, because of the size and cost limitations inherent in using them. There are three exceptions: PowerBooks, disk mirroring, and near-line storage. Having a hard drive on hand for PowerBook backups is a great idea. Having a battery-powered drive on hand is an even better idea because you can use it to back up those important files whether or not you are near a power source. Near-line storage is for those files you identified as having to be restored immediately. If you need the files back immediately, back up the files in Finder format. You can't back up files to Finder format if you are backing them up to tape. Having a hard drive specifically set up for near-line storage of essential information, therefore, is a very good idea.

Price per Megabyte (Normal Drives)

8.669-GB **APS ST 9.0** =	$0.35
4.094-GB **APS ST 4.0** =	$0.37
2.050-GB **APS ST 2.0** =	$0.49

1.015-GB **APS ST 1.0** =	$0.54
810-MB **APS Q 840** =	$0.37
699-MB **APS Q 730** =	$0.36
516-MB **APS Q 540** =	$0.39
350-MB **APS Q 365** =	$0.46

APS SR2000 Series Hard Drives

Price per Megabyte (Battery-Powered Drives)

773-MB **APS T 800 SR 1000** =	$0.97
504-MB **APS T 504 SR 1000** =	$1.09

Mirrored Hard Drives

You should use *mirrored* drives, that is two drives containing the same continuously updated data, only if you need fault-tolerant systems. Computers running electronic mail and other groupware services identified by your corporation as having zero tolerance to downtime should be on a mirrored system.

When people talk about mirroring you will hear them talk about RAID, or Redundant Array of Independent Disks. We talk about its various levels elsewhere in this book. As for the cost per megabyte for mirroring, you can't simply figure it as twice the cost of a given drive, since you have to factor in the RAID software and hardware as well. To give you an idea of the cost, we used APS's 7,200 rpm ARRAID Level 1 and "Level 5" arrays for comparison. Truthfully, we don't really think the ARRAID lives up to the full potential of Level 5, because it doesn't permit the hot-swapping of drives, which MicroNet's RAIDbank does permit.

Price per Megabyte

1-GB **ARRAID Level 1** =	$1.60
2-GB **ARRAID Level 1** =	$1.25
4-GB **ARRAID Level 1** =	$0.83
8-GB **ARRAID Level 1** =	$0.81
2-GB **ARRAID Level 5** =	$1.25
4-GB **ARRAID Level 5** =	$0.95
8-GB **ARRAID Level 5** =	$0.63
12-GB **ARRAID Level 5** =	$0.56

APS ARRAID

MicroNet's RAID Level 1 is called Raven Pro. It consists of two drives and has dual channel Fast Wide SCSI controller. In English, this means that you can connect both drives off one NuBus slot without having to daisy chain. The range of total drive space available is between 4–17 GB.

Price per Megabyte

4-GB **MicroNet Raven Pro RAID Level 1** =	$0.97–$1.06
8-GB **MicroNet Raven Pro RAID Level 1** =	$0.62–$0.68
17-GB **MicroNet Raven Pro RAID Level 1** =	$0.50–$0.55

There are a number of different solutions for each type of computer. For Quadra 700, 800, 900, and 950, the PDS40 solution is available. For all other Raven Pro configurations, use the NuBus solution. There is also a PCI solution for RAID Level 1, but it is not included in the Raven Pro family. If you have more questions, call MicroNet directly at (714) 453-6100.

MicroNet's RAID Level 5 is called RAIDbank Pro. It comes with two hot-swappable power supplies as well as six slots for drives. At least three drives must be put in the slots to implement a RAID Level 5 system. From a logical perspective, one of the six slots is always used to contain the parity information. From a physical perspective, the parity information is spread across all drives, but takes up to one total disk space. Thus, one drive is not included in your total usable space. There are two solutions available with RAIDbank Pro. The bottom line is that the PCI is faster and cheaper. Only use the NuBus solution if you cannot implement the PCI solution.

Price per Megabyte (NuBus)

4-GB **MicroNet RAIDbank Pro Level 5** =	$2.57–$2.97
8-GB **MicroNet RAIDbank Pro Level 5** =	$1.50–$1.75
12-GB **MicroNet RAIDbank Pro Level 5** =	$1.16–$1.36
16-GB **MicroNet RAIDbank Pro Level 5** =	$1.00–$1.16
20-GB **MicroNet RAIDbank Pro Level 5** =	$.90–$1.04

Price per Megabyte (PCI)

4-GB **MicroNet RAIDbank Pro Level 5** =	$2.45–$2.80

12-GB **MicroNet RAIDbank Pro Level 5** = $1.11–$1.31

8-GB **MicroNet RAIDbank Pro Level 5** = $1.42–$1.67

16-GB **MicroNet RAIDbank Pro Level 5** = $0.96–$1.12

20-GB **MicroNet RAIDbank Pro Level 5** = $0.87–$1.00

As you can see, a little negotiation should bring your list price down to around $2,500. That's at least one trip to the beach!

MicroNet's RAIDbank

BLOCK-ADDRESSABLE AND STREAMING TAPE

Tapes are advantageous because they are relatively cheap and have high capacities. The capacity of any given tape drive is defined by the tape length for that particular drive specification, its recording format, the type of tape, and the speed and stability of not only the computers you are backing up from and to but also the speed and stability of the network overall. I don't know whether you understood the last part of that sentence, so I'll explain it in detail.

Tape Length

A longer tape allows for higher capacity. That's pretty simple. DDS-1 DAT formats support 60- and 90-meter tapes. A 90-meter tape (2 GB) provides twice the raw capacity of a 60-meter tape (1.3 GB). DDS-2 DAT formats allow for 120-meter (4 GB or more) tapes. However, the raw capacity is not proportionally larger—that is, 1/3 larger than 90-meter—because the DDS-2 tape formats are *much denser* than the DDS-1 formats. These tapes, when used in conjunction with a fast backup mechanism and a fast network, can support up to 8 GB of data.

Recording Format

There are primarily two types of recording formats used by DAT manufacturers today. One method, the older of the two, is the QIC methodology of writing to the tape. This method follows the well-known block-addressable format. Much like the hard drives that have to be formatted before use, block-addressable tapes have to be formatted as well. When writing to the tape, the block-addressable driver writes in a serpentine manner, as illustrated in the following diagram.

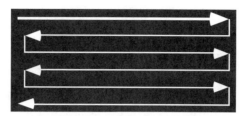

QIC Serpentine Recording Method

The other type of recording format uses the *streaming tape* process. These tapes do not need formatting, because the drive mechanism formats the tape as it writes to it. Because the tape is being formatted during writing, the capacity may vary, depending on the condition of the tape, the speed of the incoming data, and the length of the tape. Most streaming tape systems today use the helical scan method of writing to the tape. Instead of the serpentine "block" technology used by the QIC format, helical scan uses read/write heads embedded in a drum rotating at high speed against the tape, which "streams" past the heads very slowly. As the device writes to the tape, the read head is positioned so it verifies each "frame" of data after writing the frame. If the device detects an error, the data is rewritten to a new frame on the tape, after which the device reads the frame again and check for errors. This process involves a certain number of retries, the number of raw retries being determined by each tape manufacturer. On the "xth" error, the media is considered faulty, and the backup is halted until a new tape can be inserted.

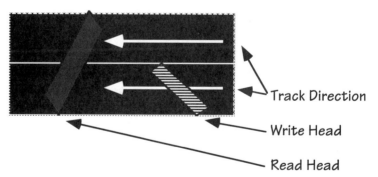

Read and Write Heads on Helical Scan Tape Systems

Tape Capacity and Backup Speed

The speed and throughput with which a backup is performed, the amount of information that can be backed up on a tape, and the amount of information that *is* backed up on a tape are all interrelated. Because the tape continually "streams" at a low speed under the tape drive heads, it is necessary to keep a constant source of information flowing to the tape drive. When the drive runs out of information to write to the tape, an "underrun" occurs. The tape will keep running whether or not there is data to write. Each time the drive mechanism has to wait for more data, it writes "padding" to the tape. Let's look at an example from the network in the following picture.

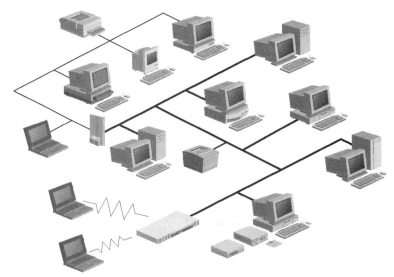

Small Network with Ethernet, LocalTalk, and ARA

This network has three media types on which the network signal travels. One type is the Ethernet network supporting sustained throughput speeds of around 4–10 MB per minute. Then there is the LocalTalk network, which supports sustained throughput speeds of around 1 MB per minute. Finally, there is the ARA network supporting, depending on the modem type, much less than 1 MB per minute. When backing up this network, the administrator decided to back up from the fastest machine he had, the PowerMac 6100 on the Ethernet side. This computer can process information coming in off the network rapidly and can transfer that information to the tape drive just as quickly. For most of the Ethernet-based computers on the network, this works fine.

The administrator then decided to back up the LocalTalk-based machines, too. The LocalTalk side of the network is a much older installation that often runs slowly and has known cabling problems. As soon as the administrator included this side of the network, he noticed that the 1 GB of hard drive space he added to the back up was taking up around 1.5 GB of tape space—with compression! Since the numbers seem backward, he decided to investigate. What he found was that the network was exceedingly slow and there were many network errors and retries occurring during the backup process. Because the DAT drive wasn't receiving a steady source of data, it had to continually stop the writing, reposition the write heads on the tape, and write "padding" while waiting for more incoming data. This constant repositioning of the write-heads was causing the diminishing return on capacity.

Now that you know about the issues that affect all tape systems, let's take a look at each one individually. There are four types of tape systems in common usage today: QIC (Quarter-Inch Cartridge), 8mm, DAT (Digital Audio Tape), and DLT (Digital Linear Tape). Note that the price per megabyte figures we use here are for best-case scenarios, which most of us will never actually achieve.

Quarter-Inch Cartridges (QIC)

The QIC format has been around since the early 1980s, when it was designed by 3M. This was the format for the old Apple Tape Drive 40SC. The capacity of these drives is generally between 40 MB and 1.3 GB. They record their data in narrow tracks along the length of the tape. They have been pushed into the background in recent years as they are dirt slow.

There are really two types of QIC media: 3.5-inch *minicartridges* and 5.25-inch *data cartridges*. These are DC 2000 and DC 6000 cartridges, to be more specific. The most common drive is the QIC-80 using a DC 2120 minicartridge for an uncompressed capacity of 120 MB, or 250 MB compressed. The QIC-160 uses a longer DC 2120XL minicartridge to store 170 MB of uncompressed data, or about 350 MB compressed. The QIC-3010 and

QIC-3020 drives look about the same but have 680 MB uncompressed to 1.3 GB of compressed storage capacity.

APS ships a unit that stores 2–4 GB on a QIC-Wide 3080XLF cartridge at a backup rate of about 30 MB per minute. Drives like this one make the QIC format a reasonable option again.

Price per Megabyte

150-MB **DC 6150 Data Cartridges** =	$0.09
250-MB **DC 6250 Data Cartridges** =	$0.07
525-MB **DC 6525 Data Cartridges** =	$0.05
40-MB **DC 2000 Minicartridges** =	$0.25
120-MB **DC 2120 Minicartridges** =	$0.11
120-MB **DC 2120XL Minicartridges** =	$0.11
2–4-GB **QIC-WIDE 3080XLF Cartridges** =	$0.01 (or less)

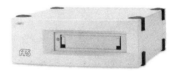

APS HyperTape Drive

TEAC

Don't confuse QIC with TEAC backup devices. These use data-formatted streaming cassettes that look like a cassette you would put in your Sony Walkman. They come in 50-MB, 60-MB, 155-MB, and 600-MB capacities. Because of their low capacities, extreme slowness, and the difficulty of finding cassettes for these systems, they should not be used for network backups.

8mm Tape Cartridges

The 8mm systems use the D8 cartridge format developed by Sony. In 1987, Exabyte Corporation licensed the technology and is currently the only producer of these tape mechanisms. The 8mm tape drives use the helical-scan method of reading and writing. Their capacities are generally 2.5–20 GB. Good uses for 8mm tapes include backing up large databases or huge graphics files.

Price per Megabyte

2.2–5-GB **8mm Tape Cartridges** = $0.01 (or less).

4mm DAT Cartridges

The 4mm DAT drives use the same helical-scan method of reading and writing as the 8mm tape drives. They generally hold 2 GB or 4 GB of data. There are several manufacturers of these drives. Originally a CD-quality audio format, the 4mm tapes have evolved to support the following formats.

60m 1.3-GB DAT

DDS (Digital Data Storage)

DDS is a backup format promoted by Sony and Hewlett-Packard and adopted by a large number of tape drive manufacturers, including Archive Corp., WangDAT Inc., and WangTek Inc. Because of the selection of different manufacturers and the low cost per megabyte, DAT is the backup format of choice. There are two DDS formats that are now supported: *DDS-1* and *DDS-2*. DDS-1 formats support 60- and 90-meter tapes. The 60-meter tapes typically hold around 1.3 GB of uncompressed data, whereas the 90-meter tapes hold around 2 GB of uncompressed data. The newer DDS-2 format supports 120-meter tapes that easily hold around 4 GB of uncompressed data.

120m 4-GB DAT

Data DAT (Digital Audio Tape)

Data DAT is an update-in-place format that treats the tape as a random-access device (similar to a disk drive). Because you will be in the ultimate minority, don't even *think* about looking for drives supporting Data DAT.

Price per Megabyte

1.3-GB **60-meter 4mm DDS-1** =	$0.01 (or less)
2-GB **90-meter 4mm DDS-1** =	$0.01 (or less)
4-GB **120-meter 4mm DDS-2** =	$0.01 (or less)

APS HyperDAT Drive

DLT Cartridges

Presently, the fastest and highest-capacity tape backup device for the Macintosh uses a technology created by Quantum involving *Digital Linear Tape*. DLT drives use a 0.5-inch streaming tape on which they record two tracks at a time. These backup deities claim backup rates as high as 150 MB per minute, but a mere 70 MB per minute is more common. Do you know what 70–150 MB per minute means? Well, for one thing, your network probably can't keep up with it. You are supposed to back up data onto these things at no less than 40 MB per minute or the heads start to wear excessively! Unless you have 100 Mbps Ethernet, the network is going to be a bottleneck. They are great for backing up file servers, though.

DLT 20-GB Cartridge

Price per Megabyte

20-GB **DLT20 Data Cartridge** = $0.01 (or less)

40-GB **DLT40 Data Cartridge** = $0.01 (or less)

APS DLT Drive

About Autoloaders

There are a few good reasons an administrator might want a tape autoloader. One reason is so the administrator can load different tape sets for backups and archives that are set to run at different times of the day. Another reason is to ensure that all backup operations can occur unattended, without having to change the tapes. Most simple backup plans don't call for these autoload systems, however, and as the aim of this book is to set you up with a simple backup plan, we won't be addressing autoloaders in detail. Instead, we will briefly mention a few we could recommend.

MicroNet's SB-DAT 48/6 Autoloader

The MicroNet Premier DAT 48/6 is one impressive machine. The 48 and 6 in the name stand for the 48 GB of storage space it makes available on its six DDS-2 4mm tapes. Available for both PCs and Macintoshes, it boasts backup rates of up to 36 MB per minute.

APS DATLoader 600

Another device (but one that we haven't put to the test) is the APS DATLoader 600 which can also accommodate 48 GB of storage space using six DDS-2 4mm tapes. Using the same HyperDAT mechanism used in APS's single-tape drive, it boasts backup rates of up to 28 MB per minute. If you are wondering, the device we currently recommend is the MicroNet device. It is speedy, reliable, and has a great readout screen.

In both cases, you can load these things with six data tapes, but a better idea is to load five data tapes and a head-cleaning cassette.

Kodak PCD Writer with Disc Transporter

The last device we'd like to mention is not something that will be on most network administrators' lists of "must-haves." If your company burns a lot of CDs, however, perhaps for software distribution for large-scale archiving, you might want a CD autoloader like the Kodak Disc Transporter/Kodak PCD Writer 600 combination. Meant to be a production machine, the PCD Writer 600's 6x drive will write 550 MB of a data to any standard CD format in about 10 minutes! Disc Transporter will autoload up to 75 blank CDs without your having to be around to deal with it!

PART SEVEN:
CONDUCTING NETWORK BACKUPS WITH RETROSPECT

Retrospect and Retrospect Remote make possible the unattended, centralized backing up of entire hard drives or just single files for every Retrospect Remote-equipped Macintosh on an internetwork. If you are backing up more than one server or one workstation acting as a backup server, you will need multiple copies of Retrospect (to be run on multiple backup workstations located throughout the network), or you will need Retrospect Remote. Depending on the number of server volumes to back up, their capacity, your network's throughput, and other factors, you might need both.

DON'T BORE ME WITH THE DETAILS . . .

Read the manual. It's a good one.

CHAPTER 13:
RETROSPECT BASICS

The Retrospect application can create backups and archives of any information accessible through either the desktop or one of its °Remote control panels. Many of my clients purchase a single copy of Retrospect to back up all file servers on the network. This sounds logical, but they don't use the °Remote control panel to retrieve information from outlying computers. Instead, they mount all the file server volumes on the desktop and back them up that way. There are two problems with this approach.

One problem is that it isn't secure to have all file servers mounted on the desktop of a computer, backing up, when you go home. Remember, to access the information, you would have to mount the servers as the Administrator, or you wouldn't be able to back up the System Folder. This gives anyone approaching the backup computer full access to all information on all the file servers.

The other problem is that this method is dirt slow. AppleShare uses a set of transport protocols that are much slower than the protocol Retrospect uses.

Thus, we strongly suggest using Retrospect Remote to communicate with the outlying computers. Remember, though, Retrospect can connect and back up any °Remote-equipped device on the network—that means devices on Ethernet, LocalTalk, and even computers currently connected via Apple Remote Access. You *really* don't want to back up computers currently connected via ARA.

TERMINOLOGY

There are three terms with which you should become immediately familiar when working with Retrospect. The terms are *SnapShot, Catalog,* and *StorageSet.* The backups and archives Retrospect creates are stored on StorageSets. When Retrospect creates or adds to one of these StorageSets, it also takes a SnapShot of the volume's contents as is and creates a catalog. This SnapShot is a picture of the hard drive's state before the backup is made. It records where each and every file and folder resides on the hard drive. If the files to be backed up need to be restored at a later date, Retrospect uses this SnapShot to automatically search the volume and restore the files to match the most recent version. This SnapShot information is stored in the backup Catalog.

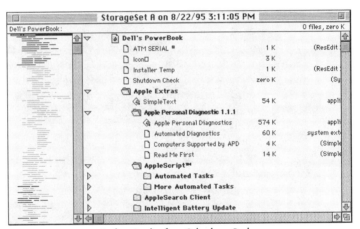

Backup Catalog for a Subvolume Backup

A Catalog is updated every time a backup or archive is performed. The Catalog is the index of files being backed up or archived. Each time a backup is performed, the Catalog is updated with the most current information. These Catalogs are either kept separate from the StorageSet, as in the case of the disk- and tape-based backups, or they are made to be a part of them, as with the file-based backups. Retrospect can work with the following four types of StorageSets:

Macintosh Files combine the Catalog with a single storage file. This means that the entire file must reside on a single volume, such as a large hard drive or an Apple-Share volume.

Macintosh Disks can use any ejectable media that can be mounted on your computer's desktop. This includes floppies, write-once read-many optical, magneto optical, Bernoulli, Zip, Jaz, and SyQuest disks. Catalogs for these StorageSets remain with the host computer.

SCSI Tape Drives can use any tape system, such as DAT, TEAC, Exabyte, QIC, DC 2000, and other systems that are Macintosh compatible and use Small Computer Systems Interface (SCSI). The Catalogs for these StorageSets also remain with the host computer.

SCSI CD-R Drives are new with the advent of version 3.0. Retrospect can now support a limited number of CD-R devices. CD-R devices are write-once, read-many devices that create what many people call "CD Masters." The problem with version 3.0 of Retrospect is that it can support these CD-Rs only in native Retrospect mode. This means that files currently can't be backed up in Finder mode and thus have no duplicate features. Once Retrospect can make Finder-readable copies of files on a CD, I will be happy. While I'm thinking of it, you might want to send them some e-mail or give them a call and tell them you want this feature added. Their phone number is (510) 253-3000. Ask for Craig Isaacs. Tell him I sent you.

THE RETROSPECT FILES

Retrospect ships with an Apple Installer Script since version 2. This makes it so much easier to install the software correctly. I can't tell you how many times I've had users install the Remote Workstation software on the same computer from which they are doing the backups. Here is a quick description of the software Retrospect installs:

This is the icon for the Retrospect application. This application is used by the administrator to do the backing up, restoring, archiving, and retrieving of computers' contents. It must be in a folder on the computer creating the backups.

This is the icon for EasyScript, Dantz Development's application that walks first-time backup users through a series of questions and ultimately helps them build a simple tape rotation system for their backups.

Retrospect Help is the help portion of the Retrospect software, accessed from the Windows menu. It should be in the same folder as the Retrospect application.

This is a Read Me file containing pertinent information about the version of the software contained on the disk and any special instructions not included in the manuals. It doesn't have to be copied anywhere but should be read, printed, and kept with the Retrospect manual.

Retro.SCSI is an INIT used to more quickly communicate with tape backup units connected to the SCSI port on the backup Macintosh. Prior to the creation of Retro.SCSI, when Retrospect gave the tape drive a block of data to write, it had to wait until that process was completed before it could prepare the next block of data for writing. Retro.SCSI lets Retrospect perform disconnect/reconnect operations with the tape drives so it can begin reading the hard drives' information and preparing the data for transfer to the tape drive while the tape drive is still writing the current block of information to tape. This allows Retrospect to continually stream information to the tape drive and thus allows for maximum throughput.

Retro.SCSI Does Not Support . . . . . . certain combinations of systems. It does not support the TEAC 35S or Gigatrend 1235 DAT. Neither does it support Macintoshes equipped with accelerator cards or a Mac Plus running System 7, although why you would want to run a Mac Plus under System 7 is beyond me.

Retro.SCSI Is Somewhat Obsolete   Retro.SCSI does not need to be installed on certain types of Macintosh computers. Beginning with the Centris, PowerBook Duo, and Quadra model Macintoshes, Retro.SCSI was rendered obsolete by the new SCSI hardware native to these computers. This continues with the Power Macintosh line as well.

This is the Retro.Startup icon, an extension file stored, appropriately enough, in the Extensions folder within the System Folder. This small extension file continually checks the time according to the computer's system clock and monitors when Retrospect should be launched to perform automatic scripting functions.

This is a Retrospect Utility Icon. In particular, this is the Update from version X icon. This small utility application is used to update the Retrospect Preferences file (found in the Preferences folder within the System Folder) from copies of the software older than the one you are currently installing.

The following files should be installed on remote Macintoshes to be backed up:

This is the °Remote control panel device (cdev). It permits the remote computer to communicate with the host Retrospect application and is used to back up individual computers across the network.

AppleTalk Data Streaming Protocol (ADSP) is an Apple Communications Toolbox tool that must be installed within the System Folder of computers that are running System 6.x software. Retrospect uses this protocol to achieve better results when passing information back and forth across the network. It is not needed in workstations running System 7.x.

INSTALLING RETROSPECT

As mentioned, Retrospect 3.x ships with Apple's Installer Script technology. To begin the installation, insert the Retrospect Install 1 disk into the computer. Open and print the Read Me file. Once you have printed it, read it and then staple it to the front of the manual. Normally, the information found in a Read Me file is worth knowing, especially Dantz's Read Me files.

Install 1 Disk

Once you click the Install Retrospect application, a really cool dialog box with Dantz's great cover art appears. After you "ooh and ahh" at the art, click **Continue**. This brings you to the screen in the next picture.

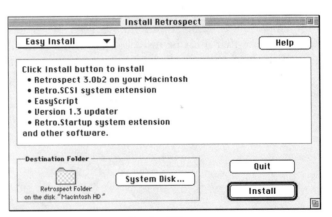

Easy Install Screen

At this point, you may choose **Easy Install** from the upper-left-hand pop-up menu, or you can be like me and customize your installation. I customize my installations because there are a few files I don't generally need. One of those files is the Version 1.3 updater file. I never liked 1.3 and hence, didn't become a rabid fan until 2.0, so I never had to update. I also don't need the Retro.SCSI system extension, because I run my backups from a 68040 machine. The two are incompatible. Thus, select **Custom Install** from the pop-up menu.

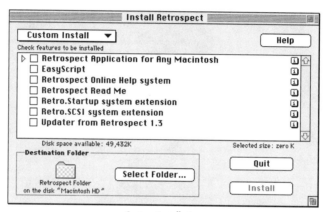

Custom Installation

I install only the appropriate Retrospect software, online help (you never know when you will have a brain-siesta), and the Retro.Startup extension. I also use the **Select Folder…** button and put my Retrospect application's folder on the desktop. It's easier to access that way. By the way, if you ever become confused about what you are installing and what it does, you can click the little "i" buttons to the right of each item. These information buttons display a great little dialog box telling you what the software is, where it goes, and what it does, as in the one depicted in the following diagram.

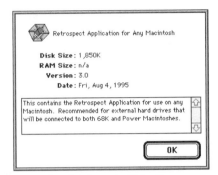

Sample Information Dialog Box

Once you click the **Install** button, Retrospect prompts you to insert the disks it needs for the installation options you chose.

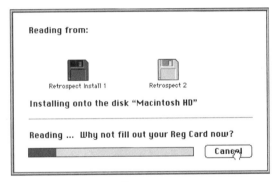

Installation Process

There are two more steps to go. Step 1 is to restart after the installation process. You don't have a choice. Step 2 is to select the Retrospect application icon and set the appropriate RAM allocation for the software. The chances are good that you will need more RAM than originally allocated. Set the allocation according to the number of files in a single volume. Here are some guidelines, provided by Dantz.

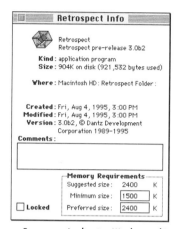

RAM Needed	Files and Folders
1800K	3,500
4000K	10,000
6000K	20,000
8000K	32,000

Retrospect Application Window and Dantz's RAM Specification Recommendations

Activating Retrospect Remote

In order for a computer to be backed up without user intervention, the °Remote control panel device must be installed on that computer. Like the Retrospect Application, Retrospect Remote also comes with an installer script.

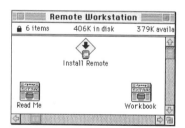

Retrospect Remote Install Disk

Installation is easy and uses only a single disk. To begin the installation process, double click on the Install Remote application icon. After "wow-ing" at Dantz's really cool splash screen, click **OK**, and you are brought to the Easy Install window. This is probably as far as you need to go. If you are comfortable with what is being installed, click the **Install** button, and the Installer application does the rest for you.

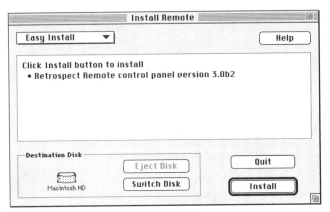

Easy Install Window

If you aren't comfortable with what is being installed, select the **Custom Install** option in the pop-up menu in the upper-left side of the window. You are brought to the Custom Install window and are shown the available installation options.

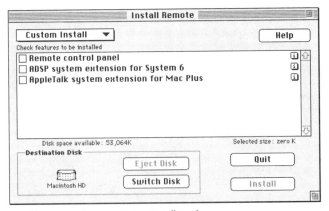

Custom Install Window

In the Custom Install window, you can obtain more information about each piece of software being installed by clicking the small "i" to the right of the installation choice. When you are comfortable with the settings, click **Install** to continue.

Step 1: Finding the Remote-Equipped Computers

You can now begin the remote user activation process and launch Retrospect. In the main window, click the **Configure** tab. The options change to reflect the services Retrospect offers for this category. Click the **Remotes** button on the right side of the screen to configure the Remote-equipped computers.

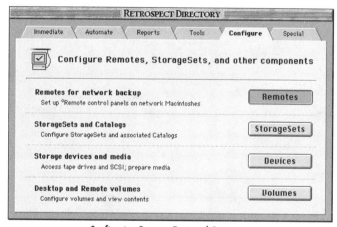

Configuring Remote-Equipped Computers

The Remotes Database window opens. Any Remote-equipped computer that has already been activated appears in the list. If the computer you are attempting to back up remotely doesn't appear in the list, click the **Network...** button to search the network for Remote-equipped computers.

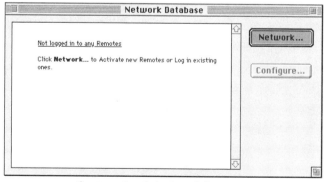

Choosing to Search the Network for Remotes

The Remotes on Network dialog box appears. It shows the network protocol currently in use, the zones on the network below that (with the zone the backup computer is in already selected), and the Remote-equipped computers within the selected zone listed in the large window on the right. The status for computers in this window will be **Not Installed**, **Not Logged In**, or **Responding**.

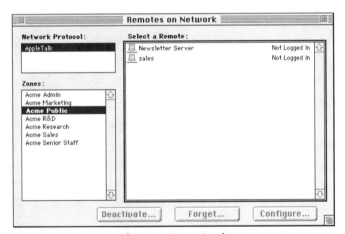

Choosing a Zone to Search

As each zone is selected, a list of Remote-equipped computers found in that zone is displayed. Those Remote-equipped computers that have not been fully installed will have a question mark within their icon and will be labeled **Not Installed**.

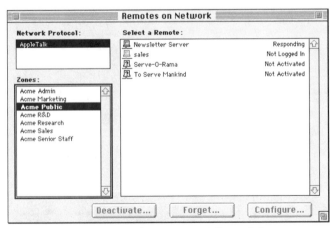

Remote-Equipped Computers Not Fully Installed

Step 2: Activating the Remote-Equipped Computer

Select the Remote-equipped computer that has not been fully installed, and the **Login…** button grays out while an **Activate…** button appears. Click the **Activate…** button. A dialog box appears prompting you to enter an Activator Code. This code is issued to you when you purchase Retrospect Remote. You should be able to find it on a list Dantz provided to you. Select a code you have not used and enter it in the field within the dialog box.

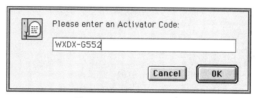

Entering an Activator Code

After entering an activator code, click **OK**. Another dialog box appears prompting you to enter a user's name for that particular computer. Enter a unique name that distinctly identifies this computer. This dialog box initially takes the computer's name from the owner's field in the Sharing Setup control panel. However, there are situations when this causes problems, such as on AppleShare servers where the **Owner's Name** defaults to Administrator. Also, users often name their computers the same things as other users do. It becomes impossible to distinguish between computers you want to back up when they have the same name.

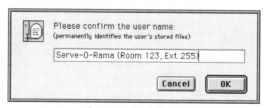

Entering a User's Name

Click **OK** after you have entered a distinct name for the computer you are activating. Another dialog box appears prompting you for a security code. I strongly suggest that you enter a unique security code for the computer, as this code prevents other copies of Retrospect from accessing the remote computer. Once you have entered a code, write it down and put it someplace where you will be able to find it again, in case you and the other administrators forget it.

Clicking **OK** brings up another dialog box prompting you to enter the code again. Read the code back from where you wrote it down and enter it the same way. You will know immediately whether you have written it down correctly.

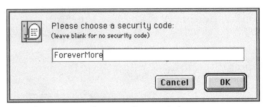

Confirming a Security Code

Quick Story   While I was teaching a backup class at a major vendor's facility, I walked by one of my student's computers and noticed his backup seemed to be going too slowly. The first thing I noticed was that the student had more Remotes in his window than the other students had. Upon closer investigation, I noticed that a couple of them didn't belong to the class. It seems he looked through the network and found a couple of "live" Remote-equipped workstations and was backing them up to his student machine. One of them happened to be the marketing director's computer with that year's forecasts on it! Moral of the Story: Password protect your Remotes.

Quick Naming Strategy   I learned this from a really cool client. Instead of naming your computers after the user, why not change the names to the room number and telephone extension of the user? Then, if there is a problem with that particular computer, you don't have to do much to find out where it "lives" in your organization or how to contact the owner of the computer!

Lynn Heiberger's Rule:

Make sure you update this information as people move around the office. You don't want to look for a user in Wing A of the building if the user and the computer have moved to Wing B.

Step 3: Selecting Volumes to Back Up

It's time to select the volumes you want to back up. Retrospect 3.x gives you some options that differ from the earlier versions of the application. In version 3 and later, you have the option of backing up the "Remote Desktop." This means you can back up *any local volume* that is mounted during the time of the backup. All mounted volumes, floppies, and locked volumes, such as CDs, are automatically excluded. This fantastic feature means you don't have to worry about making sure that the latest drives the user has purchased are now being backed up.

Another option is to back up only the startup volume, which is the volume with the system on it. All other volumes and partitions would be automatically ignored.

Finally, the last option is to go in and manually select the volumes you want backed up. The only reason I could see you doing this is if you wanted to automatically exclude certain volumes on the computer from being backed up. Personally, I think you should take the Leif Erickson approach: If it is there, take it. Remember, I'm an ex-soldier. We took everything that wasn't bolted down (we came back for that stuff later).

At this point, you have the option to include link encryption. Selecting **Link Encryption** ensures that as the data is being backed up over the network, it is scrambled so prying eyes can't find it. Personally, I think it's a waste of time. Someone who wants information on your computer is more likely to steal the computer than to try and reassemble it after capturing the data with a packet analyzer.

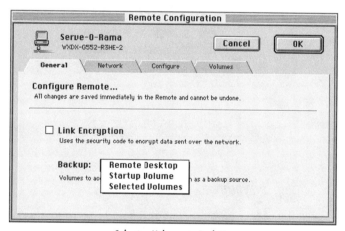

Selecting Volumes to Back Up

Click **OK**, and all volumes selected at that time are available for backing up.

Step 4: Selecting Zones to Search

A new feature of Retrospect 3.x is the ability to look for missing remote computers in zones other than the one to which they were originally assigned. To tell Retrospect which zone the computer should be in, click the **Network** tab in the Remote Configuration window.

The current zone the computer is in will already be highlighted. Select all zones to which you think the user might move the computer by clicking on them. If you have a large network, you won't want to select *all* the zones. Just select the zones that are *local* to the user. If you don't know what a local zone is, ask your network administrator or read our books on network design or network administration. Both of them discuss this in detail.

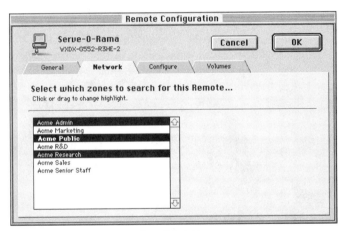

Zone Search List

Step 5: Synchronize Clocks

You might want to take this opportunity to synchronize the clock on the backup computer with that of the Remote-equipped computer you plan to back up. You want to ensure that the clocks are the same for calendaring and reporting purposes. To do this, select the **Configure** tab in the Remote Configuration window and click the **Sync Clock** button. This is also a Script option. It would be wise to set it here as well as in the Script options.

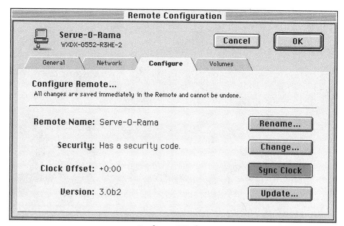

Configure Window

Once you click **OK**, you are returned to the dialog box showing the Remote-equipped computers found within a given zone. Click **OK** to proceed. You are returned to the Remotes on Network window. The Remote-equipped computer you just finished activating should now show up in this window, and the word **Responding** should be by its icon and name.

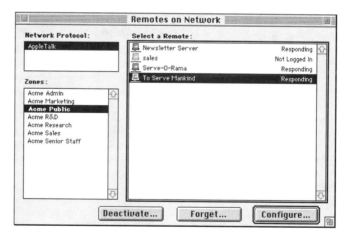

Remote-Equipped Computer Now Responding

Updating Remotes on the Network

There will be times when you need to update the °Remote control panels on your computers across the network. In the Remote on Network window, don't bother to highlight specific Remotes; select **Update All...** from the **Remotes** menu.

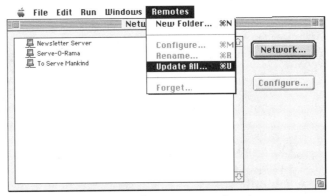

Choosing to Update °Remote Control Panels

Click **Update**, and a dialog box appears asking whether you really want to update all the Remotes listed in the window. See, I told you that you didn't have to select any of them! Anyway, click the **OK** button . . .

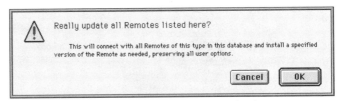

Confirming All Remotes Are to Be Updated

. . . and select the copy of the Remote software you want to use as the update source. A good rule of thumb is to use the one Dantz provided on its diskettes. You know it's a clean copy, and you also know it is the most recent version.

Note: Don't worry about any of your preferences. Updating a Remote keeps those intact.

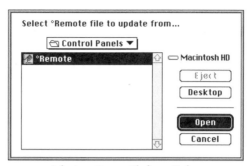

Selecting a Remote File for an Update

Retrospect cycles through the list of Remotes and updates their software, if necessary. Remember, changes won't take effect until the computers are restarted.

What If You Can't Find the Remotes?

This is a more common question than you would think. I frequently receive support calls from network administrators who can't find the Remote-equipped Macintoshes on their networks. Here are some suggestions I have given to them.

Is the Control Panel Loaded? First, establish that the °Remote control panel device is loaded on the computer and is visible on the network. You can discover this quickly by running Check-NET, LANsurveyor, SaberLAN Network Manager, or Net Watchman. If you can't see the service with any of these applications, that means the control panel didn't load during startup. You can always ask the user to open and check the Control Panels folder, too. If it isn't in the Control Panels folder, it didn't load. If the user has something like Extensions Manager or other software that manages extensions and control panels, check whether the Remote is on the computer but located in a folder called Control Panels (disabled). If it is in the Control Panels folder, the status should say "Not Logged In" or something like "Ready."

If you searched the computer with SaberLAN or other monitoring software and found no network services running on the computer (which is pretty unlikely in today's networking world), that means the user restarted the computer with the shift key down, disabling all extensions. Have the user restart the computer again.

Is Remote Access Turned Off? If the control panel is loaded, it could be that the user has turned off Remote Access. Enabling and disabling this function is handled in the next section of the book, but right now, just for you, I'll let you in on the secret. If the status states "turned off," that doesn't mean your wardrobe needs updating or that you are a nerd. It means that the Remote Access radio button is set to **Off**. Set it to **On**.

Is It a "Network" Thing?

There are some other messages the control panel's status field might display also:

"AppleTalk disabled" means that you turned off AppleTalk in the Chooser.

"ADSP not installed" means that you are running System 6 and haven't installed the ADSP extension. Switch to System 7.

"AppleTalk Closed" means that you probably have a PowerBook or Duo and it went to sleep. When your computer goes to sleep, it turns off the AppleTalk protocols and shuts down any connections that might have been running. To reactivate AppleTalk, just open the Chooser.

Is It a "Name" Thing?

"No Macintosh Name or Owner Name specified in Sharing Setup" means that you didn't name your computer. Open your Sharing Setup Control panel and give the computer a name. Then restart and you will be fine.

"Network Name Conflict" means that this computer has the exact same name for an activated °Remote cdev as another computer on the network. Rename the °Remote control panel and restart.

THE °REMOTE CONTROL PANEL

°Remote Control Panel

Retrospect uses a °Remote control panel for each Macintosh on the network (except the one running Retrospect) to communicate with the host backup computer. This software uses the ADSP protocol to communicate across the network. This means that you don't have to use file sharing to communicate as well (or TOPS—you know who you are). The AppleTalk Data Streaming Protocol (ADSP) and AppleTalk Secure Data Streaming Protocol (ASDSP) are symmetrical protocols that support sessions in which clients can exchange full-duplex streams of data. Because ADSP is symmetrical, both clients at either end of the connection maintain equal control over the session and data exchanges. Saber-LAN Network Manager, SaberLAN Update Manager, Timbuktu, and QuickMail are other software packages using ADSP to establish communication with, and send information to and from, the administrator's computer and the computers selected by the software. Apple's Open Collaboration Environment (AOCE) and AppleMail use ASDSP to send secure mail messages from a sender to the intended receivers. So, Retrospect is in good company.

When you first open the °Remote control panel, it displays certain information about the computer on which it is running. The first line of information is the Activator Code number. The second line is the name under which it is registered on the network. The status box should state "Ready." The control panel also displays the date and time the computer was last backed up and the status of that backup. The little "fold" in the bottom-right corner indicates that there is more information. The Remote records the last five backups according to each volume's name. Finally, Remote Access can be turned on and off from this location.

More Info Clicking **Preferences…** presents the user with more options.

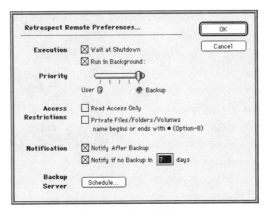

Retrospect Remote Options

Execution and Priority The **Execution** option has two choices. The **Wait at Shutdown** option sets the Remote to intercept the shutdown command in the Finder. When a user selects **Shut Down** from the Finder's **Special** menu, the Macintosh goes through its normal shutdown procedures, like turning off Personal File Sharing and closing applications. However, instead of actually shutting down, Remote presents a dialog box allowing the user to do one of three things: fully shut down, restart, or do nothing. Doing nothing causes the Remote screen saver to activate, and the workstation will await Retrospect's backup. The Remote will follow this procedure whether a backup is scheduled or not.

Run in Background allows the user to continue working uninterrupted while a backup is being performed on the computer. If this is not checked, the user is presented with a dialog box asking whether the backup should take place in the foreground—meaning that nothing else can happen on this computer during the backup process—or whether the backup should be canceled. If the user chooses to run the backup in the background, the priority can be set to either the User or the Backup. Because Retrospect's tape backup capacity is directly affected by network throughput and speed, you should have your settings either set to run in the background with highest priority to the backup or set for the backup to run in the foreground. I've proved to more than one network administrator that if users are working on decent machines (that means a IIci or better), they won't even notice when a backup is happening as it runs in the background.

Access Restrictions

Don't mess with Access Restrictions. If your users are messing with this, have them sign a waiver of liability. I'm not kidding. The network administrator is responsible for the well-being of all data on the network, on every computer.

There have been only two times in my career when I've seen users decide to begin restricting access to the files on their computers. One time was with a government agency, one of the alphabet soup variety. The agency didn't want that information backed up because it didn't want a record of the data to exist outside of the computers on which it was working. This was also an agency that, rather than having hard drives fixed, would destroy (read *incinerate*) its hard drives and buy new ones. Strange, but true.

The other time this happened was in a company that didn't trust the network administrator, and with good reason. The employees were marking folders they didn't want this person to see. If users are denying access to the administrator because of privacy issues, this should be dealt with in an ethics policy.

Gopher Early Warning System (Notification)

I call this the Gopher Early Warning System because these options are displayed on the computer after a backup has taken place. If you leave them selected, set the **Notify if no Backup in 'x' days** limit to at least 3. Why not 1? If you are not backing up over the weekend, you need your settings to be for at least three days.

I guess I still haven't told you about the gopher reference. It relates back to a time I was walking with one of my favorite network administrators, I'll call him Bob, through his office. The server had gone down while we were getting a Coke (that's when it always happens). By the time we hit the office door, his boss had paged him twice, and three people met us in the hall, telling us the server was down. Now comes the gopher part: As we walked by the final row of about 20 cubicles, each user decided to stick his or her head up out of the cubicle and tell us the server was down. It was like watching gophers come out their holes. As a matter of fact, that's what Bob called them. "Why don't you gophers gimme a break," was something akin to what he said. Anyway, since that time I've noticed that when anything on the network goes wrong, every cube-based user will be there to sound an early-warning system as the administrator walks by.

Setting a Backup Schedule

There are three basic options that the user can choose when altering the administrator's backup schedule. The default option is to use whatever normal schedule was created by the administrator. The second option is to move the computer to the top of the list for backups by setting the first radio-button to **As soon as possible**. Finally, the user can set a scheduling option to indicate that the computer cannot be backed up until after a certain time. This is great for computers that are extremely busy and should be backed up later in the scheduling process.

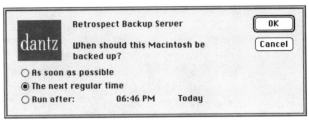

Setting a Backup Schedule

CHAPTER 14:
CREATING AN IMMEDIATE BACKUP
WITH RETROSPECT

Retrospect's main window is much like a directory of services. It is from this window that the administrator begins each interactive backup, restore, or archive.

When the window is first opened, the **Immediate** directory, the top-left tab of the window, is automatically selected. All available options for an immediate operation are shown in this window. Selecting other tabs brings up different options.

While you are learning the ins and outs of Retrospect, ensure that your servers are backed up before you begin anything "fancy," like rotating backup scripts. For this reason alone, I am going to teach you how to create an immediate backup of the local and Remote-equipped computers on your network. Remember, to maintain the AppleShare access privileges, AppleShare must be running on the file servers during the backup process.

BEGINNING THE IMMEDIATE BACKUP

Step 1: Begin the Backup Process

To begin an immediate backup, select the **Immediate** tab in the Retrospect Directory window, then click the **Backup** button.

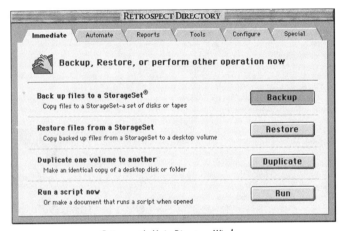

Retrospect's Main Directory Window

Step 2: Choosing the Source Volume

The Volume Selection window appears with a listing of mounted volumes and Remote-equipped Macintoshes available for backing up. The source volume is the volume from which the backup is originating. Source volumes can be mounted volumes, such as SCSI devices directly connected to the backup machine, or AppleShare volumes, from either a server or another workstation's shared folder.

Retrospect 3.x introduces a new concept, called the Local Desktop. Within this grouping, all the locally mounted volumes appear. The administrator has a choice of selecting each volume individually by clicking the twiddle next to **Network Remotes** or selecting the **Local Desktop** grouping itself, which is what we recommend. There is also a selector called **Source Groups**, but we aren't going to talk about the Source Groups at this point in time. We'll save that for more advanced backup topics.

In the following window, I selected all local and Remote-equipped volumes for backup by selecting their major grouping headers—**Local Desktop** and **Network Remotes**. This is the easiest way I know to ensure that you are backing up everything out there you have logged in to.

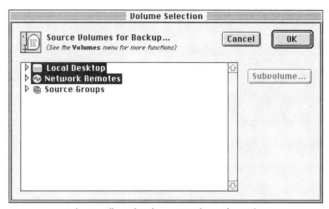

Selecting All Local and Remote Volumes for Backup

Selecting "Subvolumes" as Backup Sources

You can do it, but I don't advise it. In short, what will happen is that you will decide that you don't want this folder and do want that folder; then, when the server goes down, you will find that the rest of the network crowd wanted a different group of folders than you did. Back up everything you can. Take some advice from an ex–Green Beret—if you can find it, take it. Of course, this applies only to beer, jeeps, money in your wife's purse, and backups.

Step 3: Creating the StorageSet

After the source volumes are chosen, click **OK**. If this is the first time Retrospect has been used, the StorageSet window shows that there are no current StorageSets. Otherwise, it displays the list of currently active StorageSets. Create a new backup StorageSet to continue. Don't be surprised if Retrospect automatically prompts you to do so. It is set to prompt you if it doesn't find any existing StorageSets.

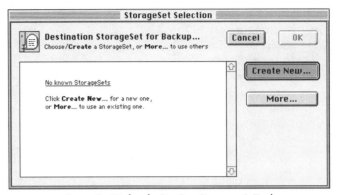

StorageSet Window the First Time Retrospect Is Used

To create a new StorageSet, click the **Create New...** button. There are four types of Retrospect StorageSets: disks, CD-R, tape, and file. To create a new StorageSet of one of these three types, select it from the **Storage type** pop-up menu and give the StorageSet a name. I named our tape *StorageSet A,* which is what Retrospect enters as your first default name. Even though we are using only one tape right now, we might as well get the ball rolling, as we soon will be creating rotating tape sets. Retrospect 3.x is smart enough to know that if your first tape is named *StorageSet A,* the next time a tape set is created, it will automatically be named S*torageSet B.* This will become useful to you later on.

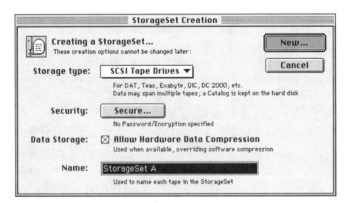

Creating and Naming a StorageSet

In my example, I chose a **SCSI Tape Drives** StorageSet. I have also left the **Allow Hardware Data Compression** checkbox selected. This way, if the hardware to which I am backing up uses data compression techniques, the software will not override it. I haven't set any special security precautions, like a password or encryption, either. I believe that physical security is much better than password security.

Once **New...** is clicked, a dialog box appears asking where you want to place the Catalog file. Select a location and click **Save**. For convenience, I usually put the storage Catalogs in the same folder with the Retrospect application. However, if you are backing up your server from the server (that is, you are backing up the file server with Retrospect running on it), you might want to put the storage Catalog somewhere else. In this way, if the server goes down, your Catalog won't go down with it. It takes about 5–6 hours to restore them from scratch. I recommend that you store your StorageSets across the network if you don't have a spare drive on which to store them. Putting them on a mirrored volume is a good idea also. In my example, this isn't the file server, so I am going to store our Catalog locally.

Selecting a Location for the Storage Catalog

Once a StorageSet is created and the Catalog file is saved to a convenient location, the StorageSet Selection window displays the new information.

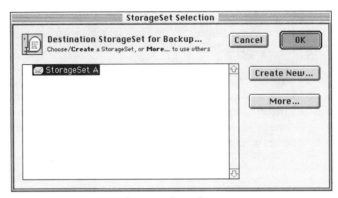

StorageSet Selection Window with New StorageSet

Step 4: Launching the Backup

If this is the first time you are doing a backup, Retrospect automatically selects all files to ensure that a full backup is created. If this is a continuation of a previous backup, then only files that have been changed or added will be selected.

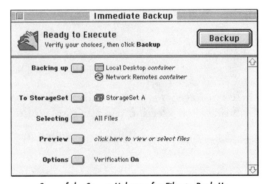

Scan of the Source Volumes for Files to Back Up

The Immediate Backup window shows the backup settings to be used during the creation of the StorageSet. There is one additional option that has been set and should always remain set—verification.

Verification compares the files in the archive to the original files at the byte level for local volumes and at the checksum level for remote volumes, after the backup has been completed. It is my opinion that all backups should be verified after completion. If, for some reason, a file or a number of files were backed up and were corrupted as a result, or even corrupted beforehand, what good is the backup? Realize, though, that this will take a significant amount of additional time. Verifying the backup adds approximately 50% more time to the backup process.

Clicking **Backup** begins the backup process. Retrospect asks you whether you really want to execute the backup. If you do, click **Yes**.

Step 5: Preparing the New Tape

If a new tape is being used, a dialog box appears prompting you to insert the new tape in the tape drive. Insert the tape and click **Proceed** for the backup operation to continue.

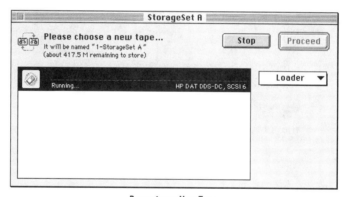

Preparing a New Tape

Step 6: Execution and Log Verification

Once a tape is in the drive and the execution of the backup begins, Retrospect displays a dialog box showing the continuing process.

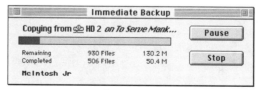

Backup in Progress

If you want to find out how quickly your backup is going while it is in progress, click the zoom box in the upper-right-hand corner of the backup progress window, and the window expands to show you more information.

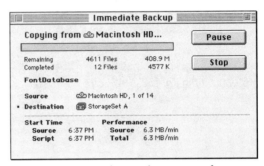

Expanded Progress Dialog Box Showing More Information

When the backup is completed, unless you have chosen the option to quit the Retrospect program, the progress dialog box remains on the screen and shows either that the backup has been successfully executed or that errors took place during execution.

You will also need to read your backup reports. For this, you'll need to reference the short chapter we wrote about it. It begins on page 279.

Chapter 15: Creating a Rotational Backup Script with Retrospect

You have your first backup under your belt and on tape. It's time to graduate to the Big Leagues. We are going to begin the implementation of rotated tape scripts. This means that in the main Retrospect Directory window, you are going to be using the **Script** button this time. From here on, you shouldn't be conducting any more immediate backups. You should always script your backups, even if you want to perform one immediately, so that you leave some kind of record of what you were attempting to back up, in case the backup fails. With a script, someone else can look at what you chose to back up, look at your options, and figure out what went wrong and at what point during the backup process it went wrong.

There are two ways to create backup scripts. The method endorsed by me and most of the staff at Dantz is to put everything into a single backup script and let the script do all the work. You can have all sources and destination tapes in the same script. This is an easy way of maintaining your backup. However, others believe that you should create a script for each backup destination. In other words, if you were going to have three backup tape sets, A, B, and C, you would have three backup scripts: one for A, one for B, and one for C. In truth, there's nothing wrong with either of these methods. But, since I'm writing this book, I'm going to show you how to put everything into a single script.

CREATING A SCRIPTED BACKUP

Step 1: Create a New Script

Launch Retrospect and once the directory window is open, click **Automate** from the top tabs. Then click the **Scripts** button to begin the scripting process.

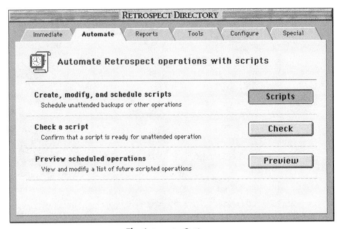

The Automate Options

The Scripts dialog box opens, asking you to either select a current script or create a new one. Click **New…** to continue.

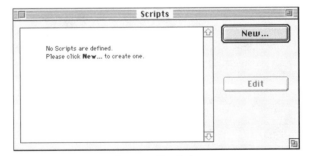

Creating a New Script

Retrospect next prompts you for the type of script you want to create. We will be creating a **Backup** script.

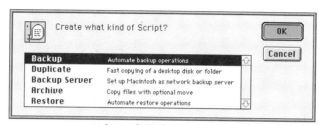

Selecting the Backup Script Option

Retrospect now asks you to name the new script. Stop and think a moment before you name the script. If you will be creating more than one script, you need to select names that easily identify the one you want to run. If you are like me, you probably will have a single script for your backups, one for archiving, and maybe a "nomad catcher" script, which I'll cover later. I called this one *Network Frontiers Backup Script* because that's what it is—it is my script for backing up our every-day work.

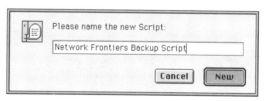

Naming the Script

Step 2: Choose the Source Volumes

After you have named your new backup script, Retrospect displays a dialog box showing the script's settings. Click the **Sources** button to choose from where you want to retrieve the information you are backing up.

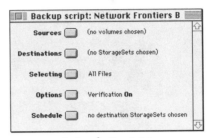

Settings for New Script

A dialog box appears listing all volumes that can be selected. There are three choices for volumes in this list: all volumes locally mounted on the computer doing the backup, all volumes local to the computers to which you signed in when setting up Retrospect Remotes, and then grouped computers. Don't worry about the grouped computers yet. We haven't created any. Select **Local Desktop** and the individual networked Remotes you wish to back up and click **OK**, or click **Local Desktop** and **Network Remotes** to back up everything that has been logged into and mounted (which is what we recommend).

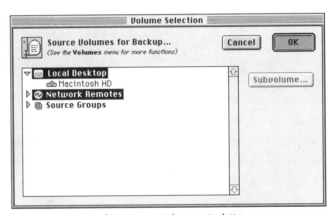

Selecting Source Volumes to Back Up

The list of volumes appears in the **Sources** area of the script in the script window.

Step 3: Selecting the Destination

Once you know what you will be backing up, set the destination for that information. To begin this step, click **Destinations** in the Backup script window.

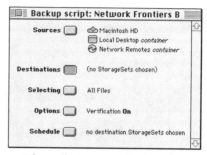

Selecting the Destinations for the Backup

Retrospect displays a dialog box with every StorageSet known to Retrospect. You should have a destination StorageSet A showing if you created an immediate backup in the previous section. Now create the other two sets: B and C. To create the next two StorageSets, click the **Create New…** button. The StorageSet Creation window appears, in which you can name your new StorageSet.

Naming the New StorageSet

I strongly suggest *not* password protecting your StorageSets. Most people forget the stupid password and then can't get back into the darned thing to restore it. However, since a lot of you moaned and groaned over this after reading the first book, I'll give you a few pointers if you *must* password protect your StorageSet. Clicking the **Secure…** button brings up a dialog box asking you which type of protection you desire. **Password Only (no encryption)** places a password on the storage Catalog. **SimpleCrypt (fast)** and **DES (more secure)** (Data Encryption Standard) encrypt the files before backup. Unless you are an alphabet soup agency (CIA, DIA, DEA, FBI, or IHASGF), you don't need either of these. By the way,

IHASGF stands for the "I Hate Acronyms Society of Greater Flatbush." I used to suggest using such encryption, but I found that too many of my clients forget the passwords. This causes major problems. But if you don't want to take my advice, select an encryption type, click **OK**, and Retrospect prompts you twice for your password. It does this to ensure that you can enter the same information both times. Here's a hint: If you can't enter it right twice in a row, give up and buy a good mean ol' dawg (*dawgs* are meaner than *dogs*) to guard your tapes.

After entering a password, Retrospect asks where you want to store the StorageSet Catalog. Select a location and click **Save**. Again, I put StorageSet B in the same place I put StorageSet A: the Retrospect Folder. It's easier to remember.

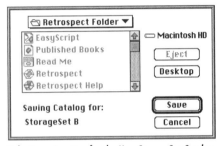

Selecting a Location for the New StorageSet Catalog

Retrospect logs this information in the StorageSet Selection window. Click **OK** to continue. You need to go through the same destination creation process to create Set C. Select them all in the StorageSet Selection window, click **OK**, and Retrospect places them in the Destination window. Ensure that they are all selected and click **OK** one last time, as shown in the following window. You end up back in the Backup script window, ready for the next step.

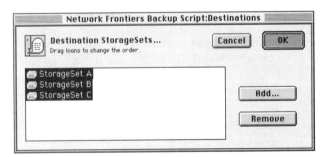

Three Newly Created StorageSets

Step 4: Setting Criteria

There should be no criteria set, other than **All Files**. Don't mess with criteria when backing up. Mess with it when restoring or creating archives. Again, take everything that's not nailed down, and come back with a crowbar for the stuff that is. If you set criteria for backups and then lose data, you are going to hate yourself in the morning.

The only folks I know who should mess with criteria are like that certain company in Thousand Oaks that won't let me mention its name and that uses really fancy-schmancy encryption utilities like A.M.E. and Empower and other things I can't mention. When using these kinds of low-level formatting tools, set a filter not to back up certain files the tools put on the hard drive. They can't be backed up, anyway, so set the filters to keep the files from showing up in the log as backup errors.

Step 5: Adding Some Options

Now that you have your sources and your destinations, take a quick stroll through the Options windows. Most of the options can be left at the default, but there are a few I want to call to your attention. In the Backup script window, click **Options** to open the Options window.

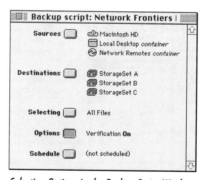

Selecting Options in the Backup Script Window

The default option is to have **Verification On**. Leave it that way. You are interested in the **More Choices** button in the bottom-right side of the window. Clicking this button leads you to fame and fortune. Well, not quite, but you do see the other available options.

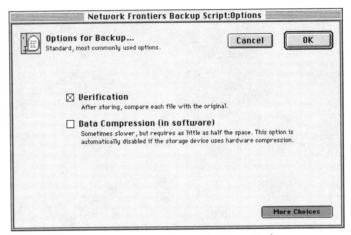

Selecting to View More Choices in the Options Window

The second option on the scrolling list is **AppleShare**. You can leave AppleShare available to users, but this risks the possibility of files being left open, which would then be incapable of being backed up. You can choose to temporarily turn off AppleShare service, which doesn't shut down the machine. It only turns off the service temporarily during the backup.

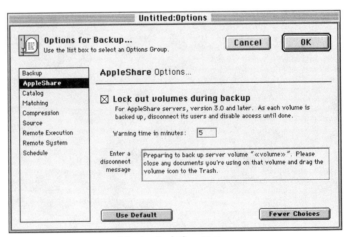

Selecting AppleShare Options

This affects only the computer running the backup. In other words, if you are not running the backup from an AppleShare server, this option isn't going to do you any good. It doesn't affect other AppleShare servers being backed up as Remotes.

There are some pros and some cons to setting this option. Let me explain both with real-world stories.

Shut It Down!   I have a client whose entire sales staff uses the same TouchBASE database. The TouchBASE file they use resides on their AppleShare file server. When people are logged on to the server, they are usually using TouchBASE, too, which means that the file is open, locked, and can't be backed up. One day, a user "dropped" the database. Bad. They lost around 5,000 client records. Very Bad. The administrator said to the boss, "I didn't back it up, because nobody would ever log off." The administrator had a new job a few weeks later. If you have critical data and you can't make people log off the server when you are doing a backup, do it for them. Being polite goes out the window if your job or reputation is at stake.

Don't Touch That Switch!   Certain computers or users need AppleShare to be active, like QuickMail file-based servers or programmers (people, sort of). If you drop QuickMail from the file server, even if it's only during the backup, QuickMail has no way of automatically logging back on. You will walk in the next morning, open your mailbox, and have about 100 urgent notices that there are problems with the file-based gateway. The other problem user is the programmer. Many programmers with whom I used to work used a product called Object Master. This was used to check their code in and out, and it resided on the file server. It seems that many programmers like to work through the night, and one night, while a couple of them were working late, Retrospect logged them off the server to perform a backup. They hadn't checked their code back in yet. Oops. They lost a lot of work, and I lost a couple of pounds of my behind the next day.

So there you have it—a pro and a con for setting this option. This is something you are going to have to decide personally. Remember, ultimately, they aren't going to fire anyone but you if the data can't be restored.

Back in the Options window, there's the world-infamous **Matching** options.

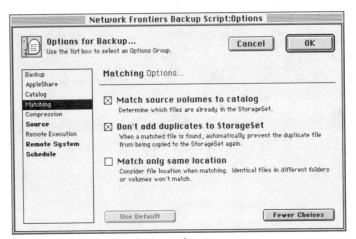

Selecting Matching Options

Unless you are using an accounting system or one of the Medi-Mac types of software, the top checkbox for turning matching on should be selected. The second checkbox tells Retrospect that if a file is already in the Catalog and hasn't changed at all, not to back it up again. If these two checkboxes are not selected (they are selected by default), every backup would be a full backup, as Retrospect wouldn't have anything to compare for the subsequent backups.

The final checkbox, **Match only same files**, is deselected by default and controls how Retrospect reacts when it finds a duplicate file. The kicker, in this instance, is that identical files—files whose name, size, type, creator, creation date, and modification date are the same—can be found anywhere on the network. That doesn't seem like such a big deal at first. However, fonts don't change; applications shouldn't change. Do you want a single copy of a font to be backed up, or do you want each and every copy of the font to be backed up? It's your choice.

Once you've made up your mind with the **Matching** choices, you should move on to the **Source** options. By default, the **Set source volume's backup time** is selected and records the time after a backup has occurred. I want you to also select **Set source folders' backup time**. We've built Server Sleuth so it can read when the folders were last backed up. This way, if a folder wasn't backed up, you'll know it when you run Server Sleuth. The third option for setting a source file's backup time is up to you.

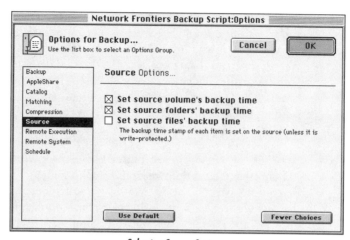

Selecting Source Options

Finally, there's one set of options left for you consider—the **Remote System** options. In the last pair of options, **Never Shut Down** or **Shut Down when Done**, the default is to shut down Remotes after they have been backed up. This means that if a user selects **Shut Down** in the Finder's **Special** menu and the Remote intercepted the shut down call by displaying its screen saver, the computer would be shut down after the backup is completed. However, this doesn't imply that all computers will be shut down, no matter what. Nothing happens to computers that haven't been given the **Shut Down** command. Thus, your servers are safe.

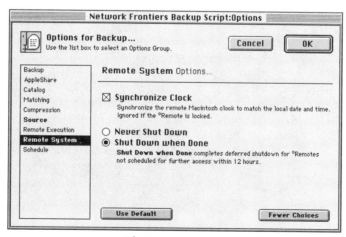

Selecting Remote Options

Notwithstanding what I just told you, I want you to think about something before you select this option. There are some computers, like the Quadra 610, that have manual shut-down buttons. If you select **Shut Down when Done**, these computers will display a dialog box right in the middle of the screen after the backup—you know, the "It is now safe to switch off your Macintosh" dialog box. This means that all night long, night after night, you will have a nice little dialog box burning a hole right through your monitor. Opt to leave the computers on; at least the Retrospect screen saver keeps running and your tubes won't burn out.

Another option is to automatically synchronize the clocks on your Remote Macintoshes. You should select this, making sure that all clocks are kept up to date on your network. It's also a great way to catch people "borrowing" software. How does synchronizing a clock do that? Many applications are "time-sensitive," like gimmees and freebees set to time out after a certain date. You can catch abusers of these types of software by monitoring the person who always says, "My clock is different from yesterday. What happened?" Why else would they be turning back their clocks?

Step 6: Setting the Schedule

It is now time to begin the scheduling operations. One of the first scheduling options is found within the **Script** options, which is why I didn't tell you to close the window we were just in. You didn't close it, did you? If you did, then shame on you for getting ahead of me, and open it back up. (Those of you who didn't close it can call us for a gold star.) Anyway, one of the scheduling options that is new with Retrospect 3.x is the ability to set an overall time clock for Retrospect's backup operations. While setting the schedules has always told Retrospect when to start a the whole backup process, there hasn't been anything until now that would tell Retrospect when to *stop* the backup process. In other words, in the past if the backups were running long, most users would break up the schedule to prevent Retrospect from running during normal business hours. Well, you don't have to worry about that any longer. With version 3, you can now set the "business hours" or "hours of operation" that Retrospect must work within. To do this, click the **Schedule...** button in the **Schedule** options portion of the window.

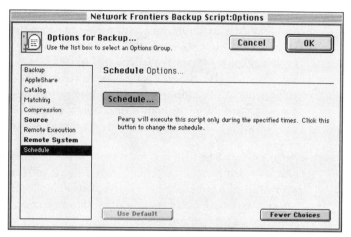

Setting Retrospect's Scheduling Options

Retrospect then displays this funky and cool-looking window where you can set the application's hours of operation for any given day. This window is a little bit unusual, so let me explain it to you piece by piece.

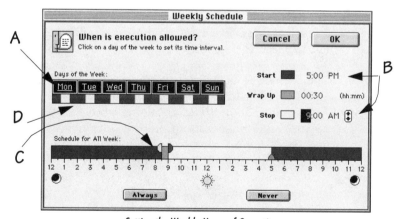

Setting the Weekly Hours of Operation

A. These are the days of the week, if you couldn't guess that already. You select the days for which you want to set the schedules, and then set the schedules themselves. I've selected all the days of the week.

B. To set the schedule, you need to know three things: when you want the earliest backups to start, when you want them to finish, and how long you want the grace period to be. Starting and stopping the backups are simple. I've set the clock here so that the backups can't start any sooner than 5:00 P.M. and must be completed by 9:00 A.M. The "wrap-up" time, or what I call grace period, is set for 30 minutes. This tells Retrospect that it shouldn't start any *new* backup procedures within 30 minutes of its quitting time. According to my settings, that means that no *new* backups will be undertaken after 8:30 A.M., and anything in progress has to be wrapped up by 9:00 A.M. Pretty cool, huh?

Note: Retrospect checks in with this schedule when deciding whether to back up the next *device* in the list. In other words, if there is 35 minutes to go in the process, with a 30-minute grace period, Retrospect will begin another backup—which could well last 30–60 minutes, depending on the capacity and throughput. So, set your grace period appropriately.

C. This shows you a sort of Gantt chart for the day, giving you a visual of what you typed in as numbers in B. This is for people who like slider bars versus people who like typing in numbers. I like it a lot. It's really cool.

D. These are the same representations as C but shown in their compacted form for each day of the week. The reason they look like a bar code is that all the days were selected together, so the daily schedules are all the same. If you had selected individual days and created individual daily schedules, this would look much different.

Does Retrospect Go into Overtime?   Nope. So what happens to computers that aren't backed up within the allotted time slot? They are backed up *first* the next time around. That's what is really cool about version 3.x and later. You don't have to worry as much about backups going overtime and running into your daily schedule. We'll cover this aspect of Retrospect later, in the "advanced backups" portion of the book. For now, let's keep going with the rest of the scheduling.

After you set your "hours of operation," click **OK** to set the changes. This returns you to the Backup script window. Click **Schedule** to set the times and dates of your backups.

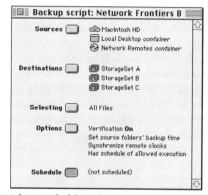

Selecting Schedule in the Backup Scripts Window

Retrospect displays schedules you have created. As this is the first time you are creating a schedule for this script, the window is blank. Click **Add...**, and Retrospect prompts you to select the type of schedule it should create for your new scripts.

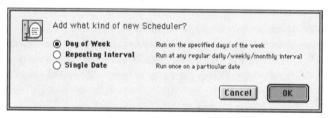

Selecting a Type of Schedule

You can choose to create a daily rotation or a weekly rotation of your tapes. I recommend rotating your tapes weekly, keeping the same tape all week long. Others recommend rotating your tapes daily, backing up to each tape every third day instead of every third week. I advocate a weekly rotation so you get into the habit of removing from the premises the tapes you aren't using. I've never encountered anyone who rotates tapes daily and moves the rotated tapes off site for two days.

The old way of creating your schedule was to create a repeating interval schedule for every day in the backup cycle (15 different schedules). What a pain. Richard the great code-master has taken pity on our poor bony fingers and given us a second option, the **Day of Week** button. This means you have to create only six different schedules. So, to begin the process, click on the **Day of Week** radio button in the dialog box and then click **OK** to continue.

I set up my repeating interval for every three weeks, with a full backup happening every Friday and normal backups happening every Monday through Thursday. Why do we always begin our full backups on a Friday? Because they both start with "F." I'm kidding. It's because it takes quite a while for the full backup to run. There are three different types of backups that Retrospect can make.

Full Backups

A full backup uses whatever StorageSet you determine and whatever storage Catalog exists for that backup. It erases both the storage media and the Catalog. It then backs up from the beginning of the storage media. All files are backed up during a full backup, whether or not they were changed since the last backup.

Normal Backups

Normal backups are what I call changed-file backups and what others call incremental backups. These backups don't erase the tape; nor do they erase the storage Catalog. Rather, they append their information to the existing information on both the storage media and the storage Catalog. Normal backups back up only those files that have changed since the last backup. The last backup need not have been a full backup, either. Anything that has changed since the last backup is put onto the storage media and into the storage Catalog.

New Backups

New backups are somewhat like full backups, but they don't erase the existing storage media; nor do they erase the existing storage Catalog. They ignore them and ask for an incrementally numbered storage media You probably have been using StorageSets called "1-Set A," "1-Set B," and "1-Set C." When a new backup occurs, the set is numbered so the new sets are called "1-Set A [001]," "1-Set B [001]," and "1-Set C [001]." There are certain reasons to use the new backup feature, but I am not going into them in this book. E-mail me, if you are interested in finding out about them.

To create your schedules, you need to set up a total of six different dates by clicking the **Add…** button in the Schedule dialog box. Three of these dates are going to be **Full Backup** dates and are scheduled for every three weeks on Friday. Notice in the following screen shot that the backup is scheduled to start on Friday at 4:00 P.M. This is before the close of business on that day, so why start it then? Because network administrators are human. They forget to change tapes. This way, the dialog box telling them to "Please Insert Tape" is flashing for a couple of hours before they go home and forget the new tape altogether.

```
┌─────────────────────────────────────────────────────────────┐
│═══════════ Network Frontiers Backup Script:Day of Week ═══════│
│ ┌───────────────────────────────────────┐                     │
│ Do Full Backup to 📼 StorageSet A Every 3 weeks on Friday,     │
│ starting 8/25/95 at 4:00 PM              ┌────────┐ ┌────────┐ │
│                                          │ Cancel │ │  OK  │ │
│                                          └────────┘ └────────┘ │
│                                                               │
│     Start:    8/21/1995 Mon        4:00 PM                    │
│                                                               │
│     Run on:  □ Monday        □ Saturday                        │
│              □ Tuesday       □ Sunday                          │
│              □ Wednesday                                       │
│              □ Thursday                                        │
│              ☒ Friday                                          │
│                                                               │
│     Weeks:   ┌─────┐                                           │
│              │ 3   │                                           │
│              └─────┘                                           │
│     Action:  ┌─────────────────┐      To:  ┌───────────────┐  │
│              │ Full Backup  ▼  │           │ StorageSet A ▼│  │
│              └─────────────────┘           └───────────────┘  │
└─────────────────────────────────────────────────────────────┘
```

Setting up a Full Backup Schedule

Your full backups don't have to be on a Friday, either. I have a few clients whose work week ends on different days. One of them starts its new production week after noon on Thursday. That's the time all the artwork has to be out to the newspapers to be color-separated. So, that's when the client starts its full backups.

The number of weeks in your rotation should be three. You are setting your backups so they rotate A, B, C, then A, B, C in a three-week cycle. It might sound confusing right now, but trust me (there's that "I believe" button again), it will work out fine. The other 12 backups, set for Monday through Thursday, will all be normal backups. You don't have to set these backups to run earlier in the day, as the tape is in the machine already. Remember, for the first week set your backups for Set A, the second week set them for Set B, and the third week set them for Set C. Once all the information is added, click **OK** to continue.

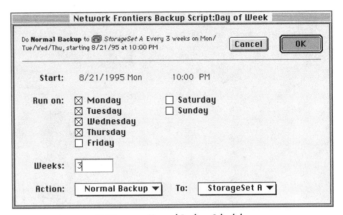

Setting up a Normal Backup Schedule

The following dialog box shows you what the Schedule window looks like after you have you have finished your schedules and the script is filled with backups.

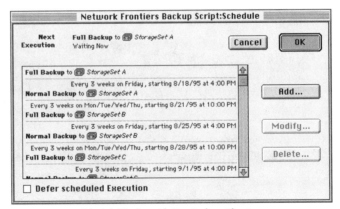

Schedule Window with New Backups Showing

Step 7: Ready for Execution

The backup is now ready for execution. The schedule shows when the next execution will take place. You are free to close the backup script. Don't shut down your computer before you go home, as the script can't run if the computer isn't on.

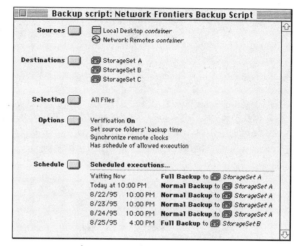

Backup Script Window Ready for Execution

SETTING PREFERENCES FOR THE LONG HAUL

Once you have written your initial backup script, enable some preferences in Retrospect. For starters, you will want to be able to take advantage of Retrospect's ability to export backup reports into a tab-delimited file ready and waiting to be imported into your favorite database. To set the preferences, select the **Special** tab and click the **Preferences** button on that card.

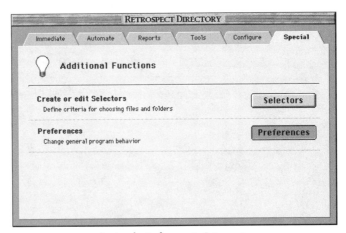

Setting the Preferences in Retrospect

Once there, you see a listing of several sets of preferences. Instead of going through and explaining each of them in order (Dantz's manual does that just fine), I will cover the ones I think are particularly important.

Setting the Log

The ability to export the backup reports is new to Retrospect 3.x. This is a great new feature, as the backup logs themselves don't give us a lot of usable information to import into a database. However, the backup report was written with this in mind.

There are three options in the logging preferences. One of them is to limit the size of the log, which is set by default to an incredibly huge 256K. That should give you enough information for just about anything you are backing up and should last most people at least a couple of backup cycles.

Another option is to always open the log when finished. I don't think that setting this would be a good idea, especially since you probably have your backups running unattended.

Finally, there's the ability to export the Backup Report. This is a *must* for anyone serious about recording the results of the backups. You will see how serious this is when we discuss the ongoing responsibilities of the network administrator, how often you should be reading the logs, and what you should be doing with them.

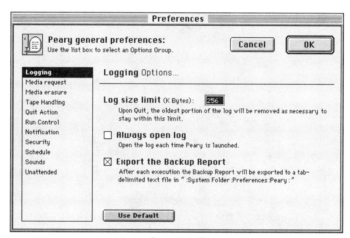

Setting the Log's Preferences

Media Options

You have two options. You can either invite the media over for your next birthday party, or they will infiltrate it with hidden cameras and you will see yourself on *Hard Copy*. Oops—wrong kind of media. Retrospect media options deal with what the application will do with tapes and removable drives when it encounters out-of-the-ordinary circumstances.

First, set how long Retrospect should wait for you to put a new tape into the drive should you forget to do so. Remember how I told you to schedule full backups on Fridays to start at least an hour before you go home? That way, the machine will sit and blink and bloop at you to put in a tape so the backup will happen. Sometimes I wish Retrospect had a feature that could send out a cattle prod–type shock to the administrator's behind informing him or her that the tape wasn't in the machine. But for some reason, this is one of my requests that Richard won't take seriously. Anyway, in the **Media request** options, set **Media request timeout** to somewhere around 75 minutes. That gives the administrator an hour to notice the screaming backup machine and yet doesn't keep the dialog box up all weekend.

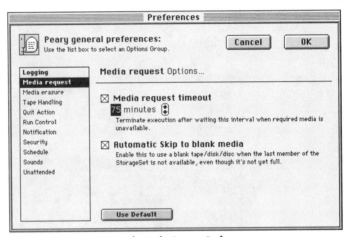

Setting the Media Request Preferences

Another setting within this is to automatically skip to blank media if the tape runs full or if the next tape in the set is not available. This means that if you have a single- or multiple-tape machine and you accidentally insert a blank tape instead of the next tape in the StorageSet, Retrospect will back up anyway, using the blank tape. The tape will be added to the StorageSet family.

Tape Handling

The last thing to set is how Retrospect handles your tapes. The default is to rewind the tapes, but that's not good enough in my opinion. After every backup, have Retrospect retension the tapes as well. Slow backups can cause the tapes to lose their tension due to all the stopping and padding that happens during slow backups. This causes the rest of your backup and restore operations to go slowly as well, as Retrospect has to spend more time aligning the tapes in the drives and compensating for untensioned tapes.

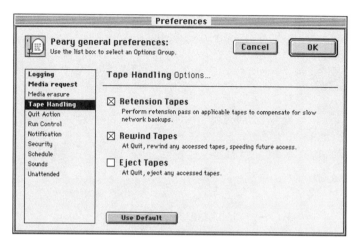

Setting Tape-Handling Parameters

Don't set Retrospect to eject the tapes when finished. Don't do that. If you have to back up again and aren't there to put in the tapes, guess what? Now, I know that some of you out there are squealing and howling and calling me everything but smart. So listen here, because I'm going to give you the down and dirty:

• Yes, I *am* aware that leaving the tapes in the drive keeps the door open and ruins the tapes much more quickly.

• Yes, I *am* aware that this also causes more wear and tear on the tape heads and that they have to be cleaned more often.

• *However,* I'd rather buy another $11.00 tape and replace it and spend more time cleaning the heads of my tape drives than potentially lose data that could cost me my job because I didn't back up. Which is worth more: the data you didn't back up because you forgot to put in the tape or the tape and drive?

So, there you have it.

Chapter 16:
Keeping an Eye on
Retrospect's Reports

Many network managers initially read their logs to inform themselves of what is happening on their networks but gradually forget to keep on reading the logs to keep informed of what is happening on their networks. I can't tell you how many times I have walked into a company and been asked, "Why is my network dying?" only to find the answer by simply reading the logs of the routers, servers, and especially the backup system.

Why read the logs of the backup system? The backup system tracks, on a daily basis, the throughput to each and every computer. If, on a daily basis, you don't change many files—there isn't that much to back up—and therefore not much to report, some daily logs from the backup system may not be helpful to read. However, the logs from the *full backups,* which should be made at least once per week, are incredibly important. If your trend in backups is to go down in average throughput over a period of time, that says something about your network's speed.

Although the "speed" issue might not point to bad routers, faulty cabling, or a lot of traffic, it does point to the users' *perception of network speed.* Anyone who has worked within a networked environment knows that the perception of network speed is as important as actual network speed. It's sort of a phenomenological point of view of the gestalt of user-knowing. How's *that* for psycho babble?

DAILY ERROR EXAMS

So, I receive this call (I won't say from whom, because it would be just too embarrassing, right, Christy?), and the administrator says, "I can't restore my server." "Have you tried?" ask I. "Yes," says she, "but there is no information on the tapes. What am I going to do?" "Are you sure your backup was set the right way?" ask I. "Yes . . . except for those errors I kept getting," says she. Yep, she was getting the infamous -1028 (**Remote not visible on network**) error on the server she was backing up. When they installed the new System Folder a while ago, somebody forgot to put in Retrospect Remote. She could have figured that out a while ago by reading the daily error logs. But, nooooooo . . . she had to wait until she needed to restore.

The point I'm trying to make here is that Retrospect won't go out onto the network, wrestle down a computer, and grab the information out of the hard drive like a Ranger student heading for a food trough. Retrospect doesn't back up information come hell or high water. It just don't work that way, folks.

There are going to be times when you have errors. Some of the errors will be nondescript, like the fact that the clipboard was open. However, some errors, like not finding the machine and therefore not backing it up, are pretty darned important.

> **Further, there's more to it than just reading that there are errors. You have to do something to fix them.**

I wonder if I'm making myself clear here.

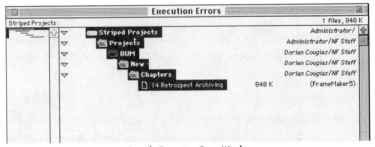

Sample Execution Error Window

EXAMINING THE BACKUP REPORT

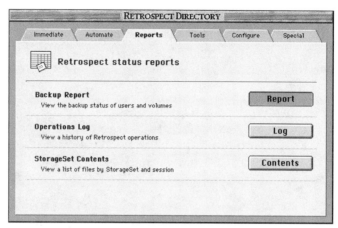

Moving to the Backup Report Window

After each backup, examine the backup report. Notice that I said *report* instead of *log*. The log is long and arduous and doesn't give you the succinct information that you need. Instead, examine the backup report itself, and if you notice any errors, go back and examine the portion of the log that pertains to the error.

Click the **Reports** tab in the main window. Retrospect opens to the general reports portion of the application. Click the **Report** button within the window. This then takes you to the backup report window shown in the next screen shot.

Backup Report Window

When Retrospect first opens the Backup Report window, the default is to show you what it calls the "standard format" backup report. This report shows elapsed days since the backup, errors per volume, the date that the backup was completed, and the script and StorageSet on which the backup can be found.

This is the place to look if an error occurred during the backup process. Notice that there was an error on the Local Desktop in the Macintosh HD volume. And no, I didn't create the error just for you. I kind of wondered what it was myself. To find the error within the log, select it within the backup report and click **Find in Log** in the top-right corner of the screen. The log appears and the volume that was being backed up when the error occurred will be highlighted.

Luckily for me, this wasn't a serious error.

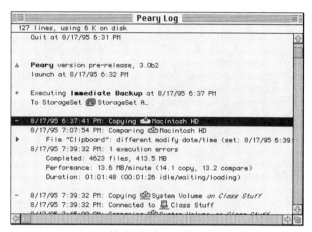

Highlighted Volume with Error

Viewing
Performance   If you want to view the performance of the server, select **View Options** from the **Reports** menu. A dialog box appears with all the settings you can choose for the backup report.

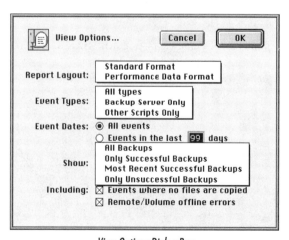

View Options Dialog Box

I like to set the view options to show me the **Performance Data Format**, with all event types and dates, and **All Backups**. What I usually receive is a backup report window that looks like the one in the next picture.

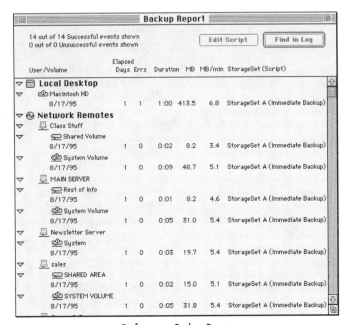

		Elapsed					
User/Volume	Days	Errs	Duration	MB	MB/min	StorageSet (Script)	

Backup Report

14 out of 14 Successful events shown
0 out of 0 Unsuccessful events shown

[Edit Script]   [Find in Log]

▽ 🖥 **Local Desktop**
▽   💿 Macintosh HD
          8/17/95   1   1   1:00   413.5   6.8   StorageSet A (Immediate Backup)
▽ 🌐 **Network Remotes**
▽   🖥 Class Stuff
▽   💾 Shared Volume
          8/17/95   1   0   0:02   8.2   3.4   StorageSet A (Immediate Backup)
▽   💿 System Volume
          8/17/95   1   0   0:09   48.7   5.1   StorageSet A (Immediate Backup)
▽   🖥 MAIN SERVER
▽   💾 Rest of Info
          8/17/95   1   0   0:01   8.2   4.6   StorageSet A (Immediate Backup)
▽   💿 System Volume
          8/17/95   1   0   0:05   31.0   5.4   StorageSet A (Immediate Backup)
▽   🖥 Newsletter Server
▽   💿 System
          8/17/95   1   0   0:03   19.7   5.4   StorageSet A (Immediate Backup)
▽   🖥 sales
▽   💾 SHARED AREA
          8/17/95   1   0   0:02   15.0   5.1   StorageSet A (Immediate Backup)
▽   💿 SYSTEM VOLUME
          8/17/95   1   0   0:05   31.8   5.4   StorageSet A (Immediate Backup)

Performance Backup Report

As we go into scripting and other backups, I'll teach you some of the basic Retrospect settings to enable so you receive the reports and the actions (such as quitting when done) that you will want for long-term backup purposes.

A Different View of the Report

Now that Retrospect can export the backup reports, we have created a small application called Retrospect Grapher. This application is designed specifically to read and then graph the backup reports that Retrospect can generate. I'll tell you right now, it is ugly as sin. But hey, what do you expect for free?

The goal of the product is to allow you to import information from Retrospect's reports and to then generate line charts showing you your computers' performance over time. This is one of the things I've been doing manually for the past year. I've been reconstructing data, through a series of applications and macros, so that I can find out when the computers on the network began to slow down. The slowdown of the computers, as graphed over a couple of months, shows me when the machines *began* needing to have their hard drives defragmented or repaired. Overall slowness of the network shows potential deterioration in patch panels, or the over-extendedness of the network. One computer dropping quickly shows an individual cable problem or some type of SCSI problem, such as a drive, a cable, or a computer itself.

The Retrospect Grapher software is pretty simple (it's a hack, of course). There is only one self-explanatory menu and there are basically two windows. The main window has three controls. Two pop-up menus help you navigate through the computers and then through each computer's volume.

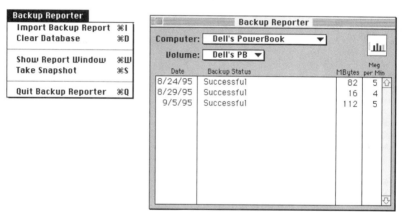

Retrospect Grapher's Menu (left) and Main Window (right)

Once a computer is selected, the volume must be selected as well. Then the Backup Reporter window will show the backup dates, status, megabytes backed up, and the megabytes per minute. Clicking the graph button will, of course, graph the data in the window.

The graphing window itself displays a single-line graph, showing all the backup dates and the performance per megabyte (in minutes) of the backup. This is the only graph that we have in the program right now. We want to put more graphs into the program as well, but they won't be finished by the time this book is finished. Why? Well, ask Pat Lee at Dantz why, and then ask Chuck, our editor at AP PROFESSIONAL, about timing. That's why. If you want a copy of the application in original form (it was created in HyperCard 2.3 and uses Boojum's graphing XCMDs and Heizer's (Lee Buck) WindowScript XCMDs), just e-mail us and we will send it to you, along with an agreement that you will abide by the other vendors' agreements not to steal their XCMDs without paying for them. We will also be coming up with a version in direct AppleScript. It, too, isn't finished yet. Anyway, I'm digressing.

When you look at the performance of the computers over time, don't freak out if the computer is running around, say, 8 MB per minute and then drops down to less than 1 MB per minute for a day or two before it goes back up. Look in the original table and figure out how many megabytes of data were actually being backed up. If you find that only a few megabytes of data were being backed up, there is your answer. Sometimes it takes more time to back up because of file overhead, and backing up small amounts of data is one of those times. If, however, you see a steady decline in performance, it is time for action.

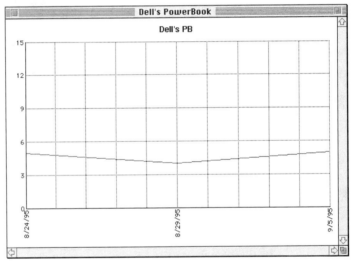

A Graph of Tom Dell's PowerBook Backup Performance

Actions

The first action I would take when looking at my backup script and finding that the computer is going slow is to run a disk analyzer on it. After that, check your cabling. We aren't going to go into detail about that, since it is well covered in our network management book, but if you are still stuck, call us.

PART EIGHT:
CONDUCTING NEWORK
BACKUPS WITH
ARCSERVE

Cheyenne Software Inc.'s ARCserve for the Macintosh can be used to back up any or all files on workstations and servers throughout an internetwork. This can be executed *locally*, where workstations and servers have their own backup devices attached, or *remotely*, where one workstation or server has a backup device attached and other computers transfer data to it over the network.

Remote backup can be accomplished in two basic ways. The first is described as *pulling*. With this *administrator-initiated* method each Macintosh is equipped with ARCserve's system extension and application, but only one Macintosh runs ARCserve itself. This machine—the administrator's Macintosh, a file server, or a dedicated backup computer—is equipped with a suitable backup drive. It is then used to "pull" data from the networked Macintoshes and write that data onto the backup media.

You can think of the second method as *pushing*. Under this *user-initiated* method, each Macintosh is equipped with ARCserve's system extension and application, used to "push" data to its own backup device or to another networked Macintosh's backup device.

In both cases and on either local or remote machines, both the ARCserve extension *and application* must be present.

All methods permit unattended backups at scheduled intervals. Which methods you use—local, remote, administrator-initiated, and/or user-initiated—will depend on a great many factors you should consider ahead of time. Some of these factors include the amount of data that needs to be backed up, the security level of that data, and your network's throughput. In the following pages we will talk about the approach we prefer, an administrator-initiated backup of all networked computers. You can apply most of what you learn to the other strategies as well.

You will have to keep track of a lot of configuration information associated with ARCserve. To help you with this, we have created the *ARCserve Worksheet*, which you'll find on the CD-ROM that ships with this book. Use it in conjunction with the other tools we've created for you.

Note: We did not write about ARCserve for the Macintosh in the first edition of this book, concentrating instead on the products of Dantz Development Corp. Dantz's Retrospect, the newest version of which is covered elsewhere in the book, is still considered the standard for Macintosh network backups, and we make no qualms about being partial to it. What convinced us we'd be doing many of our readers a disservice by not covering ARCserve this time around is the fact that it spans several platforms—Macintosh, Windows, OS/2, UNIX, and NetWare. This is a capability that is obviously important to many network administrators. We're not going to tell you to buy one over the other. We decided early on that we would not be doing product comparisons, as that is hardly our role. We'll tell you what we know, what we like, and what we dislike about both. Fair enough?

Don't Bore Me with the Details . . .

- ARCserve permits both local and remote network backups.

- ARCserve supports both administrator-initiated and user-initiated backup strategies. We recommend the former.

- Cheyenne makes ARCserve for Macintosh, Windows, OS/2, UNIX, and NetWare-equipped computers. ARCserve for the Macintosh version 1.5 provides for the cross-platform backup of Macintoshes to Novell servers and restores data that is interchangeable with ARCserve for Windows.

- ARCserve can be used to back up data to most devices that can be mounted on a Macintosh desktop, including the relatively new Digital Linear Tape (DLT) drives, DAT autoloaders and autochangers, and optical disks. It can also be used to cascade backup data across multiple DAT drives.

- ARCserve lets you manage the backup of one machine's data to a second machine's backup media remotely from a third machine! We recommend, however, that you initiate backups from a dedicated backup server.

- Setting up ARCserve on a Macintosh internetwork requires a lot of legwork, so no need to go to the gym while you are getting this thing up and running.

- Whenever a big event is about to occur on your network, such as before you add a major service like network backup, you should perform a milestone backup of everything.

- Use ARCserve's virus-detection feature to scan your data for viruses before backing it up.

- Use ARCserve's byte-by-byte comparison feature to verify your data after backing it up.

- Use ARCserve's scheduling and filters features to create rotational backup scripts.

CHAPTER 17:
PREPARING TO BACK UP
WITH ARCSERVE

The ARCserve application has the ability to back up any data accessible from the Macintosh desktop or through the ARCserve system extension, Stealth. If you want to back up only one Macintosh workstation (locally), you don't strictly need to have Stealth installed on it. To back up across the network, however, it must be present on all workstations you wish to include in the backup.

Pay attention to the use of the term *workstation.* Computers that are *servers*—such as Macintoshes running either System 7 Personal File Sharing or AppleShare File Server—are another matter. ARCserve gives you the option of backing them up via AppleShare. Servers don't need to have Stealth installed, but those that do will be backed up more quickly in some cases. We don't recommend you back up only files and folders made available through AppleShare. This leaves off the System Folder, various hidden files, and documents users have not specifically shared that way. You should back up *entire hard drives,* and that does require Stealth.

Under an administrator-initiated "pull" implementation of ARCserve, workstations must be equipped with the Stealth extension and ARCserve application, but the owners of these workstations do not use ARCserve.

Centralized "Pull" Scenario

In its simplest form, this scenario centers all of the responsibility for network backups on one machine: a file server, dedicated backup computer, or administrator's workstation. It also puts control of this vital process in the hands of one person, presumably the network administrator. Only the computer this person designates uses the ARCserve application to initiate backups. Working without supervision with its preconfigured backup scripts, ARCserve pulls the data from the hard drives of all networked Macintoshes at a scheduled time, usually when everyone has gone home.

This is the best way to implement ARCserve. You need only one backup drive, so there is not much hardware to worry about. Only one Macintosh is given the ability to use ARCserve to copy data from the others through passwords, so security risks are lessened. Although you can *use* just one backup drive here, you should always *have* two in case one dies on you. At the risk of sounding morbid, the same is true of the person who runs the backup system. Although only one person *has* to know how to use ARCserve, train more than one person.

Under a simple user-initiated "push" implementation of ARCserve, workstations are equipped with both the Stealth extension and ARCserve application, and all workstations run the application.

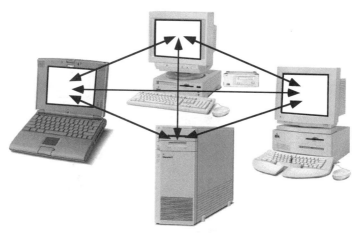

User-Initiated "Push" Scenario

Under this far more *laissez-faire* approach, any workstation can initiate a backup. It can push the data on its hard drive out to one or more backup devices on the network. It can even direct the transfer of data from one Macintosh onto the backup media of another!

If that last paragraph raised your hackles, you obviously have some experience with the foulability of users. Let *anyone* backup *anywhere?* You might be thinking that, at worst, users won't back up their workstations consistently. However, they *could* overwrite one another's data, send network bandwidth plummeting, crash their workstations, and call you *a lot*. Unless your users are all well trained and competent, these fears will point you to the administrator-initiated approach. ARCserve is easy to use, however, so don't dismiss the user-initiated backup scenario out of hand. Sometimes this option has great merit. One of the best uses we have seen of this is by graphics arts firms that regularly move huge amounts of data on and off site. These people are making their backup devices pull double duty. During business hours they are treated like output devices. The artists use ARCserve to push their huge PostScript art files to DAT drives. The tapes are then sent out of house for use by subcontractors, printers, and clients who also have in-house DAT drives. At night, the DAT drives go into service as backup devices.

Yet another possibility is a cross-platform, user-initiated backup implementation of ARCserve. Not only can workstations push data out to the storage media of other Macintosh workstations and servers, workstations can also push data out to an ARCserve for NetWare/Windows edition–equipped Novell NetWare server.

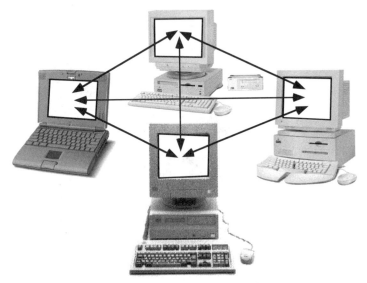

User-Initiated "Push" Scenario across Platforms

This approach is useful when Macintoshes are served exclusively by NetWare servers and when both Apple and Novell servers share the internetwork. Among the things that are really neat about this is the compatibility of backup tapes created by either ARCserve for Macintosh or ARCserve for Windows. Suppose a piano falls on your Novell server (happens all the time). ARCserve for Macintosh can be used to restore data that was recorded with ARCserve for Windows.

On NetWare-only networks, Macintoshes using ARCserve Client for Macintosh, which is sold per NetWare server instead of per workstation, can back up to the tape drive attached to networked PCs.

Should you *push* or *pull?* The answer is something you need to carefully consider, since only you know your own network's special circumstances. ARCserve gives you the power to do *either* or *both*, and that gives you flexibility in your backup planning. The "pull" scenario is safest, so that is what we will cover here.

In using ARCserve there are some terms you will encounter frequently. The first is *source*. The source is any device that can be mounted on the Macintosh desktop and contains the data to be backed up. This means internal hard drives, SyQuest and Bernoulli-based devices, optical disks, DAT drives, and mounted server volumes. The *destination* is—you guessed it—any device that can be mounted on the

Macintosh desktop to which the data from the source is to be copied. It too includes any of the aforementioned media. I actually backed up a few files from the hard drive of my PowerBook onto a diskette in the floppy drive of an Apple Workgroup Server 8150. It worked just fine.

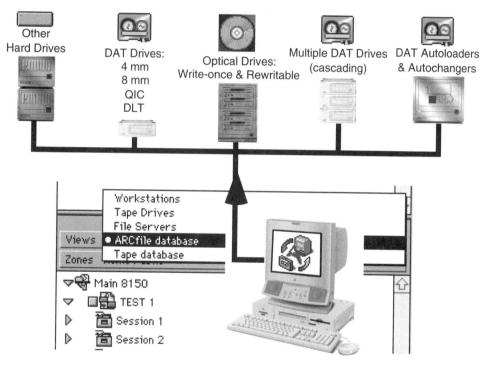

A Few ARCserve Backup Media Options

ARCfile

ARCfile is as important to know about as *source* and *destination*.

Here is where all the data backed up by the ARCserve application to media other than tape is stored (tapes are specially formatted and act just like ARCfiles). Its contents can be browsed and restored from within ARCserve. Inside each ARCfile are separate *sessions*. Each session contains, as the name implies, the results of a different backup operation between one source and one destination, with one for each source hard drive. In other words, one ARCfile into which three workstations and a server with an external hard drive were backed up would contain five consecutively numbered sessions.

ARCserve Disks

ARCserve uses an installer script, so you don't need to know much about where to put what comes on its shipping diskettes. Here are the basics:

Stealth

This is ARCserve's extension, an INIT. It advertises its presence to other ARC-serve-equipped Macintoshes on the network and lets them browse the files on your Macintosh, if they have the necessary password and access privileges. It can also launch ARCserve when a scheduled backup job is due.

ARCserve

This is, obviously, the guts of ARCserve. It lets the user back up and restore data locally and across an internetwork. From the ARCserve application you can con-figure all of the system's various options and scripts.

ARCserve Help

Installed along with the ARCserve application is a Help file that can be accessed from within the ARCserve application.

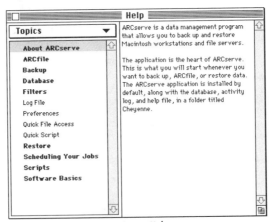

ARCserve Help

You can find it under the **Apple** menu bar item.

ARCserve Database

This is one of the three vital ARCserve components, the other two being Stealth and ARCserve itself. Here is recorded information pertaining to each backup you perform to tape or ARCfile, including its session number and which folders and files are in it. This information is recorded in the databases of both the source and the destination computers. If you are using a third computer to initiate a backup between a source and destination, the information is not recorded in the third computer's ARCserve database. You can use the ARCserve database to determine which folders and files to restore and on what backup media they reside, without having that backup media at hand.

This database will grow with every backup you perform until it eventually eats up all the computer's free hard drive space. When this happens, delete entries that are updated and/or compress the database file. This process is called *grooming*.

ARCserve Log

The log file also keeps records of your backup and restore operations. Here you can find when a session began and ended, what the source and destination machines were, the number of items copied, and how many bytes they totaled.

Both the ARCserve database and the ARCserve log are created the first time you launch ARCserve.

ARCserve Document

An ARCserve document contains options you want to keep, such as certain preferences, access privileges, and source/destination configurations. With this file, you don't have to set them up each time you launch ARCserve.

Installing ARCserve 1.5

If you already have ARCserve, you can probably skip this section of the book and move on to the chapters about backup scripting and restoration. If you don't have ARCserve and the last few pages have convinced you that you want it, go out and buy as many licensed copies as you need before proceeding. It comes in 5-, 20-, and 50-user packages. If you don't have ARCserve already and are not convinced it's for you, use the ARCserve "live trial" Cheyenne was generous enough to provide for the CD-ROM that comes with this book.

ARCserve takes up 1.5 MB of space on a workstation's hard drive. It will run with System 6.0.5 and later. For use with System 6.0.5–6.0.8, the Apple Data Stream Protocol (ADSP) driver must be installed and at least 3 MB of free RAM must be available. System 7.0 and later already have ADSP and require an extra megabyte of free RAM.

Step 1: Run the Installer

ARCserve's various component parts are placed automatically in the correct locations on your hard drive by a scripted installer.

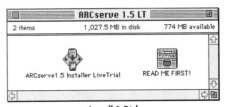

Install 1 Disk

Before you launch the installer, however, open the READ ME FIRST! document and—how should I put this—*read it first!* You would be amazed how often one warning sentence in a "ReadMe" file can save you hours of precious time. You know what I mean: *There is a known incompatibility with DiskPuffer Deluxe, which may, in some circumstances, cause your hard drive to sing "Yankee Doodle"* . . . that sort of thing. We suggest you staple a printed copy inside the cover of the manual. Among other things, the READ ME FIRST! document tells you the installer is going to create a folder under the name "Cheyenne" on your Macintosh's startup disk. The Stealth extension will look to that folder for the ARCserve application, so if you move the folder, *you must launch ARCserve afterward to alert Stealth of the change.* You can quit the ARCserve application immediately thereafter.

To begin, double-click the ARCserve 1.5 Installer icon and admire Cheyenne's artwork. Oooh . . . ahhh . . . pretty . . . Click **Continue** once you have been sufficiently impressed.

ARCserve Splash Screen from Our CD

This brings you to the main install screen.

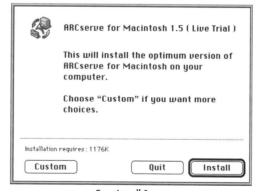

Easy Install Screen

Here you have but one real choice: Click the highlighted **Install** button. The installer checks to see if the Macintosh you are using has a 68K-based processor or the newer PowerPC chip and installs the version of software native to it. The only reason you would want to use the **Custom** button is to force the 68K version to be installed on a Power Macintosh instead of the PowerPC-native version, and why you would do this is a mystery to me. If you start to feel this urge, go splash cold water on your face. You would use the **Quit** button only if you realized you had done something stupid like begun this process without disabling virus protection first. You didn't do *that,* did you?

After you click **Install**, you are forewarned that the Macintosh will need to be restarted after this process. You probably expected that. After you dismiss this dialog box, the installer loads the proper software and leaves you with a final command and an admonishment.

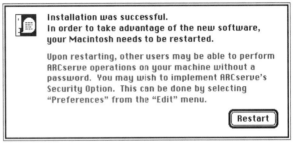

Installation was successful.
In order to take advantage of the new software, your Macintosh needs to be restarted.

Upon restarting, other users may be able to perform ARCserve operations on your machine without a password. You may wish to implement ARCserve's Security Option. This can be done by selecting "Preferences" from the "Edit" menu.

Restart

Final Installer Screen

The command is clear: **Restart**. This causes the Macintosh to reboot with the newly installed Stealth extension loaded. Deal with the admonishment *immediately* after the Macintosh comes back up. (You forgot about turning off the virus protection, so how am I supposed to trust you to remember about passwords at a later time or date?)

Step 2: Launch the Application

After the Macintosh has been restarted, notice that there is, as promised, a Cheyenne folder on the hard drive. If you want this kept somewhere else, move it now. If you're using an administrator-initiated backup strategy, we strongly suggest that you move it into the System Folder so it is less likely to be relocated later. If a user were to move it without launching it afterward, Stealth would not be able to find the ARCserve application when needed, and no remote backup of that user's hard drive would take place. If you want users to be able to use ARCserve but don't want them digging around in the System Folder, make an alias of ARCserve and put it in the Apple Menu Items folder or the Launcher (System 7.5).

When you open the Cheyenne folder, you see two icons: one for the application and one that contains its help information. Launch the application.

Cheyenne Folder After Installation

You are taken to ARCserve's main window, a sight you are going to get to know very well.

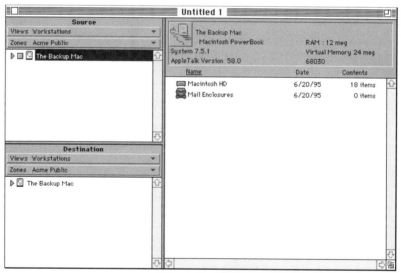

ARCserve Main Window

Step 3: Set the Stealth Password

Select **Preferences** from the **Edit** menu.

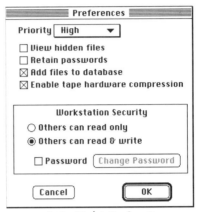

Setting Workstation Security

To permit other ARCserve network users to copy files from your Macintosh's internal or peripheral volumes but not allow them to write new files to these volumes, select the **Others can read only** checkbox. The default **Others can read or write** checkbox lets your coworkers copy files from your Macintosh's internal or peripheral volumes and write new files to these volumes. The security of either of these choices can be enhanced by selecting the **Password** checkbox and assigning a unique code.

We'll talk more about configuring this control panel farther on. For now you need only set a password. Suffice it to say that permitting ARCserve access to workstation volumes without password protection is about the same as permitting "guest" access to workstation hard drives through System 7 Personal File Sharing. If you don't think anonymous guest access is a good idea, then you shouldn't think anonymous ARCserve access is a good idea either. Even though you might be the only one who is *supposed to use* the ARCserve application in an administrator-initiated backup plan, use this security feature to ensure that you are the only one who *can*.

We have two more criteria for this password that lend themselves to our centralized scheme. First, make the password unique and use it on no other workstation. Second, *don't tell the user what it is!* In this way, the users won't be able to change any of the control panel's options on you. If that sounds unfair, think about this: Who is ultimately responsible for making sure that users' data is backed up? If you are the network administrator, *you* are.

Once you have set the password, click **OK** to return to the main window. You may now quit the application. Look in the Cheyenne folder. Two new files can seen there: "ARCserve db" and "ARCserve Log."

Cheyenne Folder After First Launch

Be sure and record the name of the workstation, its user's name, and the password either in the ARCserve Worksheet we provide on our CD or in your own notes. Also record where the Cheyenne folder is located on the hard drive if it is not in the System Folder.

Add the Rest of Your Users

The procedure we just went through works for our live trial or the 5- and 20-user *base packages* you can buy from Cheyenne. If you have more workstations than that, buy an *additional user package* and perform some additional steps. Adding additional accounts to your ARCserve system is a good news/bad news proposition. The good news is that it is easy. Here is how you do it.

Step 4: Back up the Diskette (First Time)

Wait a minute, back up a floppy diskette that contains backup software? Don't just copy it to the server or archive it later to tape? Nope. Copy that "additional users" floppy. All will be revealed, Grasshopper.

Step 5: Make Sure ARCserve Is Installed

In other words, make sure you have done everything we just talked about in Steps 1–3: installed ARCserve from your 5- or 20-user pack, moved the Cheyenne folder where you want it, and booted up the application to initialize it with the

Macintosh's zone and machine name. This has to be accomplished with an ARCserve base package.

Quit all open applications before proceeding.

Step 6: Launch the Additional Users Application

Place the ARCserve for Macintosh Additional Users diskette copy into the machine with which you are working and launch the "license. . ." application.

ARCserve for Macintosh Additional Users Diskette

Step 7: Type in the Serial Numbers (First Time)

First, enter the serial number of the base package that is *already installed* in the first field. Enter the serial numbers of any other *previously installed Additional User packages* in the subsequent fields. *Do not* enter a password for the Additional User package you are currently installing.

```
┌─────────────────────────────────────────────┐
│  Enter Base and Additional Serial Numbers     │
│                                               │
│   1.  ┌──────────────────────────────────┐   │
│       │ 5MAC 0000000                     │   │
│       └──────────────────────────────────┘   │
│   2.  ┌──────────────────────────────────┐   │
│       └──────────────────────────────────┘   │
│   3.  ┌──────────────────────────────────┐   │
│       └──────────────────────────────────┘   │
│   4.  ┌──────────────────────────────────┐   │
│       └──────────────────────────────────┘   │
│   5.  ┌──────────────────────────────────┐   │
│       └──────────────────────────────────┘   │
│   6.  ┌──────────────────────────────────┐   │
│       └──────────────────────────────────┘   │
│       ( Cancel )        (    OK    )          │
└─────────────────────────────────────────────┘
```

Type in Previously Installed Serial Numbers

Since that is about the most ridiculous thing one can imagine happening at this point, I'd better repeat myself: Don't bother entering a serial number for the Additional User package you are currently installing. I know. Weird. Click **OK** when you are finished.

Step 8: Click Add License

In the next window that appears, click the **Add License** button.

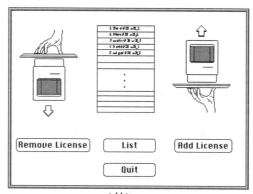

Add License

Click **Quit** when you are finished. You should see this pat-on-the-back dialog box.

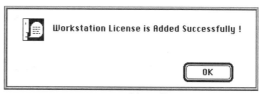

Successful Install

So that was the good news. It was easy.

Now for the bad news: You have to go around and do this for the 49 other workstations you wish to add to your ARCserve system (Steps 4 and 7 excepted). Ha, ha, ha, ha (hysterical laughter trails off . . .).

Click the **List** button in the window that has the **Add License** button, and you see the first workstation you have installed . . .

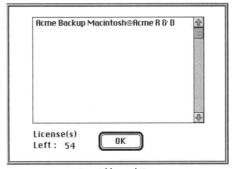

First Additional Users

. . . and subsequent installs as well.

Subsequent Additional Users

This is one thing I really hate about ARCserve. About the only good I think that will come of this cumbersome, time-consuming, and footwork-intensive process is that it will get your butt out of the chair and into the office, where you can take a first-hand look at what is going on at the network's workstations. Take this time to look for bad patch cables, viruses, broken floppy drives, out-of-focus monitors, and any of the myriad other things we tell you how to look for in our other books. Maybe in some dark office on the eleventh floor you will even meet that special one—that one with whom you will share hopes and dreams, laughter and tears, till death do you part—but probably not.

Don't forget to set and make note of the passwords in Stealth.

ACTIVATING ARCSERVE

Now that you have Stealth set up on your networked Macintoshes, you can set up a backup management document on your administrator's workstation, file server, or dedicated backup machine. Wherever you decide to put it, make sure it is on a machine that will be up and running after you have gone home. This does not necessarily mean it has to be the same machine with the backup device attached, but it usually will be. The best idea is to set aside one Macintosh as a *dedicated backup server* available for all network backup, archiving, and restoration needs.

Step 1: Name an ARCserve Document

When you boot up the ARCserve application, a window that is also an untitled document appears.

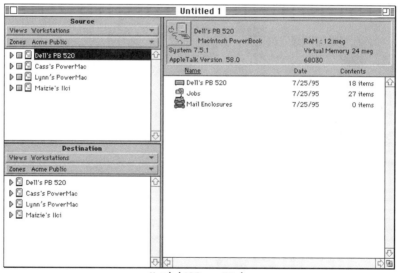

Untitled ARCserve Window

Since you don't want to go through these configuration steps each time you run ARCserve, save this document with some meaningful name, probably in the

Cheyenne folder. You can double-click this document or an alias of it to launch ARCserve thereafter.

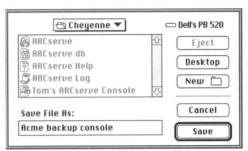

Save ARCserve Document

Take a look at the window. It has three main elements: awindow pane for source computers, a pane for destination computers, and a pane for information on whichever computer is currently highlighted. You can customize this by dragging on the separator bars. For instance, if you think the information pane is a bit redundant, you can reduce its size or even make it disappear.

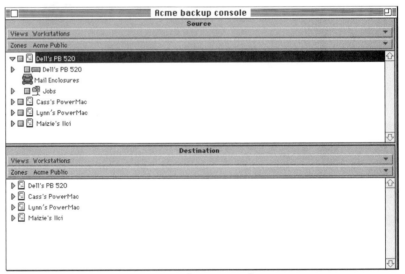

Customized ARCserve Window

We'll stick with the default so we don't confuse you. Your document reverts to the default each time you relaunch it, anyway!

Step 2: Set the Preferences

In addition to the password you set when first installing ARCserve, there are a few more options you might want to enable on the Macintosh actually attached to the backup device. To do this, select **Preferences** from the **Edit** menu.

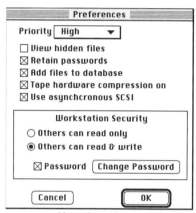

Additional Stealth Options

We plan to back up the entire hard drives of remote computers so it is not necessary to select the **View hidden files** checkbox. Hidden files will be included.

If the ARCserve document you are creating will be secure from others, you can feel comfortable in selecting the **Retain passwords** checkbox. This way the passwords for the workstations you are browsing will be remembered after the first time you type them in.

If the Macintosh is dedicated to nothing but backups, set the **Priority** pop-up to **High**. If somebody will be using the Macintosh while a backup is taking place, choose a priority of **Medium** or **Low**, depending upon the power of the machine.

If the backup Macintosh is SCSI Manager 4.3-compatible, select the **Use asynchronous SCSI** to increase backup speed. If the computer is not SCSI Manager 4.3-compliant, this option shouldn't even appear.

The options **Add files to database** and **Tape hardware compression on** are enabled by default.

Step 3: Locate the Workstations

In the Source pane, initially you see the Stealth-equipped workstations that are in the same network zone as the computer on which you are working (assuming your network has zones). Check these off on your worksheet, then choose the next zone in the **Zones** pop-up menu and do likewise.

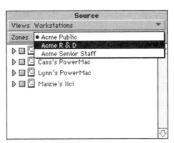

Looking for Stealth Computers

Do this until you find them all. If any are missing, skip ahead to the troubleshooting section of this chapter.

Step 4: Select the Volumes to Back Up

Once you checked to see that everyone to whom you have given ARCserve is responding, you can start selecting the volumes you want backed up. If you click on the name of each source, its mounted volumes appear in the window in the information pane. The cursor places a little green box next to it.

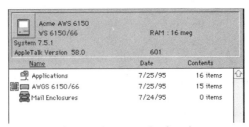

Selecting Volumes in Right of Window

You don't want to select mounted server volumes. Also, you usually do want to select the virtual partitions created by such software as PowerTalk, FileWave, and Virtual Disk, if they appear.

You can perform the same operation in the Source pane by clicking the triangle next to the source computer. *Don't just click on the box next to the source computer.* That will select all mounted volumes, including server volumes. Look at what's there and select only the drives physically attached to the source computer.

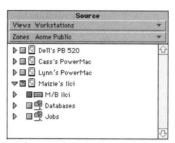

Selecting Volumes in the Source Pane

Notice that the little green box changes colors to reflect different selection options. Here's what this means:

100% green: All files and folders within a hard disk or folder are selected.

50% green: Files and folders within a hard disk or folder are selected but not sub-folders and their contents.

25% green: Some files and folders are selected, farther down on the directory tree.

0% green: You didn't select anything!

As we mentioned earlier, another option afforded by ARCserve is the ability to back up volumes that are shared on the network by AppleShare File Server and System 7 Personal File Sharing. To do this, choose **File Servers** in the **View** field of the Source pane instead of **Workstations**. To browse the server's shared contents, supply a valid AppleShare account name and password.

Selecting Server Volumes in the Source Pane

Although you *could* do this, we recommend you use the Stealth extension on your workstations and servers alike and back up their entire hard drives, not just their shared folders.

Repeat the selection process for all of your networked workstations. Since you are backing up their entire contents, you should see solid green boxes next to each of their hard drives. Again, you should see empty boxes next to AppleShare volumes mounted on their desktops.

Properly Selected Workstation

Step 5: Select Destination Device for the Backup

Next, select the device to which you want your workstations' data copied in the Destination pane. You could copy data to your backup Macintosh's hard drive, SyQuest and Bernoulli cartridges, optical disks, or DAT drives. The latter is most commonly used for network-wide backup.

Choose **Tape Drives** in the **View** field of the Destination pane to see which devices have DAT drives. Click the triangle next to the Macintosh's name to select its specific drive.

Select Tape Drives

ARCserve can make use of common 4mm, 8mm, and QIC tape formats. It also supports newer Digital Linear Tape (DLT) mechanisms from Quantum and DEC. It can write across multiple tape drives, a process called *cascading*, as long as the drives are all of the same type and manufacture. Finally, it works with auto-loaders and autochangers with mechanisms from Advanced Digital Information, Archive, Exabyte, and Hewlett Packard. While writing this book, we used a MicroNet Premier DAT 48/6 with Hewlett Packard's mechanism.

Click the tape box next to the destination tape for the green box go-ahead symbol. If you are managing all this from a remote machine, the Macintosh with the tape drive cannot be both a source and a destination. That is one good reason to set all this up on a dedicated backup server; another is the fact that you have to do tape formatting locally as well.

Step 6: Double-Check Your Selections

Before you proceed with a backup, verify your work, especially if you are doing all this remotely. To do this, choose **Sources** from the **Run** menu. You will receive a listing of all the sources you chose, their zones, and the selected folders and hard drives. Make sure what you'd intended to back up is what is selected in this list.

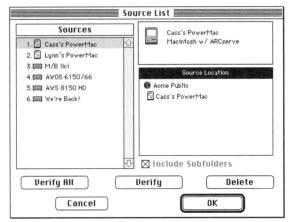

Verifying Your Sources

Next, click the **Verify All** button. You are checking two things here. First, you need to know if you have to enter a login name or password before you can gain access to any of the selected drives. Second, you need to know that all the drives are still up and running on the network.

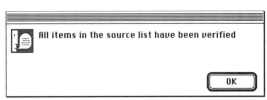

All Is Well

If you do have errors, go to the troubleshooting section at the end of this chapter.

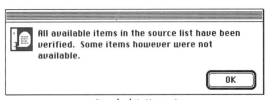

Somebody's Missing!

Do the same for the tape drive by selecting **Destination** from the **Run** menu.

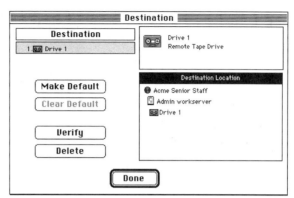

Verifying Destination

Save your ARCserve document to preserve its settings, and you are all set to perform a backup, which is the subject of our next chapter. First, however, let's go over a few things you should know.

WHAT IF YOU CAN'T BACK UP REMOTE COMPUTERS?

This *will* happen. That's why you need to take careful notes while you are installing ARCserve, so you can determine what might have changed since then. The problem can be a bit elusive, since even though a Macintosh might not be available for backing up, ARCserve will often still show it in the window. An alert dialog box saying "Yo, buddy, this machine is outta here" would be darned helpful, but alas, you see no such thing. When you realize that a Macintosh is not showing up in the ARCserve window or is not being backed up, check the following things.

Is the Macintosh On?

Needless to say, if the Macintosh is *turned off,* it won't be available for backing up. Go check to see that the remote computer is on or call the user's extension and ask the user if it is.

Likewise if the Macintosh is *not there,* it won't be backed up. PowerBooks have legs, you know.

Is the Macintosh on the Network?

Check to see that the remote Macintosh is physically plugged into the wall. You'd be amazed how often that is the problem.

Check to see that the proper network driver is selected in the **Network** control panel. If the Macintosh is on an Ethernet network, then **LocalTalk** should *not* be selected. If the Macintosh is on a LocalTalk network, then **Remote Only** should *not* be selected. You get the idea.

Network Control Panel

Make sure the Macintosh is in the *zone* in which you expected it to be located. Check to see that AppleTalk is enabled in the Chooser.

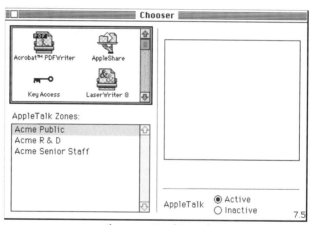

Chooser on Zoned Network

If your network has zones, make sure these can be seen in the Chooser. If not, it may be that your router is down.

If the Macintosh is running System 6, make sure ADSP is installed or, better yet, join the rest of civilization and install System 7.

Check if the machine in question is using an energy-saving feature such as the one used by PowerBooks. If the Macintosh "goes to sleep," you won't find it.

If you were using the browse-by-file servers feature to back up remote volumes, we'd tell you to make sure that either AppleShare File Server or System 7 Personal File Sharing is active on the computers that are home to the shared volumes. We don't want you doing that, however, so we won't. Forget this paragraph.

Has the ARCserve Application Been Moved?

Remember we warned you about this? If someone moves the folder containing the ARCserve application, whether it be named Cheyenne or something else, Stealth will lose track of it. You will still be able to see the workstation and its folders and files from your Macintosh because Stealth will still be running on the remote Macintosh. You won't be able to back it up remotely, however, because Stealth won't be able to launch ARCserve as required.

Again, we recommend that you put this important folder in the System Folder. If the user needs access to it, give the user an alias to use. You might also want to label the folder "Essential," using the **Label** menu item in the System 7 menu bar. Then, keep the folder locked in the System Folder, using the **Protect System Folder** checkbox in the **General Controls** control panel of System 7.5x. Installing a camera over the user's shoulder is also an idea.

Is Stealth Loaded?

If the Stealth INIT extension is deleted or moved from the Extensions folder of the System Folder, you won't see the workstation through ARCserve at all.

Why would somebody perform such a hideous feat? Usually it is because a user was "cleaning up" the System Folder or trying to track down an INIT conflict and thought Stealth was unnecessary. This is particularly easy to do with System 7.5x's **Extensions Manager** control panel.

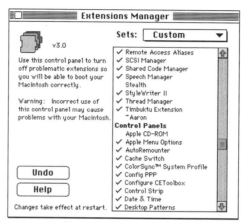

Stealth Disabled in Extensions Manager

One user in our own office chucked it because she thought it was part of a flight simulator game the authors are always playing (not realizing that we'd long since switched to Marathon, I guess). A name like "Important Thing Don't Trash" or "Death Follows Removal" might have been a better choice of names than "Stealth," don't you think, Cheyenne?

If you're not doing remote backups, don't sweat it. You don't need Stealth to back up locally.

Has the Macintosh Been Renamed?

The effects of this are easier to show than to explain. In the next illustration, note that we have a "Joe's Macintosh" in the Source pane and when we verify its selected volumes in the Source List, we find its hard drive is named "Macintosh HD." The first name is set in the Sharing Setup control panel and the second on the Macintosh desktop or through formatting software.

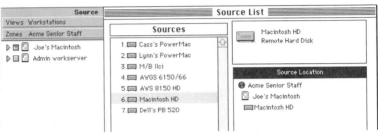

Macintosh HD and Joe's Macintosh

Then Jane comes along. She changes the name of her computer to "Jane's Macintosh" in the Sharing Setup control panel. You still see "Joe's Macintosh" in your ARCserve document until she restarts. After she restarts, you see "Jane's Macintosh" in your ARCserve document, but the "Macintosh HD" is not selected. Hmmm. So you reselect "Macintosh HD" to be sure it is backed up and verify your Source List again.

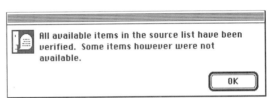

Verify Doesn't Fly

No go. You are told some items are missing. You look at the Source List and . . . whoa . . . two drives called "Macintosh HD?" You click on one and, you guessed it, ARCserve still expects there to be a "Joe's Macintosh."

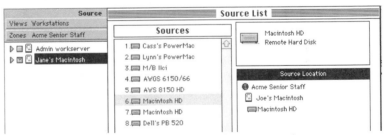

Macintosh HD, Macintosh HD, and Jane's Macintosh

Becoming a little frustrated? Wait! Jane's been busy! She renamed her hard drive "I Hate Mondays" (appropriately enough) and when she restarts her Macintosh the next day, you find the drive is once again unselected in your ARCserve document. You select it again. You verify your selections again. I'm sure you know where *this* is going.

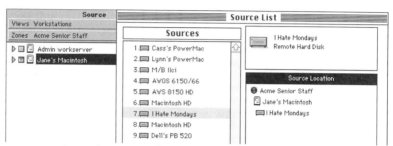

Macintosh HD, Macintosh HD, I Hate Mondays, and Jane's Macintosh

Lookee here! Now ARCserve sees two drives called "Macintosh HD" and one called "I Hate Mondays."

So, your options here are:

A. Use the **Delete** button to clear all the entries you know are outdated from the Source List.

B. Keep careful records of each workstation so you will notice these types of changes. Record the changes and redo your ARCserve document.

C. Establish a uniform naming convention for networked computers and don't let users deviate from it.

D. Don't worry about what's in the Source List. So long as the volume under its current name is there, the rest don't matter.

E. All of the above.

Don't be surprised if you see that one in the Apple Certified Service Engineer (ACSE) test. The answer is E. Of course, there are problems inherent with all these solutions. Response A begs the question: How do you know which entries are outdated? Response B comes back to that only halfway. Just how much record keeping should you be expected to do, especially if you have hundreds of nodes? Response C provides a solution that would make your life a whole lot easier but is neither very realistic nor very "Mac-like." Response D is the easiest, but this effectively nullifies the effectiveness of the **Verify All** command in the Source List, since you are not told *which* Macintoshes in the list aren't responding. It also means your backup logs will always report errors.

What is needed is something to identify each Stealth extension uniquely, regardless of what the Macintosh or its hard drive is named. A name, a serial number, a symbol—we're not picky. This you do not receive with ARCserve. Run a network scanner like Apple's venerable old Inter•Poll and you know what you'll find? Stealth registers itself on the network as a generic "MacINIT."

Has the Password Changed?

If you've followed our advice and used a unique password when setting up the Stealth extension, and one that you did not make the user privy to, this shouldn't come up. If you didn't follow our advice, go figure out what the user changed it to.

Is Something Else Running in Background?

When it is time for a backup to occur, Stealth will attempt to launch ARCserve on the workstation so that it can run in background. Sometimes if something else is already running in background or if there is not enough free RAM, ARCserve can't run. Check to see that this is not happening.

CHAPTER 18:
BACKING UP LOCAL AND NETWORK-BASED MACINTOSHES WITH ARCSERVE

At this point you should have ARCserve for the Macintosh installed on all the networked workstations on which you plan to use it. You should also have documented a good deal of information associated with that installation and have set up your first ARCserve document that retains information about your networked Macintoshes. After reading the previous chapter, you should also be well aware of how ARCserve works, what it looks like, and what you need to watch for when using it. Now you get to use it.

THE ARCSERVE WINDOW

As you'll remember from the previous chapter, all the workstations, file servers, and backup devices ARCserve can see are found in the main window generated when you launch the application. In your case, you have probably launched ARCserve from the document you previously saved.

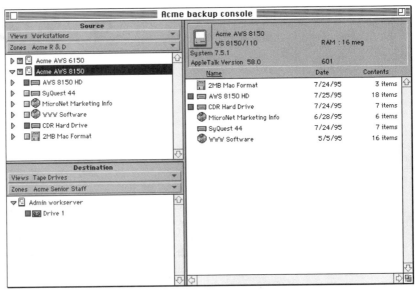

An ARCserve Document

Two primary commands concern us in this chapter, both of which are found in the **Run** menu. They are **Run Now** and **Schedule Job**.

Notice that there is also a **QuickScript** command with **Full Backup** and **Incremental Backup** subcommands. These are for local backups. They are designed to let you do immediate backups of all volumes *attached to your local computer* without manually setting the source and destination (assuming you have a DAT drive). Most of what we talk about here regarding network-wide backups applies to local backups as well.

PERFORMING A MILESTONE NETWORK BACKUP

Before you start doing anything "cool" with ARCserve, perform a milestone backup. This backup will be a moment in your computers' lives frozen in time. If there are problems with the backup plan you prepared, you should catch them here. More important, however, this first network-wide backup will serve as a yardstick by which to measure later backups. Of almost equal importance is the fact that it will give you something to fall back on should something terrible happen before you get this system nailed down.

If you are unwilling or unable to commit to a network-wide backup at this point, at least back up your servers. Remember, in order to preserve AppleShare access privileges, *AppleShare must be running* while the backup is taking place.

By now you should have decided from where your administrator-initiated backup will be controlled. Our recommendation is that you run it from a dedicated backup Macintosh equipped with a DAT drive. You might not have a Macintosh to spare, however, in which case you could use a file server, your administrator's workstation, or both. In this section, we perform both local and remote backups by running ARCserve on a destination AppleShare file server with an attached DAT drive.

Try to do this first backup when no one else is around, so no one interferes with the process ("Forget the beach this weekend, honey. I've got ARCserve!").

As this is a milestone backup, you want to back up *everything*. Don't waste time thinking about whether you need to back up *this* folder but not *that* folder. There was a Vietnam-era T-shirt Dorian's type (Green Beret) used to wear that carried the slogan "Kill 'em all, let God sort 'em out." A little strong for civilian life, but with some slight modifications it can be applied in this situation: "Back 'em all up, let the user sort 'em out."

Step 1: Open the ARCserve Document

We're assuming that you followed our instructions in the previous chapter and that nothing has changed since you created your ARCserve document. If you are unsure, go back and verify your work before proceeding.

Step 2: Format the Tape

If you are backing up to a DAT drive, format the destination tape so that ARCserve can work with it. To do this, choose the **Format Tape** submenu in the **Tape Utilities** item from the **Utilities** menu. This cannot be done remotely.

You are asked to give the tape a name. "Milestone 1," "My First Backup," (aw shucks), or something with the date in it might be good.

Step 3: Customize Script Settings

The **Script Settings** command can be found under the **Customize** menu.

Script Settings

In the window that appears, the **Backup Database (tape only)** checkbox should be selected by default. Make sure it is. Also in this **General Settings** window is a checkbox for **Virus Detection**. Some geek's digital malice is not something you want to save on your backup media. We strongly recommend that you enable this feature even though it will increase your backup time. This will tell ARCserve to examine each file and log and to not back up infected ones.

Before you leave the Script Settings window, switch to the **Destination Settings** window by clicking on the pop-up menu in the upper left. You see the **Data Authentication** pop-up in which we recommend you select **Compare**, even though this too will increase your backup time. Doing so will instruct ARCserve to make a byte-for-byte comparison of the data on your hard drives with that on the tape. If what ends up on tape is not exactly what was on the hard drives, ARC-serve will log this as an error. If you don't do verifications, you won't know if something is wrong with your backup. This is important because *corrupted* backups are about as good as *no* backups.

Do one more thing before you click **OK**. Click the **Set Default**. This ensures that the important settings we just went over are always selected in yet-to-be-created ARCserve documents.

Step 4: Run the Script

Go ahead! You've earned it. Select **Run Now** from the **Run** menu.

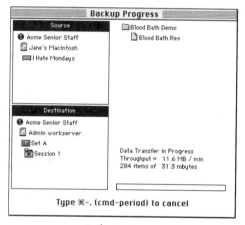

Backup in Progress

At the destination, ARCserve displays a status window in which you can watch the progress of each session. Of course, you'd actually watch this only if you had forgotten to renew your subscription to *MacWEEK*. At the source, hopefully not the workstation on which you just booted up Hellcats, things will be going pretty darn slowly. How slowly depends upon the processor priority you gave ARCserve when setting up. If you were running this remotely, you'd see the same progress window on the remote that is displayed on the destination computer.

Step 5: Check the Log

No backup operation is complete without taking a look at the log. This can be accessed with **Show Log File** from the **Utilities** menu.

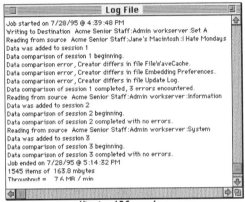

Viewing ARCserve Log

Here you will see information on errors, start/stop times, and other performance statistics that are useful for future backup planning.

Step 6: Copy Preferences to Floppy

This step is not very elegant, but it is required. Copy the "ARCserve Preferences" file from the Preferences folder of the System Folder onto a floppy diskette. You'll need it for restorations if the destination machine kicks the bucket.

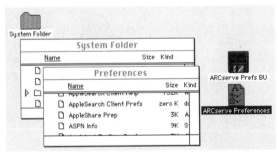

Backup Copy of ARCserve Preferences

CREATING A ROTATIONAL BACKUP SCRIPT

Now that you know you can successfully complete a network-wide backup with ARCserve once, it's time to make a habit of it. To do this, you need to set up backup *scripts*. The script is not really any different from what I have up to now been calling your "ARCserve document" except that it also contains a repeating time interval and special file inclusion/exclusion filters.

There are a couple of types of backup scripts. The first is the *full backup* script. We just did a full backup. It includes everything, including the kitchen sink, the pipes attached to it, and the water main from the street. Because it includes everything, a full backup takes the longest to do. The second type is the *incremental backup* script. It includes everything *except* those files that have not changed since the last backup. Because significantly less data is written to tape, it takes a lot less time to do this type of backup.

I'm not thrilled with the idea of incremental backups. I'd much rather apply ARCserve's numerous filters to archiving and restoring and not worry about missing anything when it comes to daily backups. The trouble with doing full backups everyday is that it might take too long. Depending on how much data there is out there on the network to be backed up and what hours your people work, you might have users coming in before your backup script has completed in the morning. ARCserve will run in background but this slows down the workstation. To avoid this, some find that they can do full backups only on Fridays, so that the process can run into Saturday.

I'll tell you how you might do incremental backups later, but the steps we perform here will be for full daily backups.

There are also a couple of ways to use your backup scripts. One is to use a different script for each of your generational backups. These could be called "A," "B," and "C," or even "Grandfather," "Father," and "Son." I prefer to use one script called "daily backup" and leave it at that. Either way works fine. The former may make it more obvious that the backup tape needs to be rotated off site at the end of the week. The latter might be better insurance against times when they are not rotated off site, since it executes regardless of which generation tape is in the tape drive. Whatever your preferences and needs are, here is one way to create a rotating generational backup script.

Step 1: Rename the ARCserve Document (First Time)

Again we're assuming that you followed our instructions in the previous chapter and that nothing has changed since you created your ARCserve document, so go back and verify your work if you are not sure.

Once you've done your first milestone backup, you are never going to want to work without a script again. Besides performing its functions automatically, the script gives you details on what went wrong should a backup not work, and you'll always want access to that. So, now it's time for a little graduation. Choose the **Save as** command from the **File** menu to give your ARCserve document a new name, representative of the new script functions it is to perform, as in "Daily Network Backups."

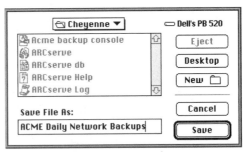

Rename Document as Script

Your humble little document is now a script! Try not to bawl if you are in public.

Step 2: Format the Tape (First Time)

You weren't *really* going to use the same tape we just saved the milestone backup on, were you? Good, good. You are taking that one off site ASAP, aren't you? Aaaaah. Glad to hear it.

Step 3: Customize Script Settings

Once again, select **Script Settings** from the **Customize** menu.

```
╔═══════════════════ Script Settings ═══════════════════╗
║ ┌──────────────────────────────┐                       ║
║ │ General Settings        ▼    │                       ║
║ └──────────────────────────────┘                       ║
║                                                         ║
║      ☐ Shut down local machine after job               ║
║      ☒ Shut down remote machines after job             ║
║      ☐ Reschedule failed jobs in  ┌────┐ ┌─────────┐   ║
║                                   └────┘ │Month(s) ▼│   ║
║      ☒ Restore into new Folder           └─────────┘   ║
║      ☒ Backup Database (tape only)                      ║
║      ☒ Virus Detection                                  ║
║      ┌─────────────────────────────────────────────┐   ║
║      │ Duplicate Files  ⦿ Replace ○ Rename ○ Skip  │   ║
║      └─────────────────────────────────────────────┘   ║
║      ┌──────────────────┐                               ║
║      │   Set Default    │                               ║
║      └──────────────────┘                               ║
║   ┌─────────────────────┐   ┌──────────┐ ┌──────────┐  ║
║   │  Factory Defaults   │   │  Cancel  │ │    OK    │  ║
║   └─────────────────────┘   └──────────┘ └──────────┘  ║
╚═════════════════════════════════════════════════════════╝
```

General Settings

The **Backup Database (tape only)** and **Virus Detection** checkboxes should be selected by default in the **General Settings** window. Select **Shut down remote machine after job**, and users' workstations will be turned off after the backup is completed at night. This doesn't work well with those Macintoshes that must be physically shut down: the ones that throw up the "It is now safe to switch off your Macintosh" screen. I haven't chosen **Shut down local machine after job**, because the local machine is a file server I want left "up."

I don't see much need to set the **Reschedule failed jobs in "x"** option. If a workstation isn't backed up, usually because the user forgot to leave it on or you forgot to put a tape in the drive, you'll know about it when you see the log and take corrective measures then. Otherwise the next night's backup should catch it.

This all assumes that you don't want to back up when your users are around. Suppose you do? Then theoretically, this is a great feature! Imagine you didn't back up a workstation at night because it was a PowerBook that was taken home. If you rescheduled the job for eight hours later, you might back up the PowerBook when the owner came back in and put it on the network the next day.

Next, switch to the **Destination Settings** window by clicking on the pop-up menu in the upper-left. In the **Data Authentication** pop-up, **Compare** should be selected by default.

```
┌──────────────────────────────────────────────────────┐
│ ═══════════════════ Script Settings ═══════════════   │
│ ┌────────────────────────────┐                        │
│ │ Destination Settings    ▼  │                        │
│ └────────────────────────────┘                        │
│          ☐ Overwrite ARCfiles                          │
│          ☒ Overwrite Tape                              │
│          ☒ Session Password    ┌──────────────────┐    │
│                                │ Change Password  │    │
│          ┌─────────────────────┴──────────────────┤    │
│          │☒ Allow Tape Cascading to               │    │
│          │  ☐ Cheyenne tapes ☐ Unknown Tapes ☒ Blank Tapes │
│          └────────────────────────────────────────┘    │
│          Data Authentication ┌ Compare      ▼ ┐       │
│                                                         │
│  ┌──────────────────┐                                  │
│  │   Set Default    │                                  │
│  ├──────────────────┤        ┌──────────┐  ┌────────┐ │
│  │ Factory Defaults │        │  Cancel  │  │   OK   │ │
│  └──────────────────┘        └──────────┘  └────────┘ │
└──────────────────────────────────────────────────────┘
```

Destination Settings

Whether you select **Overwrite Tape** depends on how much data you have to back up. For instance, if you have enough room on a tape to store five times the amount of data on your network, don't bother to choose it. Each night's backup (Monday through Friday) will be written to tape after the previous night's backup in consecutively numbered sessions. If the total data on your network is about a tape's worth of information, you can overwrite the older data by reformatting the tape.

We recommend setting ARCserve's **Session Password**. What if a company competitor obtained one of your backup tapes and restored your customer database onto one of its computers? This feature helps prevent this type of thing. A potential problem is that ARCserve requires the password when it launches to do the backup, so if you are not around to enter it . . .

```
┌──────────────────────────────────────────────────────┐
│ ═══════════════════ Script Settings ═══════════════   │
│ ┌────────────────────────────┐                        │
│ │ Scheduling Settings     ▼  │                        │
│ └────────────────────────────┘                        │
│                                                         │
│   Session password for restore  ┌──────────────────┐   │
│                                  │ •••••••          │   │
│                                  └──────────────────┘   │
│   Default Destination Name       ┌──────────────────┐   │
│                                  │ AServe Dest      │   │
│                                  └──────────────────┘   │
│                                                         │
│  ┌──────────────────┐                                  │
│  │   Set Default    │                                  │
│  ├──────────────────┤        ┌──────────┐  ┌────────┐ │
│  │ Factory Defaults │        │  Cancel  │  │   OK   │ │
│  └──────────────────┘        └──────────┘  └────────┘ │
└──────────────────────────────────────────────────────┘
```

Scheduling Settings

. . . choose **Scheduling Settings** in the pop-up menu. Here is a place to type that password so that ARCserve can execute even when you are not present. Note here also that the **Default Destination Name** is "AServe Dest." This is what ARCserve names tapes it automatically reformats. Click **OK** when you are finished.

Step 4: Schedule the Jobs

Choose **Schedule Job** from the **Run** menu.

Schedule Job

Select the first day that the first generational backup tape will be used in the calendar and drag it to the pane at the upper right, presumably a Monday. Next, select the **Repeat every "x" Days(s)** checkbox and set it for one day. Set the time for when you expect none of the company's employees to be at their workstations.

Step 5: Monitoring the Backup (Repeating)

In the previous steps, you set up a single rotational backup script that automatically performs full backups on your networked workstations at night, Monday through Friday. What the backup script can't be expected to do is check up on its own work. You must do that by checking the backup log every day.

Some Notes on Multiple Scripts and Filters

As I said earlier, you might want to have multiple scripts instead of just the one we created here. For instance, you might want a script for each week in your rotation. You might also want scripts that contain different options, such as a Monday through Thursday incremental backup script and a Friday full backup script. Making these are easy once you have set up the first one. Simply duplicate the original backup script through the Finder to preserve your previous work, rename it, and alter the settings that you want changed.

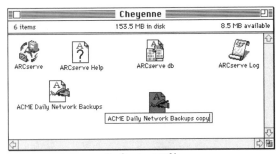

Duplicating ARCfile

Here's how you could set up the types of scripts I mentioned earlier. First, name the duplicated ARCserve document something like "Full Backup." Next, reset the schedule for the first Friday of the week that Tape One of the generational backups will be used. Set the interval for every three weeks.

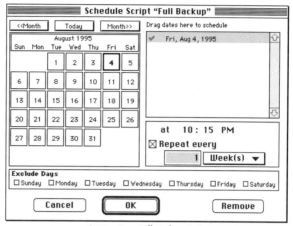

Setting First Full Backup Script

Duplicate this new script and rename the copy "Incremental Backup." As with the script you just made, you'll need to set the repeat interval for three weeks. This time, however, you'll be working with four dates in the script, one for Monday, Tuesday, Wednesday, and Thursday.

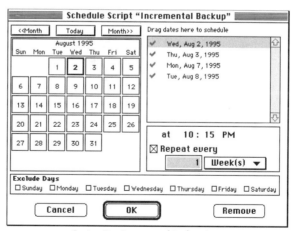

Setting First Incremental Backup Script

But that's not all! Set the criteria that tells ARCserve what to back up and what not to back up. Do this by choosing **Add Filter** from the **Customize** menu.

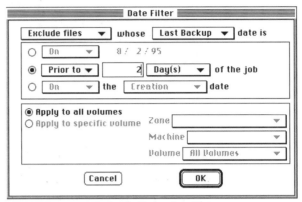

Setting the Backup Date Filter

One filter you might set is under the **Date** submenu. Direct it to **Exclude Files** whose **Last Backup** date is **Prior to** 'X' **Day(s)** of the job. We'll talk more about filters when we reach the chapter on archiving.

You can review your scripts without having to open them individually by selecting **Queue Manager** from ARCserve's **Utilities** menu.

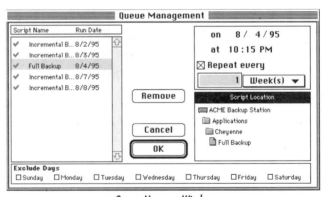

Queue Manager Window

Here, too, you can reset the scripts' execution intervals.

PART NINE:
THE BIG PAYBACK:
RESTORATIONS WITH
RETROSPECT

There is where you earn your stripes. If you can restore your computers' information within the allotted time frame, you are a hero. If you can't, well, there's always a fry cook position open at my friend Joe Bob's Country BBQ & Bar.

Don't Bore Me with the Details . . .

- Hey, folks, sweat the details here. Big time.

- Take your time. This isn't something you want to rush.

- Practice these steps once or twice so you know what to do when the real McCoy comes your way.

Chapter 19:
Creating Dr. Dorian's
Famous Retrospect
Restoration Drive

Here is something to put in your belt. If you need to rebuild a hard drive for restoration, and then re-install System 7.5, and then reinstall Retrospect Remote, it will take you 15 minutes (the Install application on the CD takes approximately 11 minutes *all by itself*). That doesn't sound too bad until you consider what that costs your company in downtime. A server that would normally have 50 connected users would cost your company the following while you are re-installing System 7.5:

# of Users	$$ per Hour	$$ Loss after 15 Minutes
10	$25.00	$62.50
20	$25.00	$125.00
30	$25.00	$187.50
40	$25.00	$250.00

So, why am I showing you these numbers? Because I'm going to convince you that you want to buy or rehab a hard drive for the purpose of restoring computers across the network. If you already have an extra hard drive, you can purchase a casing for it for about $90. If you don't have one, an 80- or 120-MB hard drive can be obtained for around $150. You can buy a 328-MB hard drive for only $300. Thus, for the price of a single drive, you can eliminate the downtime costs you would incur by having to manually reinstall the system before a restoration. These kinds of arguments are easily winnable with bosses.

WHAT SHOULD GO ON THE DRIVE

The following window shows the contents of our restoration drive. We created the drive by buying a casing from APS, because theirs is battery-operated, installing a copy of System 7.5.1, which will boot *any* computer, and then tossing on a couple of additional applications.

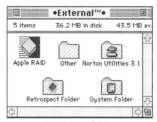

Our External Drive

The applications we added are the following:

- **Apple RAID** software so that if the Workgroup Server you are restoring was set for either RAID 0 or RAID 1, you can reconfigure the drives before the restoration process. Apple RAID can also be used for reformatting pretty much any hard drive running on a Macintosh.

- **Norton Utilities** because it never hurts to have Norton around. Just be sure you go to restore and don't play with Norton forever, trying to fix the hard drive instead of restoring it. (Remember the cost table you used to obtain the drive in the first place?)

- **Retrospect** in case the server you are restoring was also the backup server. If that happens, you'll need to rebuild your catalogs from tape. Having Retrospect on the hard drive will keep you from havin to reinstall the application. If you are really smart, you will have the hard drive online somewhere and will be continuously running a duplicate script to put the tape catalogs in the Retrospect folder.

Also, we put the °Remote control panel into the System Folder of the external drive and gave it its own serial number and name (we call it EMERGENCY DRIVE). This ensures that we can back up over the network to the extern and won't have to worry about reinstalling a °Remote INIT.

CHAPTER 20:
REBUILDING THE RETROSPECT
STORAGE CATALOG

We are going to assume you are restoring the same computer on which you made your backups. This probably means that, along with losing everything else, you also lost the StorageSet catalog containing the crashed hard drive. To re-create the StorageSet catalog, open the Retrospect application and click the **Tools** tab on the top of the Retrospect Directory window. A list of options appears. Click the **Repair** button to re-create the StorageSet's catalog.

Tools Options in the Retrospect Directory

Immediately after clicking the **Repair** button, a dialog box appears with a list of choices in the form of radio buttons. Click the top button in the list if you created your backup on a tape. Click other buttons in the list for other options. For our purposes, we are assuming that you made your backup on a tape system.

Choose a catalog repair function:

- ● Recreate from tapes
- ○ Recreate from Macintosh disks
- ○ Recreate from CD-R discs
- ○ Repair Macintosh File StorageSet

- ○ Update existing catalog file

OK

Cancel

Select Recreate from Tapes to Rebuild a DAT-Based StorageSet

After you select the **Recreate from tapes** radio button and click **OK**, the Media Selection window appears prompting you to insert the tape from which you want a catalog recreated. If there isn't a tape in the tape drive, **no media** is displayed in the window.

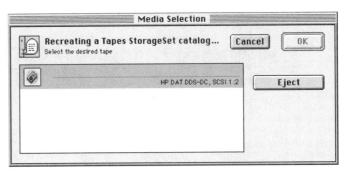

Media Selection

Recreating a Tapes StorageSet catalog...
Select the desired tape

Cancel OK

HP DAT DDS-DC, SCSI 1:2 Eject

Empty Tape Drive in the Window

Once a tape has been inserted, that tape's name appears in the dialog box. If this is the correct tape, click the **OK** button to continue. If not, keep inserting tapes until you find the right one. You have to remember the name of the tape because there is nothing in the window to remind you.

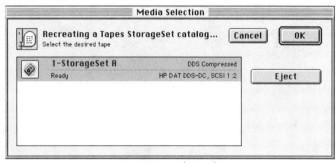

Correct Tape in the Window

After you select the tape, Retrospect asks you where you want it stored. I usually suggest storing it in the Retrospect folder. Whatever you do, *don't put it on the hard drives you are restoring.* Not a good idea.

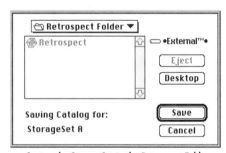

Saving the StorageSet in the Retrospect Folder

After you save the file, take a break. The progress window will run for a while. When it is finished finding all the files on the tape you put in the drive, a dialog box appears asking if there are any more tapes in the series. If not, click the **No** button and you are finished. If yes, guess what you click? Did you answer "the **Yes** button?" Good.

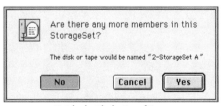

Finished with the Set of Tapes

Remember one thing: The longer the tape, meaning the more sessions you have on it, the longer it takes to restore the Storage Catalog. Look at the log report for the following tape.

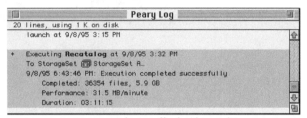

Wow, more than a coffee break's worth!

Three hours, and that was a week's worth of backups for only 18 computers! Plan on spending some time recreating the catalog if it goes down. *Now* will you create a duplicate script to protect your catalogs, or will you at least put them on a mirrored drive?

Chapter 21:
Preparing a Computer for Restoration with Retrospect

There are a few things to do before you can begin the restoration process for your servers or workstations. One of them is to prepare the server or workstations' drive for installation. The chances are good that when the server went down, so did the drive or drives. If the drive didn't go down and the server did, the drive probably has a few problems associated with it. There are a couple of steps you can take when your server goes down. One of them is to start futzing around with Norton to see if the drive is okay. Another option, and the one that we prefer, is to have your drive formatting software on hand, and before you restore, reformat your hard drive. You read that right. We suggest that before you perform any restore, you automatically reformat the hard drive. We recommend hard drive reformatting so that you'll *know* the hard drive isn't having any problems during and after restoration. Too many times I've walked through a restoration with a client only to have it fail several times because the hard drive had bad sectors.

When reformatting a drive, turn to your backup planner sheet and ensure that you are reformatting the drive to the partition sizes and types that they were *before* the server or workstation went down. Consider this—if the server had a drive that was mirrored when it went down, and you didn't mirror it before you restored, you'll have extra drive space. If, however, the drives were striped into a single larger volume, say with two 2-GB hard drives striped into a single 4 GB, you won't have the same capacity on the volume during restoration. You will come up short. Thus, do some checking before you restore your volumes.

REFORMATTING WITH APPLE RAID

Apple RAID is a great software program. It is not just for formatting drives for use with RAID either. One of the features of the program is that you can launch it and search for drives that don't show up on the desktop. The following picture shows the Apple RAID software. Notice that the volume selected on the left points to a physical drive on the right, and there are two other drives. The top disk is already formatted for RAID, but doesn't have any volumes associated with it. Another volume is showing that there is a media failure on the disk, and that it needs to be initialized before it can be used.

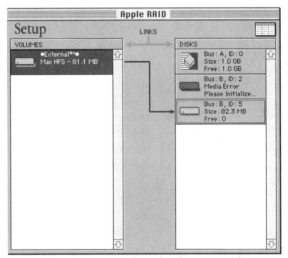

Media Failure on Drive that Didn't Show up on Desktop

Whether or not you are using RAID 0 or 1, you can use the Apple RAID software to format the drive for use with either a workstation or a server, because an alternate format is the standard Macintosh HFS volume.

Initializing a Drive

If a drive doesn't have the Apple RAID-type icon on it in the Apple RAID window, then it cannot be used to create either a mirrored or striped volume. If the drive is blinking in the window, as in the previous picture, you have no choice but to initialize it before you do anything else. Fortunately, initialization is extremely easy. Select the device and then select **Initialize...** from the **Disk** menu.

Selecting to Initialize a Selected Disk

A dialog box appears warning that any data on the drive will be lost. Heck folks, if the drive is having a media failure and you are going to restore, you are going to overwrite the data anyway, so don't worry about it. Go full speed ahead. A warning, though: If your drive is having *really bad media problems,* Apple RAID might not be able to initialize it. We have seen the following dialog box more than once.

Warning that a Drive Can't Be Initialized

When you see a dialog box like the previous one, it is *not* time to grab Norton or your favorite formatting tool. It is time to put a new drive in and reformat that.

If your drive formats correctly, though, you won't see any dialog box saying so. It merely shows up in the Disks list with the same type of icon as other correctly formatted drives.

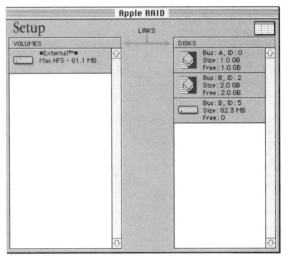

New Drive Formatted Correctly

CHECK THE DRIVE'S SCSI ID

Before you go any further, ensure that the drives you are adding to your computer don't conflict with the SCSI devices already installed. One of the most confusing computers is the Workgroup Server 8150. This server has two SCSI channels, but really only uses one of them. The following table shows SCSI channel A (also known as 0) and channel B (also known as 1). The internal drive is always hooked up to A:1 or 0:1, depending on how your software wants to describe the channel. The internal DAT drive and CD drive are automatically set to B:2 for the DAT and B:3 for the CD (1:2 and 1:3).

ID	SCSI A/0	SCSI B/1
0	Internal Drive	
1		
2		Internal DAT
3		Internal CD
4		
5		
6		

This means that you are left with B:1, B:2, and B:4–B:6 for adding additional external drives. When adding your external drives, don't worry about whether or not you are setting them for channel B/1. They are *automatically* set to that SCSI channel, and that is where the problem lies. Many folks don't understand that the CD and DAT drives are hooked up to the same SCSI channel as drives that are installed externally. Oh, well. They learn soon enough.

CHAPTER 22:
RESTORING A SERVER
WITH RETROSPECT

This section is for all you folks out there who have listened to us and have put Retrospect on a mobile drive that you can move from place to place if necessary. There are fewer steps you will need to take when restoring, as compared to losing your Storage Catalogs as well as your drive. As you can see by the following windows, our drive not only has an active and working System Folder, it also has the appropriate Retrospect folder with the Catalogs in it. Remember we taught you to put your Catalogs inside the Retrospect folder for ease? Well, here you go.

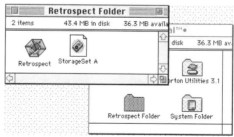

Storage Catalogs Easily Located in the Retrospect Folder

Step 1: Beginning the Restore Process

To begin the restore process, launch Retrospect. The **Immediate** tab will already be selected. The second option down, **Restore,** is the restoration option. Click **Restore** to begin the restoration process.

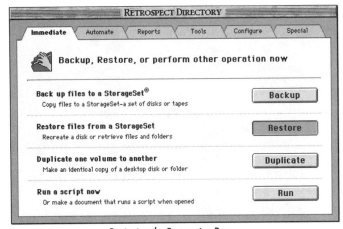

Beginning the Restoration Process

After clicking **Restore**, a dialog box appears prompting you to either **Restore an entire disk** from a backup of any volume, **Restore files from the latest backup** which should be used for finding files backed up in the last day, or **Search for and retrieve older files** which looks through multiple StorageSets for files. Retrospect looks at things completely different at this point. Clicking the **Restore an entire disk** button brings us to the volume Snapshots and automatically highlights the **Restore entire disk** pop-up menu choice.

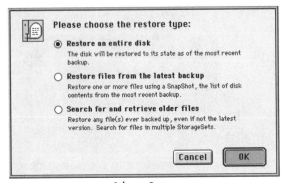

Select to Restore

Clicking **Restore files from the latest backup** brings us to the volume Snapshots and automatically highlights the **Replace existing files** pop-up menu choice. Clicking **Search for and retrieve older files** opens the search to *every* volume that was backed up to a given StorageSet. I can't tell you how many times I've been called in to help users who have decided to *search* instead of *restore* at this point, and who have then messed up their drives so badly that they had to erase all the information and start from scratch.

The easy way to remember what to do here is to simply remember that you are *restoring* your hard drive, nothing more, nothing less. So, ensure that the **Restore an entire disk** button is selected, and click the **OK** button to proceed.

Step 2: Select the StorageSet

The first thing you should restore is the old System Folder that holds all the important network connection information, as well as the invaluable Users & Groups file from the AppleShare file server. Without this file, all user and group access privileges would have to be rebuilt after restoration. When you look for the source Snapshot for this computer, don't become confused because the new drive is named something different from the old drive. In the following dialog box the old drive was named AWS 8150 HD. The new drive is now named Internal.

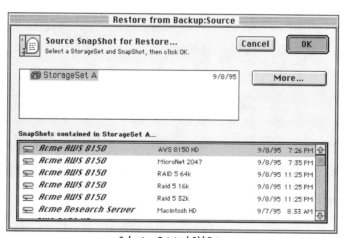

Selecting Original Old Drive

The best thing you can do for yourself at this point, which is the same thing you should have considered when formatting your hard drives, is to refer back to the

Backup Planner chart you initially created when preparing for your backups. That chart will tell you which of the drives was the startup drive (it should be listed first on the chart), and it will list the old drive's name. Once you are sure about the drive you want, click on the drive's name in the list and click **OK**.

Once you click **OK**, a dialog box appears asking you to select the destination of the restore. Select the drive you have just set up and formatted. Unlike previous versions of Retrospect, you don't need to change the restoration preferences. Retrospect automatically assumes that you want to restore the information from the tape to the drive, completely erasing whatever is there. Since this is a newly formatted drive, there shouldn't be anything there at all.

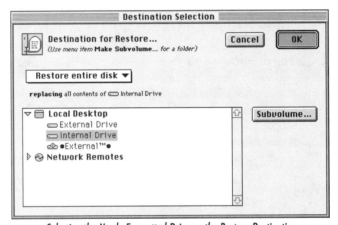

Selecting the Newly Formatted Drive as the Restore Destination

The dialog box shows that you will be replacing all contents of the newly formatted drive with the contents of the original drive. When you click **OK**, you see a dialog box asking if you really want to do this. Click **OK**, and you see *another* dialog box asking the same thing. We call these the "really, really" buttons.

Step 3: Select Files Chosen to Locate the System Folder

After the **OK** button has been clicked, the Restore window appears listing the source of the restoration, its destination, the number and space required for the restored files, and the restoration options being used. Click the **Files Chosen** button to find the System Folder.

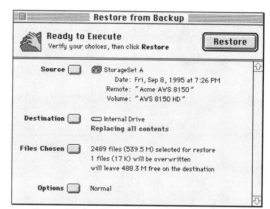

Restore Window Showing Current Restoration Options

When the Browser window appears, everything will be highlighted and marked for restoration. Since you don't want *everything* at this point, unmark the entire list and set your own choices.

![Restore from Backup:StorageSet A window]

All files are selected by default; this is not what you want.

Type Command-A to select everything within the list, and then click the **Unmark** button on the top right of the window. You are doing this because you don't want to restore *everything* within the list, only the System Folder. Once everything has been unmarked, you can either scroll through the list of folders and files until you find the **System Folder**, or you can select **Find...** from the **Browser** menu.

Find Menu Item

There are two ways to go about finding the System Folder.

1. One way is that if you are using the **Find...** menu item, type in the words "System Folder" in the dialog box and set the pop-up menus to find **Folders** whose **Name Is At Start** "System Folder". You aren't finished yet. There is a big difference between looking for a folder and looking for an *enclosing folder*. In Retrospect's parlance, if you search for a folder you will find exactly that and nothing more, just a folder. However, if you search for an *enclosing folder*, you will find not only the folder you specified, but you will also find and highlight all the folders *within* that folder. That's a big difference. I'm sure you don't just want the System Folder per se. I'm sure, since I'm writing this and telling you what you want, that you want the **Enclosing Folder** to be the **System Folder**. Clicking **OK** begins the volume search for the System Folder. Once found, the System Folder and all the folders within it are highlighted.

2. The second option, and the option that I prefer, is to let Retrospect find the System Folder for you, and ensure that it is finding the *blessed* System Folder. You can surely use the first example if you are positive there aren't two (or more) System Folders on a computer. However, I like to ensure that I'm using the right one, and for a few extra clicks of the mouse I can get what I'm looking for the first time out. To use this method, click the **More Choices** button in the bottom left of the window.

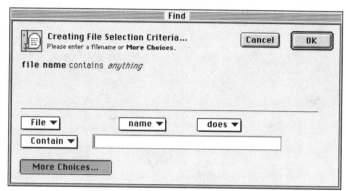

Clicking More Choices

Another dialog box appears, which is actually an expanded version of the previous one. The **Include** line is highlighted already for you. Clicking that small arrow brings up the pop-up menu shown on the right in the following picture. In actuality, the pop-up covers the arrow when you select it, but this is a book, and I wanted to show you the whole window as well as the pop-up.

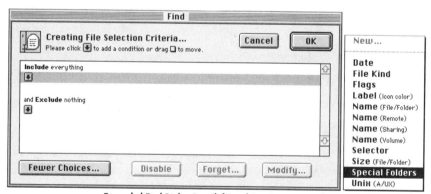

Expanded Find Dialog Box (left) and Pop-Up Menu (right)

Anyway, one of the pop-up menu options is the **Special Folders** option. When you select that option, yet another dialog box appears and is already set to find the blessed System Folder.

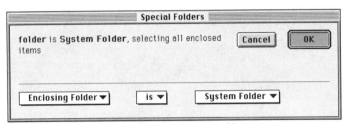

Finding the Blessed System Folder

Clicking **OK** brings you back to the selected files window where you see the System Folder highlighted. Click the **Mark** button to select it for restore.

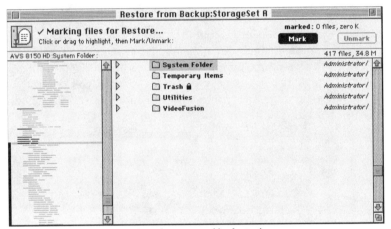

Marking the System Folder for Backup

You can then close the window because you are ready to proceed with the next step of the backup process.

Step 4: Restore the System Folder

When back in the Restore window, click **Restore** to execute the process. After you click the **Restore** button, Retrospect asks you if you really want to execute the restore. It does this to make sure of your intentions.

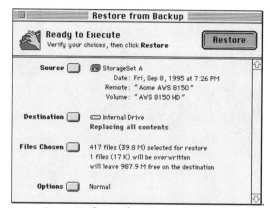

Restore Window Ready to Restore System Folder

If you haven't placed your tape in the tape drive yet, Retrospect prompts you for the first tape it needs to perform the restoration. If Retrospect needs any additional tapes after that, it prompts you for those, too.

During the restoration process, Retrospect displays a dialog box like the one in the following screen shot, showing you your progress. Once it has reached the final stage, it will remain on the screen letting you know that the restoration was successful. We clicked the zoom box to check the progress during the restoration. As you can tell, it didn't go very quickly.

Dialog Box Showing Optional Performance

After completion, you will have the new drive ready for restarting. The System Folder will be in place, and there's nothing else that needs to be removed (like the Temp folder if you are restoring via the same disk). You will need to set the startup disk via the Startup Disk control panel to be that of the new server's drive.

Setting the Startup Disk

Step 5: Beginning the Rest of the Restoration

After you have restored the System Folder, restart the server running from the newly restored System Folder and drive.

We taught you to restore the system first to ensure two things:

1. The system itself wasn't corrupted.

2. You have the right system. To ensure this is true, open the Sharing Setup control panel. Is it the computer you want? I don't know how many clients, no doubt in haste, have restored the wrong server, only to have to do it all over the right way.

Once the server has been restarted, launch the AppleShare File Server software. You will probably see a dialog box that says some access information has been lost. No kidding! How about a couple of drives worth? That's okay, as you are about to restore that access information. You are ready to begin the restoration process when you have the AppleShare windows up on your screen. The connection window should look something like the following, with the volumes available in the top and nothing in the bottom.

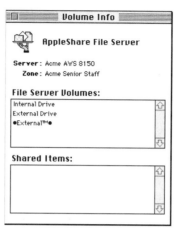

Volume Info Window

While the server is running, launch Retrospect and begin performing the rest of the restoration process.

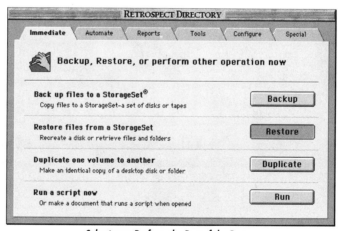

Selecting to Perform the Rest of the Restore

Immediately after clicking the **Restore** button, a dialog box appears prompting you to either **Restore an entire disk** from a backup of any volume, **Restore files from the latest backup** which should be used for finding files backed up in the last day, or **Search for and retrieve older files** which looks through multiple StorageSets for files. This should be familiar, but to refresh your memory, clicking the **Restore an entire disk** button brings us to the volume Snapshots and automatically highlights the **Restore entire disk** pop-up menu choice. Clicking **Search for and retrieve older files** brings us to the volume Snapshots and automatically highlights the **Replace existing files** pop-up menu choice. Clicking the **Search** button opens the search to *every* volume that was backed up to a given StorageSet. Remember, you don't want to search for anything. You are **restoring** your hard drive, nothing more, nothing less. So, ensure the **Restore an entire disk** radio button is selected, and click **OK** to proceed.

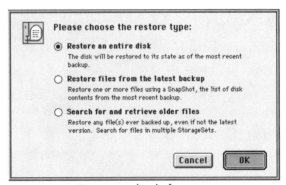

You want to select the first option.

Step 6: Select the StorageSet

The same SnapShot as you used the first time should already be selected. This is the SnapShot you want.

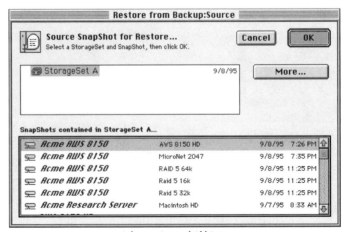

Selecting Original Old Drive

Once you click **OK**, a dialog box appears asking you to select the restore destination. Select the drive you have just set up and formatted. Unlike previous versions of Retrospect, you do not need to change the restoration preferences. Retrospect automatically assumes that you are going to want to restore the information from the tape to the drive, completely erasing whatever is there.

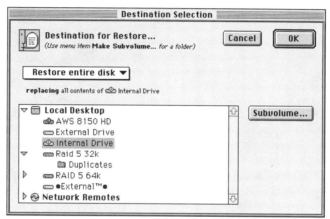

Selecting Newly Formatted Drive as the Restore Destination

The last time you were in this window you restored data to the server and also restored a few files for Retrospect. Don't freak out if a few extra drives are in the Local Volumes window this time. Notice they are grayed out, and notice that the names of the grayed out drives in the window correspond to the drives that were originally on the server you are restoring. That's normal. Either delete them now or later—it's up to you. After you have ensured that you clicked the same drive as the one you restored to last time, click the **OK** button.

The dialog box shows that you are replacing all contents of the newly formatted drive with the contents of the original drive. When you click **OK**, you see a dialog box asking if you really want to do this. Click **OK** to receive another one as well. Click **OK** to proceed.

Step 7: Executing the Restore

When back in the Restore window, click **Restore** to execute the process. Once you click the **Restore** button, a dialog box asks if you really want to execute the restore. Click **OK**. Finally, because you are overwriting the contents of the drive, Retrospect prompts you one more time. Click **OK** to continue.

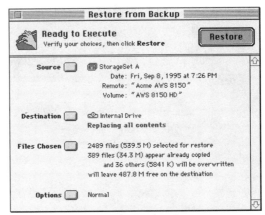

Restore Window Ready to Execute

When Retrospect finishes, there will be a few execution errors, as some of the files were active during the restoration process and can't be overwritten. It is a good idea to browse through the log, although most errors can be ignored for now.

Step 8: Restoring Other Hard Drives

Once the rest of the first hard drive is restored, go through steps 5–7 for other drives. After the final restore, you should restart the computer one more time, this time holding down the option and command keys to rebuild the desktop.

Step 9: Reconfiguring AppleShare

Your volume now has all the original folders and files in the hierarchical setup they were in when you backed up. The Retrospect folder will be there as well.

Restart the server one more time. When you restart, hold down the option and command keys to rebuild the desktop. After that is finished, launch AppleShare and reset the mount-point folders to being shared. For some reason AppleShare can't remember that very first folder. But once it does, it will remember everything else. You'll know you are at a share point when you select the volume and see the access privileges for the folder already selected. At that point you can click the **Share** button and you are home free.

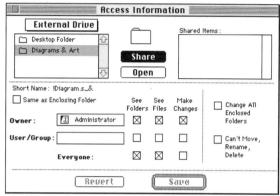

Share-Point Selected

CHAPTER 23:
RESTORING A WORKSTATION
WITH RETROSPECT

This section will focus on restoring workstations across the network. Since workstations don't hold as much data as servers do, and since they can take longer to restore, you can afford the time to restore them across the network. Again, we rely heavily upon our trusty utility hard drive for occasions when we have to perform remote restorations. We use a large utility drive because we need to store a lot of extra files on it as well. Most of these extra files are connectivity files. We have Ethernet Installers for every Ethernet card known to geeks on this thing, and yes, we are often forced to use them to gain access to the Ethernet network.

Step 1: Beginning the Restore Process

After you reformat the user's hard drive and attach the emergency drive, you are ready to restore to the brand new drive. In Retrospect's Main Directory window, click the **Immediate** tab. The second option down, **Restore**, is the restoration option. Click the **Restore** button to begin the restoration process.

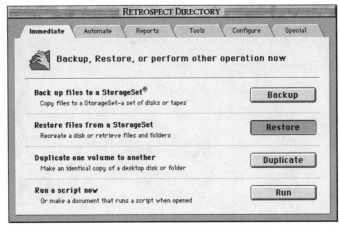

Selecting to Restore

After clicking the **Restore** button, the dialog box appears prompting you to either **Restore an entire disk** from a backup of any volume, **Restore files from the latest backup**, or **Search for and retrieve older files**. (For an explanation of the other radio buttons, see page 354.) Ensure that the **Restore an entire disk** radio button is selected, and click **OK** to proceed.

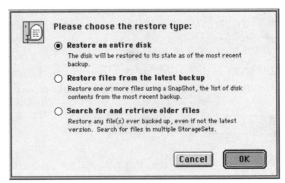

Select Restore an Entire Disk

Step 2: Choosing the Storage Set

The next step in the restoration process is to select the StorageSet and SnapShot to be restored. The source window has a listing of all current StorageSets. Choose the appropriate one and then select the SnapShot as well.

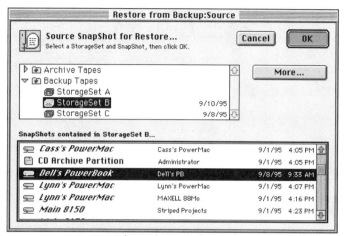

Selecting the Source SnapShot

Step 3: Selecting the Destination Volume

Initially, Retrospect sets the restoration destination to replace the entire contents of the hard drive with the entire contents of the backup. When looking through the destination list, you won't find the original drive. You will find the Emergency Drive, although it won't have the newly formatted drive showing in the list the first time. That's easy to correct though. Double click the Emergency Drive's icon so the Remote Configuration window appears. In the Remote Configuration window, tab to **Volumes** and choose the new drive from the list.

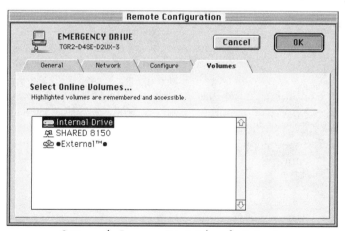

Setting up the Emergency Drive's Volume for Restoration

Once you have clicked **OK**, you are returned to the Destination window.

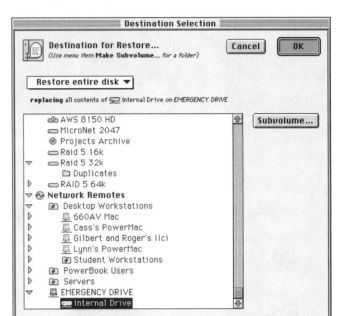

Destination Window with Emergency Drive Available

When you click **OK**, you see a dialog box asking if you really want to do this. Click **Replace** to continue the process.

Step 4: Executing the Restore

There is one last item to check before you click the **Restore** button. If you backed up this computer as a Personal File Server, restore it as a Personal File Server. The way to tell if you backed it up as a Personal File Server is to click the **Files Chosen** button in the Ready to Execute window. A directory of all files and folders you backed up appears. If the spaces by the folders are blank, then the computer was *not* backed up as a Personal File Server. However, if there are owner and user/group names there, you have to restore this computer as a file server, picking first the System Folder, restoring it, restarting, and then restoring everything else.

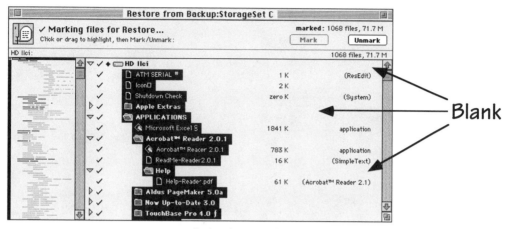

Checking for Personal File Sharing

When back in the Restore window, click **Restore** to execute the process.

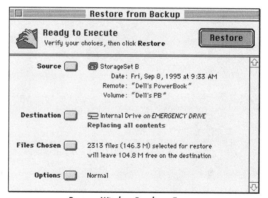

Restore Window Ready to Execute

A dialog box asks if you really want to execute the restore. Click **OK**. As you are overwriting the contents of the drive, Retrospect prompts you with the really, really ready dialog box. Click **OK**. If the tape is already in the drive, it's time to get a coke or have a smoke. There's nothing you can do until the restoration is complete. After that, restart the computer and rebuild the desktop.

CHAPTER 24:
RETRIEVING FILES
WITH RETROSPECT

Retrieving files is a thankless job; one that goes right up there with plant watering and hedge trimming, and about as exciting. To retrieve files quickly and semi-painlessly, you need some rather good detective skills, like being able to figure out where the files came from in the first place. This is because the *user* surely doesn't know. Thus, while we are traipsing through the retrieval process, we'll also teach you a few things about how to sift through the muck and find those elusive files.

Step 1: Preparing to Retrieve

Click the same button to retrieve files as you did to restore them. Therefore, in Retrospect's Main Directory window, click the **Restore** button in the **Immediate** options to begin this process.

This time, though, unlike restoring entire hard drives, you are faced with two choices; to restore a file that was lost or corrupted *since the last backup,* or to restore a file from whenever. By the way, "whenever" is a real date in the minds of users. If you ask them when they last worked with the file, they will often answer "whenever," or "Idunno." If you are wondering, "Idunno" is longer ago than "whenever." We are going to work with the "Idunno" assumption, using the **Search for and retrieve older files** option within Retrospect's restore dialog box. Therefore, click the bottom radio button and then click the **OK** button.

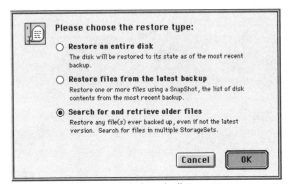

Selecting to Search through All Known Tapes

Step 2: Selecting the StorageSets

When retrieving files, one of the things you *don't* want to do is to select a single StorageSet. Instead, open the search criteria to all files that have been backed up or archived in that last whenever. In the following dialog box, we selected all three backup tapes, but not the archive tape since we knew that the file hadn't been archived yet. If you remember our archive tapes, they are for files that are then removed from the hard drives. Therefore, it was only necessary to look through the regular backup tapes.

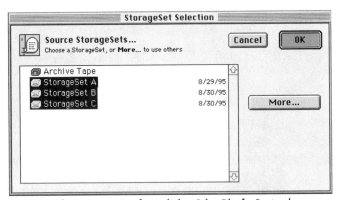

Selecting StorageSets from which to Select Files for Retrieval

Whichever StorageSets you select, Retrospect then searches through their Catalogs looking for matching files. Again, more StorageSets give you more options for the file searching.

Step 3: Selecting the Destination Volume

This is where the power of Retrospect comes in handy. If Joe-Bob or Freddy Bartholomew from down the hall wants a file back, you can put it directly from the tape onto their hard drive. If they don't have a folder set up for retrieval, you can always make one. The dialog box in the following screen shot shows that I selected the Acme Research Server for the location of the retrieved files.

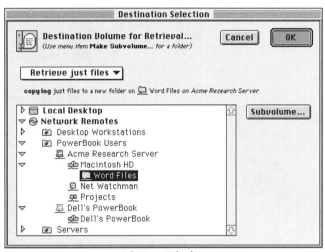

Selecting a Subvolume

The window doesn't show that in order to select the Word Files subvolume, I had to first create it. That's easy and provides a great place for you to put files you are retrieving to the user's local hard drive. Notice, too, that I set the pop-up to **Retrieve just files**. I did that because all I was bringing back were a couple of files that had been accidentally trashed.

Step 4: Setting Your Search Criteria

Once you select your sources and destination, you still aren't ready to retrieve your files. Retrospect automatically opens the search criteria window for you.

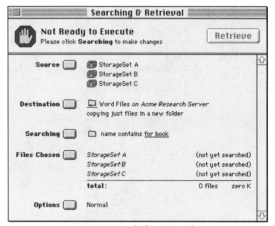

Not Yet Ready for Retrieval

At this point, click the **Files Chosen** button to manually search through the folder hierarchies and look for your files (not recommended), or click the **Searching** button and give Retrospect a few parameters for your search, which is what we did in the following picture. With the search window open, and knowing that the term "for book" was a part of the file I wanted, I set up the search string to find only folders with "for book" somewhere in the title.

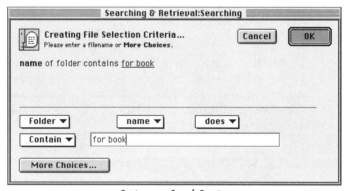

Setting up a Search Routine

Clicking the **OK** button yielded two sets of found files. There were three sets total (one for each StorageSet), but one of the StorageSets didn't have the folder I was looking for. Therefore, I opened up both sets and checked the file dates to ensure that I was restoring the most recent version. There will be times when you *don't* want the most recent version, and therefore should make sure you involve the user who is looking for these files. Once the files are chosen, ensure that they are marked for restoration with check marks next to their names.

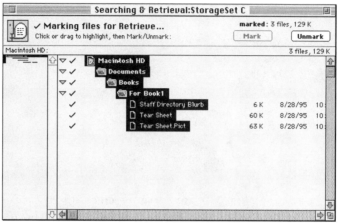

Files Selected and Marked for Restoration

Also go through the other StorageSets and unmark all files so you only restore the files you want. When finished with this, a dialog box like the one in the following picture, shows which files are ready for restoration. There's only one button left to click. Click **Restore** and let the user know the files are on their way.

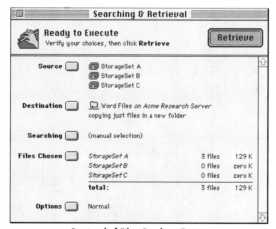

Retrieval of Files, Ready to Execute

PART TEN: RESTORING WITH ARCSERVE

Backing up is somewhat like brushing your teeth. You do it daily, but you see the benefits only twice a year. In brushing your teeth, the payback comes when the dentist says that you don't need the drill. In backing up, the payback comes when you restore.

In this section, we'll look at restoring locally and remotely, both with and without the ARCserve database and preferences.

Don't Bore Me with the Details . . .

- Make sure you have practiced restoring a few times before you are called on to do it "for real."

- Keep a copy of the ARCserve preferences file on a floppy diskette.

- Keep all your restoration tools—such as manuals, tapes, and system software—together and ready for use.

- If you backed up with Personal File Sharing or AppleShare running, you must restore with them running as well.

CHAPTER 25:
RESTORING A SERVER
LOCALLY WITH ARCSERVE

Let's assume that the worst has just happened. Your server's hard drive has just gone "kablooie"! Your users are screaming. Customers are whining. Management is huffing and puffing. All eyes are on *you*.

First, chill out! You are prepared for this situation. That's why you have a backup system and that's why you purchased this book. You have read this chapter and practiced these steps at least a couple of times (hint, hint), so this is nothing new.

Second, decide how to do this thing. If the affected server is also the backup machine, you are going to do a local restore. If you have a dedicated backup computer or the backup drive is somewhere else, you might need to do a remote restore. I say *might* because the backup station might have a peripheral backup device. If it does, take it to the server and do a local restore. Restoring over the network takes longer and slows down network performance.

Third, gather together your stuff. Your "stuff" includes the new hard drive sitting on a shelf waiting for just such an eventuality. It also includes your ARCserve manual, its printed-out ReadMe files, and this book! It includes the most recent backup tape. It includes Apple system software and peripheral hardware drivers. Finally, if the server was also the backup station, you need the floppy that contains the ARCserve preferences file. A small medicinal flask of Scotch might also be useful but should be administered only after the server is restored.

Restoring Servers Without ARCserve's Database and Preferences

We are going to work through the worst possible scenario here. Your AppleShare file server's startup hard drive is totally "dead" and you have had to install a new one. This server is also the backup station and has a peripheral DAT drive. You have lost the floppy with the ARCserve preferences file, and you don't know which session on the backup tape includes the data from the old drive. Piece of cake! Let's get started.

Step 1: Get the Hardware Working

Install the new hard drive according to the manufacturer's instructions.

Whether it is a new drive or you are just trying to revive the old one, you probably need to initialize and format it next. The easiest way to do this is with the Disk Tools floppy, included as part of Apple's system software that ships with each Macintosh. Boot up from this floppy so you can work on the server's hard drive.

Apple HD SC Setup

Run Apple HD SC Setup to initialize the hard drive, then copy the stripped-down System Folder from the floppy onto the newly formatted hard drive If you are working from System 7.x system disks but you are planning to restore System 7.5x software, update the SCSI driver, using the version of Apple HD SC Setup on the System 7.5x diskettes. Use the **Update** button to do this.

If the drive you had sitting on the shelf came from a company like APS, it's probably already formatted and has a System Folder on it. Trash everything on it except that System Folder.

At this point, you have a bootable server drive. If driver software allowing the server access to its peripheral drives needs to be installed, install that now. When everything is in place, rename the System Folder "Temp" and restart the server from its internal drive.

Step 2: Reinstall ARCserve

If you have any questions about how to do this, go back and read "Preparing to Back up with ARCserve" on page 291 or the ARCserve manual.

Step 3: Restore the System Folder

Restart the server, as is required by ARCserve's installer, and you will have a *Temp* and a *Cheyenne* folder on the hard drive. Rename the Cheyenne folder *Temp2*. Next, put the most recent backup tape in the tape drive and launch ARCserve.

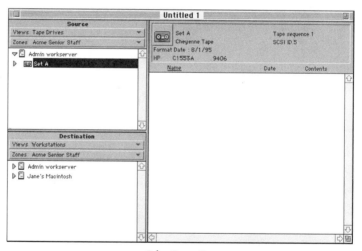

Select Source Tape

In the ARCserve document window, choose **Tape Drives** from the **View** pop-up menu of the Source pane, then click on the backup tape. You are asked whether you wish to merge the sessions on the tape. You do.

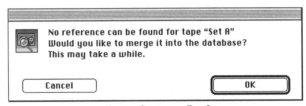

Merging Sessions on Tape?

After you click **OK**, you are asked which sessions to merge. Make sure that the **All Sessions** radio button is selected and click **OK**.

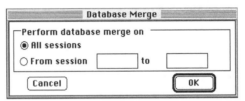

Merge All Sessions

ARCserve is appending the data relating to the sessions on the tape to the newly installed ARCserve database on the hard drive. Once the merge has been completed, you will be able to search through the backup tape's sessions to find the server's former System Folder. Once you have found the session containing it, select the System Folder as the source and the new hard drive as the destination.

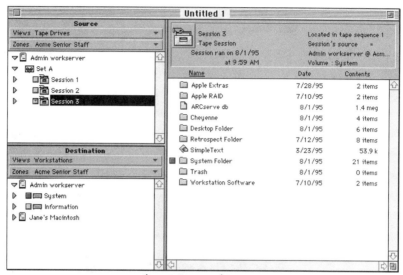

Choosing Source and Destination

Before continuing, make sure that the **Restore into new Folder** checkbox is *not* selected in the Script Settings window.

Deselect Restore into New Folder

Choose **Run Now** from the **Run** menu. After the System Folder is restored, quit ARCserve and move the System file from the Temp folder into the Trash.

In addition to making sure that the **Restore into new Folder** checkbox *is not* selected in the Script Settings window, make sure that the **Skip** checkbox *is* chosen in the **Duplicate Files** box. No point in overwriting the System Folder we just painstakingly restored.

Restart the Macintosh to proceed.

Step 4: Restore the Rest of the Hard Drive

With the server now running from its old System Folder, launch ARCserve and AppleShare File Server (or System 7 Personal File Sharing, as the case may be). This software must be up and running before you restore the remaining files and folders, so as to preserve their access privileges.

Next, select the entire session from the **Tape Drives** view in ARCserve's Source pane, with the new hard drive as the destination.

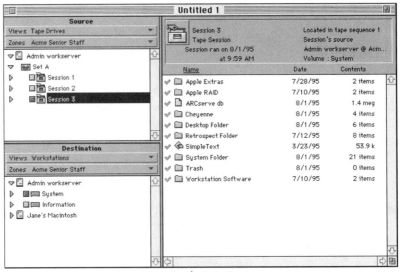

Restoring the Entire Session

Choose **Run Now** from the **Run** menu. When the restoration is complete, reboot the Macintosh. If you are running system software earlier than System 7.5, hold down the command and option keys as it restarts to rebuild the desktop.

Step 5: Reconfigure AppleShare

Once the server comes back up, launch AppleShare File Server. With AppleShare running, boot up AppleShare Admin.

Next, reassign the appropriate Users and Groups for root access to networked volumes. Do this by selecting **Access Information** from AppleShare Admin's **Privileges** menu.

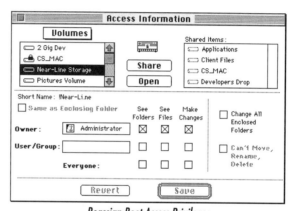

Reassign Root Access Privileges

Here you can use the **Share** button to reassign privileges and publish the shared volumes and folders on the network.

You would need to do the same thing on a workstation using System 7 Personal File Sharing, except that these access privileges are set through **Sharing** in the Finder's **File** menu.

If you need to know more about the nuances of access privileges, buy our other book in this series: *Managing AppleShare & Workgroup Servers*.

Step 6: Reconfigure ARCserve

Trash the Temp and Temp2 folders, and boot up the original copy of ARCserve that has just been restored to the server's hard drive. This will alert Stealth to its location and permit you to use your old ARCserve database file. You can quit the application immediately after launching it.

WHAT IF YOU HAVE THE ARCSERVE PREFERENCES?

If you *have* saved the ARCserve preferences file, things go a bit more easily. The only step that changes is step 3, which goes like this:

After you have restarted the server, as required by the ARCserve installer, you should have a *Temp* and a *Cheyenne* folder on the hard drive. Rename the Cheyenne folder *Temp2*.

Next, load the floppy diskette onto which you had backed up the ARCserve preferences file and drag this file into the Preferences folder of the Temp folder.

Put the most recent backup tape in the tape drive and launch ARCserve. Select **Restore Database** from the **Database Utilities** submenu in the **Utilities** menu. If you set a session password when backing up, you are prompted for this now.

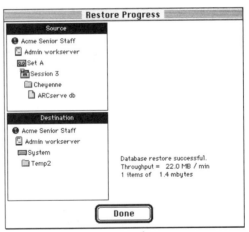

Restore Database

Click **Done** when the process is complete. Go back to the ARCserve document window and choose **Tape Drives** from the **View** pop-up menu of the Source pane. Click on the backup tape and search through its sessions to find the server's former System Folder. Once you have found the session that contains it, select the System Folder as the source and the new hard drive as the destination.

Make sure that the **Restore into new Folder** checkbox *is not* selected in the Script Settings window, and choose **Run Now** from the **Run** menu. In addition to making sure that the **Restore into new Folder** checkbox *is not* selected in the Script Settings window, make sure that the **Skip** checkbox *is* chosen in the **Duplicate Files** box. There is no point in overwriting the System Folder we just painstakingly restored.

After the old System Folder has been restored, quit ARCserve. Before moving on to step 4, move the ARCserve preferences file from the Preferences folder of the Temp folder into the Preferences folder of the newly restored System Folder. Throw the Temp folder into the Trash and restart the Macintosh.

CHAPTER 26:
RESTORING A WORKSTATION
ACROSS THE NETWORK
WITH ARCSERVE

Now that you have the all-important local server restoration down—which really means both servers running AppleShare File Server *and* workstations running System 7 Personal File Sharing—let's apply these steps to the remote workstation. We will use the same basic situation. Hard drive: "kablooie." User: screaming. Management: huffing.

We will once again assume that you don't have a floppy with the ARCserve preferences file on it, but of course we both know that you really do.

Step 1: Get the Hardware Working and Install ARCserve

Install the new hard drive according to the manufacturer's instructions and reformat it. Next, install a full version of Apple system software on it. You will need more than just the gutted System Folder from the Disk Tools diskette to get back on the network. If you set yourself up with a mobile hard drive that contains the Apple system installers, this should go fairly quickly.

Restart the Macintosh from the workstation's new hard drive. If you booted from the mobile hard drive previously, select the new hard drive's name in the Startup Disk control panel.

When the workstation comes back up, type a unique name in the Sharing Setup control panel . . .

Sharing Setup Control Panel

. . . and make sure that you have the correct connection type selected in the Network control panel.

Network Control Panel

You know the rest of the drill. Rename the System Folder *Temp*. Install ARCserve. Restart the Macintosh.

Step 2: Restore the System Folder

After you've restarted the workstation, rename the Cheyenne folder *Temp2*. Launch ARCserve so Stealth knows where it is. You can then quit immediately.

Next, load the most recent backup tape into the Macintosh with the backup drive and launch ARCserve there. In the ARCserve document window, choose **Tape Drives** in the **View** pop-up menu of the Source pane, and click on the backup tape. Search through the backup tape's sessions to find the workstation's former System Folder. Once you have found the session that contains it, select the System Folder as the source and the remote workstation's hard drive as the destination.

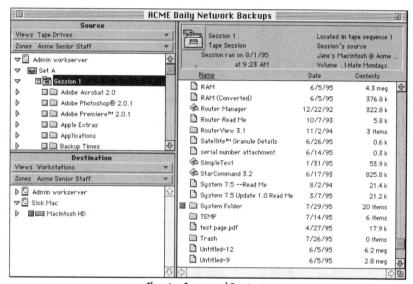

Choosing Source and Destination

Before you go on, make sure that the **Restore into new Folder** checkbox is *not* selected in the Script Settings window, and choose **Run Now** from the **Run** menu.

After the old System Folder has been restored to the workstation, move the System file from the Temp folder into the Trash. Restart the workstation to proceed.

Step 3: Restore the Rest of the Hard Drive

With the workstation now running from its old System Folder, select the entire session from the **Tape Drives** view in ARCserve's Source pane, with the remote workstation's hard drive as the destination.

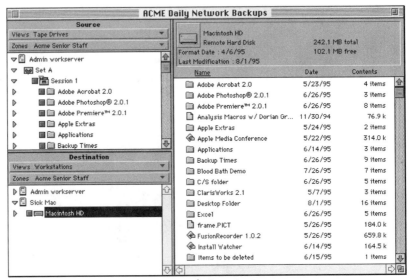

Restoring the Entire Session

Make sure that the **Skip** checkbox is chosen in the **Duplicate Files** box of Script Settings, and choose **Run Now** from the **Run** menu.

When the restoration is complete, reboot the workstation. If it is running system software earlier than System 7.5, hold down the command and option keys simultaneously as it restarts to rebuild the desktop.

Step 4: Reconfigure ARCserve

Trash the Temp and Temp2 folders. Next, boot up the original copy of ARCserve you just restored to the workstation's hard drive. This will alert Stealth to its location. You can quit the application immediately after launching it.

So now that you know how to do restorations with ARCserve, where did you put that flask . . . .

PART ELEVEN: ARCHIVING WITH RETROSPECT

Network administrators often confuse the process of archiving information with the process of backing up information. The two are quite different. Backing up information is for the purpose of being able to restore a computer that has crashed or to retrieve information recently lost. Archiving information is for ridding the network storage systems of information that is no longer immediately needed (cleanup archival) or for maintaining complete records of what was created on the computer systems for the purposes of later retrieval (continuous archival). We will now spend a little time with archival operations, defining the differences between the two types of archivals just mentioned: cleanup and continuous.

Don't Bore Me with the Details . . .

- Backups are for restoration. Archives are for retrieval.

- There are two types of archives: continuous and cleanup.

- The goal of continuous archives is to maintain complete records of what was created on a network.

- The goal of cleanup archives is to remove old information from the computers and to make room for new information.

- Schedule your archives at a time different from your normal backup so that the archives don't interfere with the normal backups.

CHAPTER 27:
THE BASICS OF ARCHIVING
WITH RETROSPECT

Archiving happens in our office daily. Lynn comes in, decides that I'm a pig, and moves my stuff around so that I can't find it. We call it archiving. Many people call that archiving in their offices, too. Let's hope that isn't what you call archiving for the information on your network. The real goal of archiving, along with cleaning up the files on the network, is to transfer the files to a medium that is not as costly to maintain as on-line storage, to provide security for the information, and to still have the information somewhat available if users need access to it.

The best way to archive to provide for the future accessibility of the information is to archive information from your server's hard drive space to a CD, keeping the files in Finder format. When I wrote the first version of this book only a year ago, that seemed a bit costly. One client of ours was paying $150 per CD for an archive to be created from tape files. Today, however, with MicroNet's HD Master 2000 Series CD-R drives, making a CD is cheap, easy, and fast. The writable CDs themselves are around $7.50 each if you buy them singly, even lower if you buy them in bulk. Each CD holds 650 MB of data. With a server set up with the MicroNet MBR-7 CD Jukebox, you can have access to 5,200 MB of data at once! (That's 650 MB of data, multiplied by 8, factoring in the server's internal CD.)

Hence, we will teach you not only about removing the data from the on-line storage (hard drives) on your servers, but also about retrieving that data for users.

PICKING INFORMATION

There are many ways to go about selecting the information you need to archive. The best way we know to do this is by the project. Projects are neat and simple. You can organize them in a "Projects" folder, have all your users put their project information into the Projects folder, and then, when you have enough data to archive, archive the individual projects to CD. Remember, you aren't deleting the data; you are just moving it to CD so it is locked for the future. Once your users know that the data will still be available, they won't go crazy and try to hoard it.

Step 1: Beginning the Immediate Archive

As this is an archive in which you are going to pick the data you want to put onto CD, don't script the archive. Instead, manually run it. To begin the process, tab over to the **Tools** portion of Retrospect (they put it there because they ran out of room elsewhere—I have that on good authority). Once there, click **Copy** to begin the process.

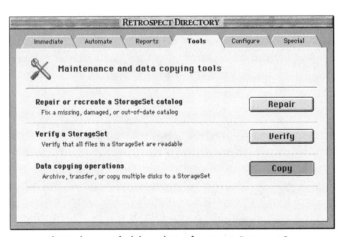

This is where you find the archiving functions in Retrospect 3.x.

After you click **Copy**, a window appears with three choices in it. The first choice is to create an archive. That is the radio button to select. The other two lead to the wrong door and there is a ravenous tiger waiting there to eat your data. Just kidding. The others have to do with copying information from one StorageSet to another or "fast adding" disks. Fast adding disks doesn't work the way I want it to, so I leave it alone. Anyway, make sure that **Archive** is selected and then click **OK** to continue.

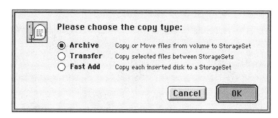

Selecting to Archive Data

Step 2: Select the Source Volume for the Archive

Now that you have created the archive backup, select the volume or volumes from which to gather the information to be archived. Since we are talking about archiving individual projects in this portion, it should be relatively simple to find the data; search for the volume in which the information is located, as we did in the following screen shot.

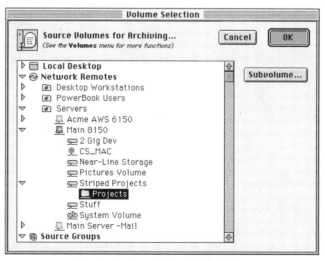

Selecting the Source Volume for the Archive

Creating Your StorageSets

Throughout the book, we have talked about storage media. In the previous book, Pat Lee from Dantz Development and I both commented on how each and every archive should have duplicates of information stored for safekeeping. The process of making archives is more than just backing up to a regular tape. When creating a file or set of files for the future, you may need to do so to fulfill a legal or an ethical obligation, or, if you are a small business like we are, you might need to store the key data on which the company relies, such as copies of our books. The next diagram shows the flow of information in an archive process. The information comes from the servers or other computers as shown on right, is transcribed onto DAT tapes and CDs, and then is stored in various locations in those formats.

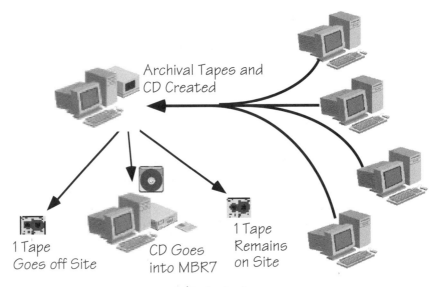

Archival Tapes and CD Created

1 Tape Goes off Site

CD Goes into MBR7

1 Tape Remains on Site

Archive Creation Process

Therefore, plan for at least two sets of archive DATs for the information you are archiving. One DAT will go off site, and the other will stay on site as a backup to the CD. The CD, once created, should be put into something like the MBR7 from MicroNet, which is the device we like the best. You can stack around five of them together before the machine becomes too slow; that's 35 CDs, or 22,750 MB of information on hand. Not bad, huh?

Step 3: Create Your Archive StorageSets

You have seen enough windows on creating StorageSets throughout this book. Do I really need to show you another one? Okay, I will. When creating a StorageSet for your archive, create only a Tape StorageSet. Yes, I know that Retrospect supports CD-R writing. The problem is that it supports writing to CD-Rs in *native Retrospect format*. This means that users can't mount the CD and browse through the information on it. There are a whole bunch of political reasons for why that was done, but hey, I don't work for Dantz, and I can only ask for the same things that you folks do. If you want to write directly to a CD-R in Finder format, you will have to call Dantz yourself at (510) 253-3000. Just don't say that I sent you.

Archive Tape StorageSet

Anyway, you should create two archive StorageSets: one for on site and one for off site. I usually don't put security on them, since I'm putting the tapes in a lock box or shipping them off to DataSafe. I also name them something that makes sense, such as, *Archive Tape* or *Off-Site Storage Tape*. That way, I know what is in the contents of the StorageSet just by looking at the title.

Once you have created your StorageSets, select only one of them for the initial archive. Since you can write to only one tape at a time, you might even want to create only one StorageSet initially and then go back and create the second StorageSet when you are ready to make your duplicate tape. This is what we do. In the next window, we show selecting a single archive StorageSet as the destination for the archive you are about to create.

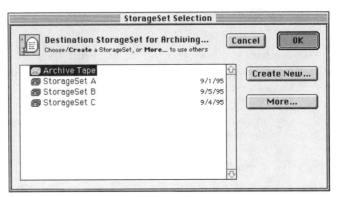

Selected StorageSet

Step 4: Sifting the Data

Now you are ready to sift your data. For the project type of backup, don't worry about setting any special selection filters. You will do that manually when you open the volume you select as your source. To do this, click the **Preview** button in your execution window. You'll see a Finder-like window showing the complete hierarchy of the volume or subvolume you selected as your source. Go through the volume folder by folder and highlight and then mark each folder for archiving. Mark the folder by highlighting it and either typing Command-M or clicking the **Mark** button found in the top-right corner of the screen. Only folders that are marked will be archived (or even backed up, for that matter).

When selecting your information for archiving, be careful not to exceed 635 MB of data. Even though you are going to create a 650-MB CD, you have to remember that stuff about block technology and block sizes that you learned in the AppleShare book. Add in some overhead, and you will find that 630–635 MB of data comes out looking very much like 650 MB of data on the CD. You will know you have selected too much data when you go to write to the CD's volume and Retrospect tells you that what you selected won't fit. Trust me, it's easier to measure the differences before you get farther along than it is to measure them later. The following picture is our Projects subvolume window showing all the project folders I decided to archive.

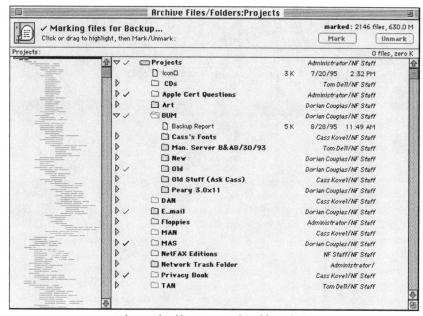

Volume with Folders Custom-Selected for Archiving

If You Aren't Sure . . . If you aren't sure what data you should be archiving off the server,

don't archive the data off the server!

Don't ever remove information from an on-line server if you are unsure about what you are doing. Take precautions. This is easy enough to do and doesn't take much extra time. It involves three programs:

- Adobe Acrobat

- RE:Mark

- Your e-mail system

From within Retrospect, bring up the files you think should be archived. Now, instead of just going full speed ahead and running smack dab into a torpedo, select the Adobe Acrobat PDF writer instead of your normal printer driver and print the page. E-mail the page to everyone who owns a folder you are thinking about archiving. Also e-mail a copy to everyone who is the group leader for groups that belong to folders. In the page shown in the next screen shot, for example, Lynn Heiberger is one owner, and the Administrator (I know, the administrator *shouldn't* own these folders, cobbler's children and all) is the owner of another folder. The group in question is NF Staff.

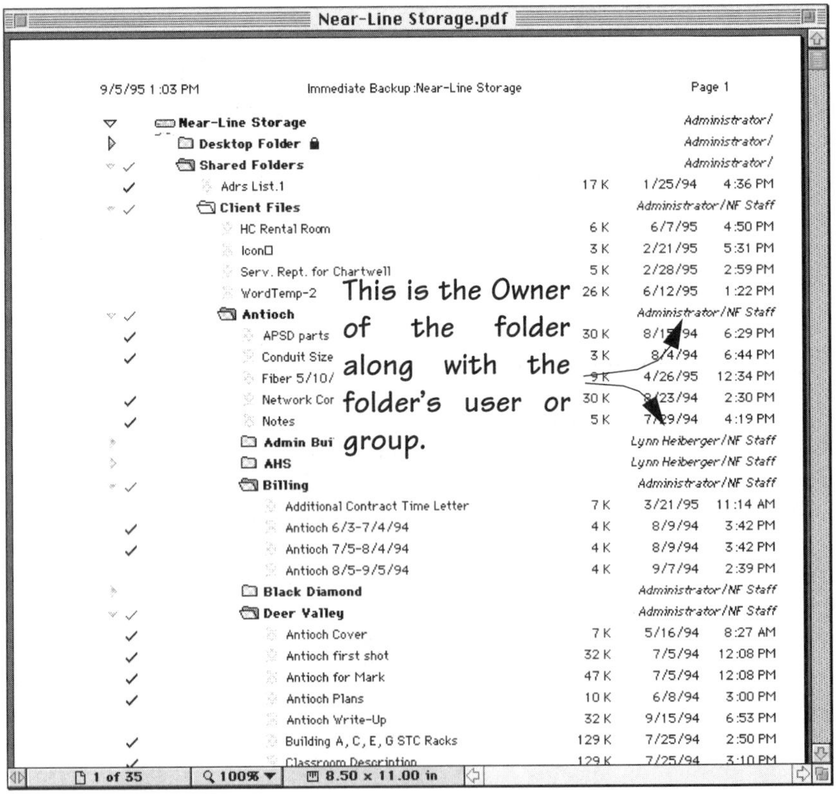

PDF File of the Files to Be Potentially Archived

Next, ask the recipients to annotate those folders *that they don't want archived*. There is some psychology at work here. If you ask people to take action on folders they *want* archived, they will never do anything, because either they won't think it is important, or it won't be important enough for them to spend the time marking up the folders. However, if you tell them that they have to actually take an action to *prevent* information they are currently using from being archived, that will motivate them to respond. If they don't, you have a great excuse for why you did what you did. If you think that I'm kidding, remember all those record deals by mail when you were a kid? Those folks made a lot of money betting that people wouldn't stick the records back in the container and send them back. It's the same thing here.

Step 5: Setting the Options

This is sort of misleading at this point. Basically, you are going to check to see that one of the options that could be set is *not* set. Click the **Options** button in the execution window, and you see the dialog box shown in the following picture. This is the way it should look. The **Move files** checkbox *should not be set* the first time you create your archive; it is safest to leave the files right where you found them.

Once you have mastered your CD and have checked it out, it is safe to create a second archive StorageSet and *move* the files from their original location to the second tape. Doing it this way gives you three copies: one on the CD, one on the original archive DAT, and one on the final archive DAT. If you lose all three, well, that's how many strikes it takes to make you out, which is what you'd probably be if you lost all three sets of an important archive.

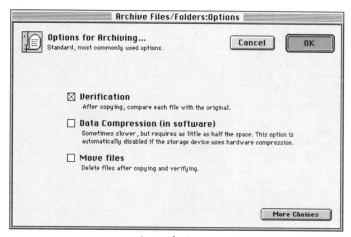

Setting the Options

Step 6: Create the First Archive

You are ready to go. The execution window should look something like the one in the next picture. Load your blank tape and click the **Archive** button.

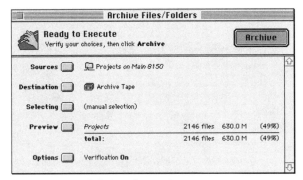

Archive Window Ready to Execute

PREPARING THE INFORMATION FOR CD PRESSING

To press the CDs, we use the MicroNet HDMaster 2000 Pro—the coolest CD building device we have found so far. This SCSI device is a 4x CD mastering machine, *and* it has an internal 2-GB hard drive. Why, you might ask, do you need an internal hard drive on a CD mastering device? Well, for starters, you can't write directly from tape to the CD-R. Therefore, you need to create a separate drive from which the CD-R can record. This is usually accomplished by creating a special soft partition on the drive. By having a 2-GB drive, you can create up to three different CD mastering partitions. Once you start creating your own CDs, you'll find that you *want* to have multiple partitions going at once, as you'll want to create CDs with as much information on them as possible. Therefore, you'll probably have a couple of them going at one time. Don't worry, though—this part is way too easy.

Step 1: Set up the CD Format

Yep, just like it says, the first step is to set the kind of format your CD is going to have. To do that and the other setup steps, launch the handy-dandy software that comes with the CD-R. The main window is shown in the next picture.

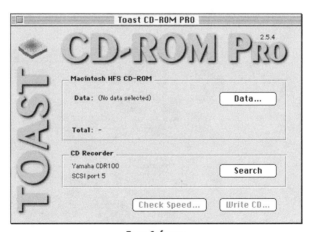

Toast Software

There are basically two menus with which you will be working. You will use the **CD-ROM** menu to choose the CD format you are creating. Don't get fancy and do something weird like creating a Macintosh/ISO hybrid with Audio Tracks. You don't need that right now. Of course, that's the kind of format of the CD that is in the back of this book. For your archive (which is what we do with our archives), set the format to straight Macintosh HFS.

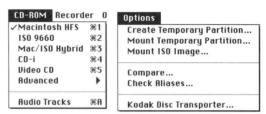

Toast Menus

Step 2: Creating the HFS Partitions

The next step in the game is to create, and then mount, a temporary partition to hold the contents of the archive before the CD is mastered. Do this from the second menu, the **Options** menu. Select **Create Temporary Partition...** and a dialog box like the one in the next picture appears. All you need to do at this point is enter a name in the **Name** field and then select the MicroNet volume in the **On Volume** pop-up menu. Don't mess with the size field. Click **OK** when you are ready, and the partition will be created and mounted automatically.

Setting Options for the CD Mastering Partition

RESTORING FROM TAPE TO THE PARTITION

You are ready to restore the information you archived to tape. You aren't going to restore it to a server. You are going to restore it to the new CD mastering partition you just created. In actuality, it takes much longer to explain it (and a lot longer to write out the process) than it does to actually do it.

Step 1: Begin the Restoration

Open Retrospect and tab over to the **Immediate** section. Once there, click the **Restore** button to begin the restoration process.

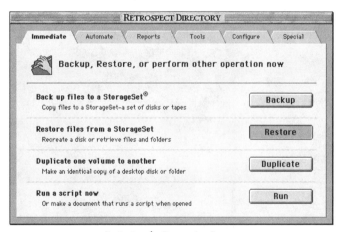

Beginning the Restoration Process

Step 2: Set the Restore Type to Search

Your restore type should be a search. If you are doing this sequentially, you'll be restoring the information archived by Retrospect all of about 10 minutes after you archived it. Looking for files by their StorageSet and backup time yields the quickest restoration results. Thus, after you choose to conduct an immediate restore, you will see a dialog box that gives you three restoration options. Click the bottom of the three to set the restore to search mode.

Setting the Restoration Options to Search Mode

Step 3: Set Your Source

Your source should be the archive tape you just used. Find it and click **OK**.

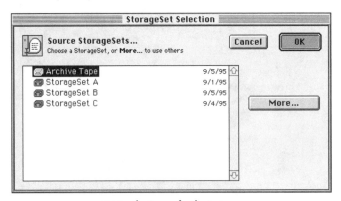

Setting the Source for the Restore

Step 4: Set Your Destination

This one shouldn't already be apparent like the source. What you are going to do now is find the new soft partition you just created and restore whatever is on that tape to the temporary partition. Because you are working with a partition per se, Retrospect treats it like a real volume. Therefore, when you go to locate the volume, you should see it in the local volumes window. The choice for restoration is going to be to restore the *entire* disk. In other words, whatever else was on the temporary partition will be replaced by the contents of the archive tape.

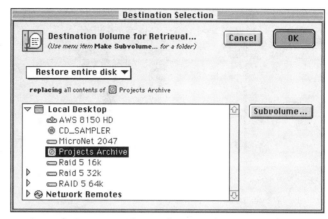

Setting the Destination Volume and Restoring the Entire Contents to It

Step 5: Set Your Search Criteria

Here's where your search criteria will help you. I set the search criteria for "today" on the archive. Simply enough, this will return all files archived today.

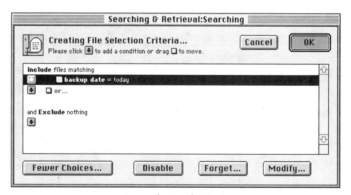

Setting the Search Criteria

Trust but verify. This motto has never let me down. Check the search results to make sure that you are getting what you think you're getting. After you press the

CD, it's too late to say, "I need this on there as well." You press CDs once (unless, of course, someone is creating a desktop mountable multisession CD reader).

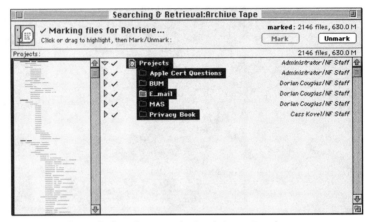

Checking the Source the Search Criteria Found

Step 6: Set Your Options

Set one option when restoring your information to the CD mastering partition: restore with minimal folder structures. All folders that aren't necessary to the hierarchy, which might have been there on the original source, are omitted.

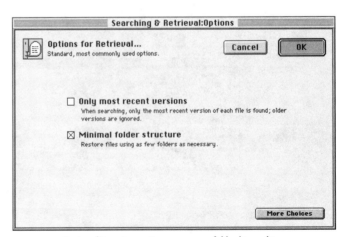

Setting this option omits unnecessary folder hierarchies.

Step 7: Restore!

There you go! There is nothing more to the restore other than clicking the button and getting a cup of coffee or playing Marathon. Click the **Retrieve** button and go relax for a while. Your system should run somewhere around 24 MB per minute throughput, which gives you a few minutes to kick back.

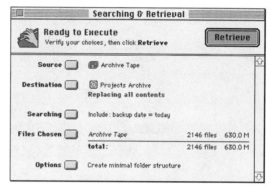

Retrieving Archive to a Partition

PRESSING THE CD

Once the data has been written to the CD mastering partition, ensure that a few things are cleaned up before you press the CD. First, remove your folder labels. The data is now on CD and doesn't have to be restored to the server's hard drive in case of failure. Also, you wouldn't want the labels to trigger any false alarms.

Information as Restored to CD Mastering Partition

Launch Toast and check for errant aliases. Errant aliases on a CD are not good. The **Options** menu has an item for checking aliases. Just direct the dialog box to the CD mastering partition, and the Toast software will do the rest. Once you are sure that the volume is clean and that the icons are in the order and view you want, you are ready to rock and roll.

Toast Software Main Window

The Toast window doesn't have many buttons. You have already looked in all the appropriate menus. Now let's push the last couple of buttons and take another coffee break. Click the **Data** button to select the partition with the newly restored information on it. A dialog box appears in which you can select the appropriate volume and then click **OK**.

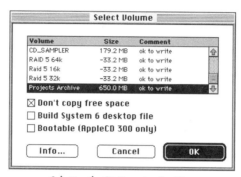

Selecting the CD Mastering Partition

If you are cautious like I am, check your backup speed. If the backup speed isn't fast enough, the CD won't be written correctly. Fortunately for people like me, there is a button just for that purpose. You can either take a coffee break and wait to check the whole volume (my excuse to kill some civilians in Marathon), or you can check part of it and go from there.

Speed Check for the CD-R

Once you are ready, click the **Write CD…** button in Toast's one and only window. Of course, insert a blank CD-R into the drive (that helps), but other than that, you are on your way.

ARCHIVING THE INFORMATION FROM THE SERVER

Here's a great section for you. Remember the first section on this topic, "Picking Information," on page 400, about creating that initial tape archive? Well, guess what? Now that you have your CD, you need to move the information off the server(s) it came from and onto your second archive tape. Doing so will provide you with the three copies of the archived information: your original tape archive, your new CD, and the second tape archive to store off site.

Go through the process of archiving again, which should be "remembered" for you by Retrospect. The only change this time is that you set that last option to move the files onto the tape and then delete them from their original locations from the Options window. Your execution window should look something like the one in the next picture.

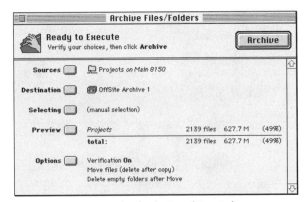

Execution Window for the Second Tape Archive

The options should be set to not only move files but also delete empty folders after the move. The only folders that won't be deleted are folders with files that could not be deleted by Retrospect. Some files can't be deleted because they are locked or potentially in use, which means that you will probably want to do some manual cleanups after your final archival.

CHAPTER 28:
CONTINUOUS ARCHIVES WITH
RETROSPECT (FOR RETRIEVAL ONLY)

Continuous archival is much easier to explain and perform than cleanup archival, so we will start there. The goal of continuous archival is to provide members of the network community and others who might want access to the information with a complete transcript, if you will, of what was created on the network.

Continuous archival is not to be used in place of backups, as archiving creates too many sessions per tape and radically slows down restoration.

We work with a lot of advertising agencies and production houses. These types of businesses need to maintain multiple, generational copies of files they create. Network administrators in advertising agencies, especially, tell me how clients often request versions of documents "like the one the artist did yesterday." The only problem, most of the time, is that the artist *changed* that file because the client didn't like it. Thus, in essence, there *isn't* a file "like the one the artist did yesterday" as it was changed and saved. *This* is the type of problem that a continual archive is designed to prevent. By running a *backup* every day and backing up only those files that have changed, the network administrator can provide a "running collection" so to speak, of files that have been changed. By doing this, the administrator provides members of the network community with the ability to request "file x on date y." Any file can be restored from any given day's activity, because that day's activity was recorded during a backup. Ad agencies aren't the only companies that need this kind of "generational" retrieving capability. Programmers, government agencies, and any other company requiring exact records might need this type of archiving capability.

Notice that I said "running a *backup* every day" and didn't say anything about an archive. That's because you really won't be *archiving* in the truest sense. In other words, with this type of process, you won't be *removing* the files from the computer after you have backed them up. You will be leaving the files on the computer and will be backing them up continually to tape so you have a record of the changes. That is a really big difference.

Step 1: Creating the Continuous Archival Script

Because continuous archives are just that, continuous, script them so they can run unattended in the background during times when you aren't too busy, like during the lunch hour. We called our script the Lunch Archive. To begin the process, launch Retrospect, select the **Automate** tab, and click **Scripts**.

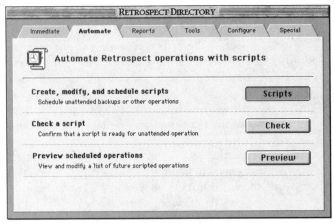

Selecting Scripts in the Automate Window

After you click the **Scripts** button, the script window appears. If this computer doesn't have any other scripts running on it, the window should be blank. Whether it is or is not, click the **New...** button to create the new script.

Another dialog box appears, asking you which type of script to create. I know this might sound silly to you, but even though you are going to use this script for archival purposes, don't click the **Archive** button. Instead, click the **Backup**

Server button. There are a couple of reasons for this, which will make a heck of a lot more sense as you progress. The biggest reason is that with archives, you are incredibly limited in the available scheduling options. The other reason is that you really aren't going to be *archiving* in the sense that you remove files from the computers as you put them on the tape. That is for later. What you are doing now is creating a running backup that never resets. This archive creates the kind of backup that makes users lazy—the kind wherein they can come and say, "I need file *x* from three days ago. Do you have a copy?" With this script running, you will.

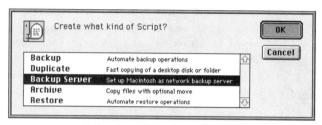

Backup Server Selected as Backup Type

Once you have selected the script type with which you are going to work, you need to name the script. As mentioned before, we call ours simply "Lunch Archives" because that's exactly what it is. Name your script so that if others need to make some additions or corrections to the script, they know with which one they need to work.

Step 2: Selecting the Sources

The sources with which we are going to work in this book are the different volumes on our servers. You aren't limited to just one computer when you create your continuous archive. You can select any volume on any computer in the network, as long as the remote computers are using the Retrospect Remote software. There are, however, a couple of caveats you might want to be aware of before you select *everything* on your network.

• Do you *really* want to create an archive for *every* computer on your network?

• Do you want full copies of your *databases* being archived every time they change, which they probably do daily?

• Do you want to include the System Folders and applications on the network?

• What about the print spooler's folders? Should those be backed up?

Once you have your answers to these questions, and probably a few more that are relevant to you but we haven't thought of, it's time to select the sources for the backup. To do this, click the **Sources** button in the archiving script.

There shouldn't be any sources already selected for this script, so click **Add...** to continue. For the purposes of this book, we are going to select the volumes on our server grouping. However, you can select any volumes or computers you wish.

Groups   Groups are really cool. Groups serve a special purpose. By creating a group, you can enter the *group* into a backup script instead of the individual computers or volumes. The reason this is great is that if you change any of the individual members of the group, you don't have to go back and change the scripts themselves, because the *group* was chosen instead of individual computers. You can create a group by selecting **Make Group** from the **Volumes** menu. The following picture shows me dragging all the desired servers into the server group.

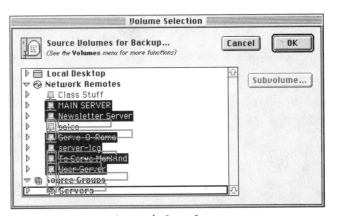

Creating the Server Group

Once the group is created, select the group itself instead of the volumes. Then click the **OK** button.

After you click **OK**, you are presented with a list of sources you have chosen. Normally, these sources are all still highlighted. If for some reason you clicked on the window and deselected any of the volumes, make sure that you select the ones you want to archive before you click **OK**. The volumes that are chosen for the archival script are the ones you select in this window. The same applies with the group. Since it was the group you chose, it should still be selected.

Step 3: Selecting the Destination

Now it is time to decide where you want to *put* the information you are backing up every day. This will depend on your budget and the amount of storage space you have on your network. Take it from me, it is ultimately much cheaper and easier for you if you archive your files to tape rather than to another hard drive or to optical disks. Tape formats are around a penny per megabyte, with any other storage medium being much higher in cost. You have two choices: You can use the same tape drive on which you are performing your regular backups, or you can buy a separate tape system for these backups. There are benefits and drawbacks to both methods.

Same Tape System
The first method is backing up to the *same* tape system you use for your regular backups. The benefit here is that you don't need to purchase another system; you can use the one you have. The drawback is that you will have to swap the tapes from the ones you use for the normal backup to the one you are using for the archival backup. This also means that you will have to run the script during the day, when people are working—so that it's finished before the normal backup occurs. Running this type of backup during the day isn't so bad, as all you are backing up are the files that have changed, and that shouldn't be very many.

Different Tape System
The second method is backing up to a *different* tape system than you use for your regular backups. The benefit here is that you don't have to worry about swapping your continuous archive tape for your normal backup tape. You can put a tape in and not worry about it until you have run out of room and need to put in another tape. Of course, the drawback is that you will have to purchase another tape system to do this. You might think that it's impossible to get your boss to approve another tape system, but that isn't so. Remember, bosses love math. They want to tell you that you can't purchase things, based on the cost. You need to be able to explain to them that you *do* need to purchase things, because of *cost savings*. If you have trouble with this, give us a call and we might be able to help.

If you ask me, I would tell you that the best thing to do would be to buy yourself one of the MicroNet 6-DAT changers. This device lets you install six DATs at once, as well as a seventh if you are using a Workgroup Server that has an internal DAT drive. By installing the 6-DAT changer, you can have your normal backup tapes *and* a couple of your archive tapes running all at once. What a great device this thing is!

Either way, you need to name your StorageSet and save the catalog to disk. To begin this part of the process, click the **Destination** button in the script window.

If you don't have any other scripts written or haven't backed up immediately, you shouldn't have any StorageSets in your window. If you don't, you should put down whatever you are doing and go back and create a regular backup script. Once you are finished with your *regular* backup scripts, come back and create your archival scripts. Back to what we are doing, whether you have any or not, click the **New...** button to create one for this particular script.

After you have clicked the **New...** button, a dialog box appears, asking which type of storage you want to use, what security and compression options you want to use, and what name to assign the StorageSet. If the computer from which you are running Retrospect has a tape system attached to it, that is the kind of Storage Type to choose in the pop-up menu. This is the kind you will probably want to choose, anyway.

A Word About Security

If you think, for some reason, that you need to secure this archive, think about alternatives other than the ones present in this window. Clicking the **Secure...** button allows you to assign a password or encryption methods. The problem with these is that most people forget the password. Then they can't get back into the tape to use it. If you are really worried about security, back up from a computer in a locked room, and when you remove the tape, physically secure it in a safe or external storage system.

Naming

We named our StorageSet "Archive," a derivative of what we named our script. It's easier to remember that this archive goes with this script. It tells what is on the tape as well. Clicking **New...** saves the name and options you set here. As before, you will want to save this in your Retrospect folder.

Creating the Archive StorageSet

Clicking **OK** in the following window saves the StorageSet to the StorageSet window, which in turn saves the set to the script. You won't need to create any more StorageSets for your continuous archives. You aren't going to be rotating tapes here you are just going to be adding, and adding, and adding to the same tapes.

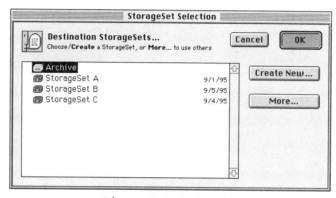

Selecting a Destination StorageSet

Step 4: Setting the Criteria

Now it is time to set some criteria for what you want and don't want to be backed up. Remember, never set criteria on your normal daily backups that you are using for restores. Set criteria only for the times when you will be creating your archives! To set the criteria, click the **Criteria** button in your script window.

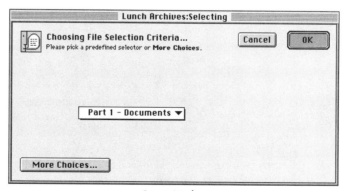

Criteria Window

When the criteria window appears, set your criteria to documents only. This rules out any applications being backed up. However, if you don't want applications to be in the continuous archive, this is not the best way to exclude them. The reason is that most application folders also come with support documents. Therefore, you should keep all your applications in an "Applications" folder so they are better organized, and you can exclude that folder from backups. We chose to include only documents, to ensure that any stray applications won't make it onto the tape.

Step 5: Setting the Options

There are two options I want you to change in your lunch archival system. Click the **Options** button, and then click the **More Choices** button on the bottom right. Once you are at the following window, deselect the checkbox for allowing early backup. This is a lunch-time archival. Therefore, we want the backups to happen when we schedule them. Also, since all you are probably backing up is servers, anything else doesn't really make sense.

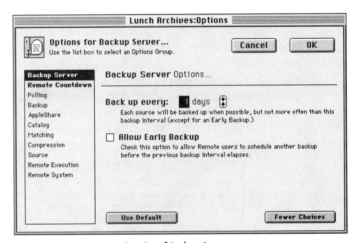

First Set of Backup Options

The next thing to set is the **Remote Countdown** options. I'm not going to show you the window, because it is a waste of space to do so. Just make sure that the counter is set to zero. This means that there won't be a dialog box warning the end user that a backup is going to happen. As you are backing up servers, there's no reason to give an unattended machine a warning dialog box—wouldn't be prudent. Anyway, just trust us right now and you'll find out that we aren't steering you wrong.

Step 6: Setting the Schedule

Create a custom schedule that sets the backup times during the lunch period. To do that, click the **Schedule** button. Next, click the **Custom Schedule** radio button and then the **Custom...** button. Gee, I'm getting tired here. You think they could have put a few more buttons in there (just kidding, guys—you know I love you).

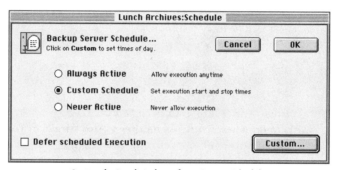

Setting the Lunch Archives for a Custom Schedule

Once you have made it to the epitome of the nerve center of the scheduling window (hey, after all those button clicks, I've gotta build it up here), you are a click or two away from nirvana. The following window shows the finished schedule, and we will go through the settings in this window.

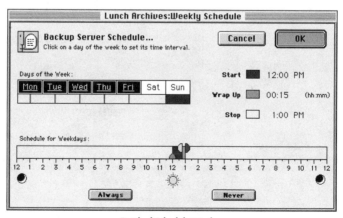

Finished Schedule Window

- Set your schedule for Saturday to be blank (no backups), because your full backups will probably overflow into Saturday, and you don't want anything to interfere with those.

- Set Sunday to be a full day for backups, because your servers aren't doing anything else, most likely, and this will give you a leg up on backing up information correctly.

- Set your weekday schedules to back up during the lunch period. Giving a few minutes of leeway for a document backup to be completed.

Finished!

Your script is now complete! You can click the close box on the top left of the window, and the script will run when it is supposed to. Make sure that the tape is in the computer before you run it, though!

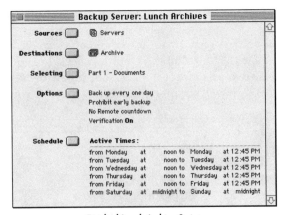

Finished Lunch Archive Script

CHAPTER 29:
CLEANUP OR PICKUP SERVICE
ARCHIVES WITH RETROSPECT

Another kind of archive you can perform on your network is much more simple than the one we just discussed. I call it the "pickup service" archive; others have called it the "cleanup" archive. The goal of this archive is to gather information the users of your network have decided they no longer need readily available. The reason that it is sometimes called "pickup service" archive is that you will be working with your users and establishing an *archive* folder on their hard drives. Whatever they put in the archive folder is archived on a regular basis. When users finish projects, they can put them in the folder for later use. This doesn't mean that when users decide they want to throw something away, they should put the information into the archive folder instead of the trash. I've seen people do this. It isn't necessary.

One of the more interesting things I've seen some of my clients do is take the information on the tape and, instead of putting it somewhere never to be seen again, republish the information on a CD and put it back into use on the network via a CD Jukebox! I think that is kind of a cool idea!

Step 1: Create the Script

Launch Retrospect and select the **Automate** tab button to begin creating the archive script. Once there, click the **Script** button to begin.

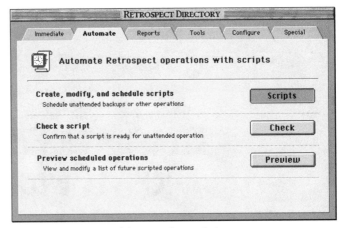

Selecting to Create a Script

If you don't have any scripts written yet, nothing appears in the script window. If you do, the script names appear here. Either way, create a new script by clicking the **New...** button. You are going to create an archive script, so this time you will click the **Archive** line. Click **OK** to continue.

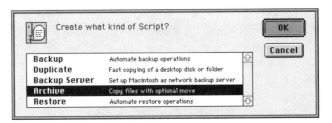

Selecting the Type of Script to Create

You are ready to name your script. We call ours simply Cleanup Archive because that is what we are doing, archiving information from our users' local volumes so they have more space. Once you have decided on your script's name, click **New** to name the script.

Naming the New Script

You are now finished with the initial script creation. You will continue on for a few more steps, selecting the sources, destination, options, and schedule.

Step 2: Source Selection

Once you have created the script, you will be shown the script itself. It is now time to make a few choices. The first choice you will make is which of your network's computers you want to collect information from. To do this, click the **Source** button in the script window. If there are no currently selected sources (and there shouldn't be, because you are just beginning to create your script), Retrospect will automatically bring you to the following Volume Selection window.

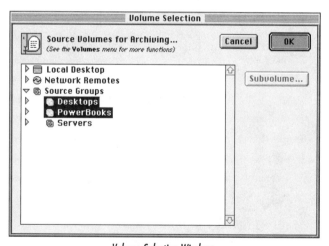

Volume Selection Window

You should be able to find the network-based computers in this list. They are the computers listed in the **Network Remotes** grouping. You will want to select only the **Network Remotes**. To make life simpler, you might want to organize your network remotes into servers, desktop computers, and PowerBooks (like we did in the previous window). That way, by selecting a source group, you don't have to worry about whether the users added to or removed from the group. The group itself is selected and the scripts don't have to change. Once you have selected the computers you want to archive, return to this section and select them from the Volume Selection window.

Step 3: Selecting a Destination

You should be able to see all the archiving sources you picked in your script's window. Now it is time to tell your script where you want to put the information. Whether or not your StorageSet window is blank, create a new destination for your cleanup archival tapes. Click the **Destination** button and then click **Create New…** to create a new destination.

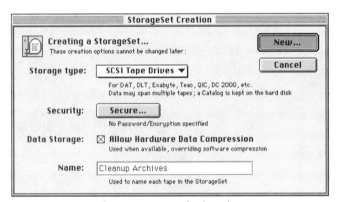

Selecting a Destination for the Archive

We decided to use a DAT tape for our destination. We named it Cleanup Archives just like the script. You don't *have* to use a DAT for this type of archive. One of the clients who performs this kind of archive actually writes the archive directly to a CD-writable disk. The only problem I have with that, though, is that the archive isn't in Finder format, which means that the users can't get to it. I prefer the method of writing the information to a DAT and, when the DAT is full, creating the CD from the information. However, as my wife likes to inform me regularly, mine is not the only opinion on this planet.

After you have decided on your archive type and name, decide whether you are going to place security on the archive. In my opinion, why *would* you? This is information that the *users don't even want* on their computers any more. Take it from me, don't use security. If you are worried about security, lock up the tape in a media safe.

The next thing to do is figure out where you want to save the catalog for the archive. I usually save the archives in the Retrospect folder itself. That way, I know where everything is.

After you have placed your local archive wherever you decided to place it, the archive will be added to the StorageSet database. Make sure that it is selected in the StorageSet window and then click the **OK** button to continue. You are about a third of the way to completing your script.

Step 4: Setting Your Criteria

When we set up our users' computers, we told them to create a folder called "Archive" on their desktops. Actually, we sent the folder *to them*, using Saber's Distribution Manager. We used Update Manager because we knew that if we sent the folder to the users, it would be installed in the same location with the same name on every computer. This makes looking for it on the user's computer so much easier, because you can set your criteria to find only that folder or any other folder called Archive.

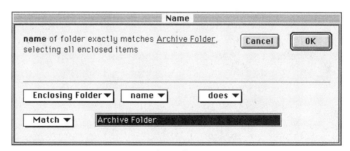

Setting the Backup Criteria

Step 5: Setting Your Options

Don't mess with the criteria selection for this type of archive. Make sure that you selected only users' folders as sources, which will act as a criterion itself. To set the options, click the **Options** button in the script's window.

The first option to set is **Move files**, which tells Retrospect that it should move files from the original source to the destination. Thus, after Retrospect writes the information to tape, it will delete the information on the original source's computer. After you have set that option, click the **More Choices** button to continue, because there is one more option I want you to set.

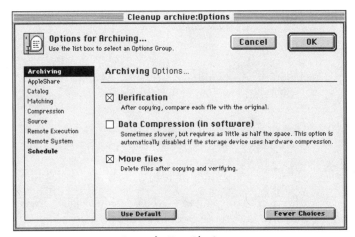

Setting the Move Files Option

Once you are in the "more choices" portion of the options window, I want you to look down the list and find the **Source** option. Click that option, and a window like the one in the following screen shot appears. There is an option I want you to *deselect*. I want you to ensure that there isn't a check mark in the **On Move, don't delete empty folders** checkbox. You *do* want to delete empty folders in this case. If you don't, users who place entire folders of information into their archive will have empty folders inside the Archive folder every morning. As you want the folder to be completely empty after each archive, you *don't want* this option selected. Don't worry about this affecting the Archive folder itself. Yes, even though the folder will be emptied, *this* is not the folder that Retrospect will delete. It will empty the others within it.

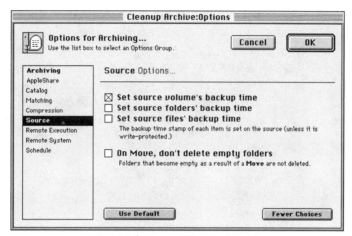

Ensuring that Empty Folders Are Deleted

Set one more option: **Schedule**. Set the schedule options so the archives run from 1:00 P.M. Friday through 4:00 P.M. Friday. You don't want this archive to interfere with the other archives, and Fridays are a great day for cleaning.

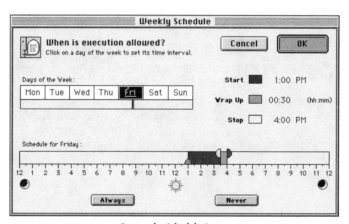

Setting the Schedule Options

Click **OK** when you are finished with the options.

Step 5: Setting the Schedule

Back in the script window, set your schedule, which is the last step before your script is complete. To begin the process, click the **Schedule** button. You shouldn't have anything in your schedule window, because you haven't created a schedule for this script yet. To do so, click the **Add...** button.

The schedule for your archive is simple. Archive every Friday. Click the **Day of Week** radio button in the scheduler dialog box, and then click **OK.**

When it opens, select only Friday's checkbox, telling Retrospect that you want an archive to be performed on that day only. Also ensure that the *time* you set your archive to run is *before* your regularly scheduled backup. This is because you don't need the information in the Archive folders to be backed up. You are already putting it into an archive. Also, you can't have your backup and your archive running at the same time. Therefore, it makes sense to run the archive before the backup. Note that we back up on weekends, as well as weekdays. That is because we are hard-working consultants who never sleep, never have fun, and always work so that we can create great training materials. (How's that for marketing hype?)

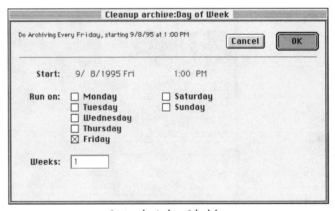

Setting the Archive Schedule

After setting your archive schedule, click the **OK** button. You are then presented with the schedule window again. Click **OK** one last time.

Finished!

Bingo Boingo, your archive script is finished!

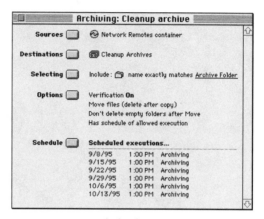

Finished Archive Script

PART TWELVE:
ARCHIVING WITH
ARCSERVE

In addition to having the ability to perform regular unattended backups, ARC-serve can be used to perform continuous archives. In this section, we will discuss how this is accomplished and how the process differs from backing up.

Don't Bore Me with the Details . . .

- Run continuous archives at a time that won't conflict with regular backups.

- Give ARCserve a low priority on the workstation for archiving.

- Script your continuous archives much as you would your backups.

- If in doubt about what to archive, stick to the "back 'em all up" approach.

CHAPTER 30:
CREATING CONTINUOUS ARCHIVAL
SCRIPTS WITH ARCserve

In applying the word *archive* to ARCserve, we are stretching the definition a bit. If the application were really going to archive data, it would first back it up to the destination and then delete it at the source. Cheyenne leaves the "delete it at the source" part up to you and your users. ARCserve can be successfully applied to what we described earlier as *continuous archiving*, however.

Before setting up your continuous archive script, you need to consider when it will run. You don't want it to conflict with your daily backup script, so it should run either before or after that takes place. This might mean that it will have to run while your users are around, and it might mean that it needs to run when you are not. Because of this, configure continuous archives to run unattended and to run without bothering the users.

To make sure that ARCserve doesn't hog users' CPU time, give it a setting of **Low** in the **Priority** pop-up menu of ARCserve's preferences on each workstation.

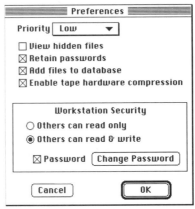

Priority Is Low

Users will be aware that they are being backed up—the slowdown is noticeable—but they can work without an overwhelming drop in Macintosh responsiveness.

Step 1: Create the Continuous Archive Script

Create an ARCserve document similar to the one for daily backups. You can copy that document and change its settings, or you can start from scratch. Name it something like "Continuous Archive" so others will know what it is.

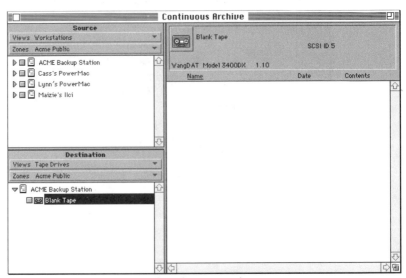

Unconfigured ARCserve Archive Script

Step 2: Select the Sources

The sources for your continuous archive will be all those Macintoshes, both work-stations and servers, with data of which you need to have a running record. This might include all Macintoshes on your network, just a few select workstations and servers, or just servers. It depends on your network's work flow. Give this some thought and talk about it with your users.

Once you have identified which Macintoshes should be a part of the system, determine what hard drive contents are important as well. Do you really want to create an archive for each computer on the network? Is that necessary? Do you want entire databases archived every time they change? That probably means daily! Do you want to archive the System Folders and applications from through-out the network? They are static for the most part.

In just thinking about it, you have probably identified a few more items to exclude from or include in archives. Browse each workstation in the Source pane of the ARCserve document window and make sure that your choices are reflected there.

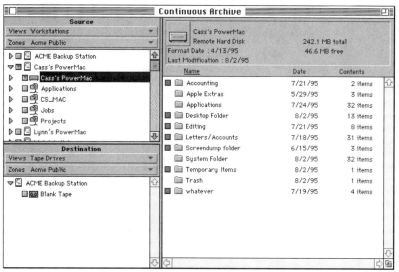

Selecting Data at Source

If your users are cooperative and diligent, you can make this really simple by mak-ing them agree on a few conventions. If users agree to store all their applications in a folder called *Applications,* all their programs will be in one place and you can exclude those folders from the archive. If you agree not to back up a folder called *Personal,* users would have a private place to keep their resumes, games, and funny QuickTime movies (depending on your company policy). If users create a folder called *Documents,* all important data could be stored there, and this folder would have the highest priority for archives.

The trouble with this is that users are sometimes careless. Even if they have agreed to have only applications in the Applications folder, that may not be the case. Users will often save documents in the same folders containing the programs in which the document was created, as that is the application's default when saving. Even if they have agreed to have important data stored in the Documents folder, they will often save documents to the desktop. (You should therefore always back up the Desktop folder.) How much emphasis you place on these concerns will depend on your unique environment and the value of the data with which you are working. When in doubt, stick to the "back 'em all up" approach. It is better to have too much safe data than to have lost data.

Elsewhere in this book, we talk about "clean-up" or "pick-up" service archives. Under this scenario, users create a folder with a name like *Archive* on their hard drives for data they don't want to trash but may never use. After a certain number of days, they can delete what is in this folder with certainty that you have picked the data up and saved it to tape. The trouble with this is that if something destroys that one tape and the same data is no longer part of the generational backup, it's gone. Nevertheless, you might want to consider this plan.

Finally, designating what will be excluded from or included in your archive at this point works only if your choices are few and their folder structure is static. If you have a whole bunch of workstations containing a whole bunch of folders and folders that change, do this with ARCserve's filtering functions instead. In this case, we recommend simply choosing the workstation's entire hard drives when performing this step. We'll set the criteria later.

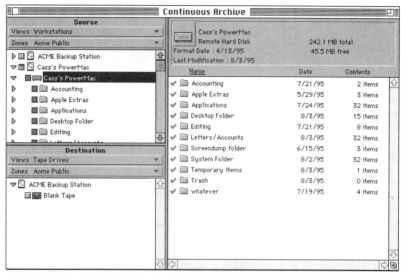

Selecting All Data at Source

Step 3: Select the Destination

There are several places this data can ultimately go, but DAT or removable media is the cheapest. The media at the destination will not be erased, as you might do with generational backup media, but will instead be formatted once and then have data added to it until it runs out of room. Both a high-capacity and inexpensive (per megabyte) media is therefore important.

Perhaps the most obvious solution is to make the destination for the continuous archive the same device that is used by the daily backup. This means that you will have to switch the archive tape with the backup tape and vice versa every day. Another solution is to use another backup device to handle archiving. This is a good method, as you can just set it up and forget it, at least until the tape fills up. This costs more but usually not as much as lost data that takes personnel hours to re-create, if it can be recreated at all. The choice approach is to use a device such as the MicroNet Premier DAT 48/6. This thing has six tapes in one unit. That gives you room for daily backup tapes, archive tapes, user-accessible immediate backup tapes, and even a head-cleaner tape.

Whatever you decide, select the media in the Destination pane of the ARCserve document window.

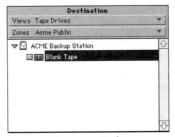

Destination Media

Since it is a blank tape (in our example), format and name it. We suggest that you name it the same thing as your script, "Continuous Archive," to avoid confusion.

Step 4: Verify the Script Settings

If the ARCserve document from which you are working is a copy of the backup document you already created, your Script Settings will already be chosen. If you start from scratch, reset a few things. Either way, there are some changes.

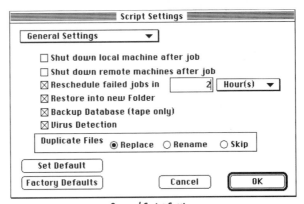

General Script Settings

As with the backup scripts, enable **Virus Detection** and **Backup Database (tape only)**. You might also want to enable **Reschedule failed jobs in...** in case something goes wrong with the backup machine during the regular schedule. Next, use the pop-up menu at the upper left to switch to **Destination Settings**.

```
┌─────────────────────────────────────────────────────┐
│ ══════════════════ Script Settings ══════════════════ │
│  ┌─────────────────────────────┐                      │
│  │ Destination Settings     ▼  │                      │
│  └─────────────────────────────┘                      │
│         ☐ Overwrite ARCfiles                          │
│         ☐ Overwrite Tape                              │
│         ☐ Session Password  ┌ Change Password ┐       │
│                             └─────────────────┘       │
│    ┌───────────────────────────────────────────────┐ │
│    │ ☒ Allow Tape Cascading to                     │ │
│    │   ☐ Cheyenne tapes ☐ Unknown Tapes ☒ Blank Tapes│ │
│    └───────────────────────────────────────────────┘ │
│    Data Authentication ┌ Compare        ▼ ┐           │
│                        └──────────────────┘           │
│  ┌──────────────────┐                                 │
│  │   Set Default    │                                 │
│  ├──────────────────┤      ┌─────────┐  ┌─────────┐   │
│  │ Factory Defaults │      │ Cancel  │  │   OK    │   │
│  └──────────────────┘      └─────────┘  └─────────┘   │
└─────────────────────────────────────────────────────┘
```

Destination Script Settings

Here again, we suggest that you enable **Data Authentication**. Do not select **Overwrite Tape**, however. You want new sessions appended to the previous sessions. There is one other option worth mentioning. Imagine that you have more than one tape's worth of data to back up and won't be around to switch tapes. You also don't want to buy a big-time DAT autochanger. Throw together a couple of DAT drives by the same manufacturer, such as APS HyperDATs, and select **Allow Tape Cascading to** and the appropriate tape checkbox. The backup will automatically flow to the next tape in line once the first is full.

Step 5: Set the Filters

Although we can't *make* you apply filters to archiving only, we would if we could. It's a good thing we don't know where you live (better not send in that registration card). When you do daily backups, back up *everything*. Life's too short.

When you do need or want to apply filters in archiving, ARCserve gives you an extensive list of choices. These choices can be made general and applied to all sources or can be made specific and applied to individual sources.

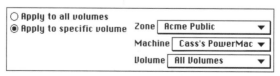

Applying Filters

Whatever your choices, they fall under the category of either *inclusions*, stuff you want to back up, or *exclusions*, stuff you don't want to back up. *Exclusions take precedence over inclusions*, so be careful. If you told ARCserve to include, for instance, all files with names containing the extension .FMP but told it elsewhere to exclude any files created by Claris's FileMaker Pro, some of your database files would not be backed up. We suggest that you avoid mixing exclusions with inclusions.

Cheyenne does a nice job of explaining ARCserve's filters in the manual, so I'm not going to go into detail here. Essentially they are:

ARCserve Filters

- Include or exclude files or folders created, modified, or backed up before, on, or after a given date or dates.

- Include or exclude files whose total size, resource fork size, or file fork size is equal to, greater than, or less than a given size.

- Include or exclude files of a certain file type or associated with a specific creator code (meaning, made with a certain application).

- Include or exclude files or folders whose name matches, starts with, ends with, or contains a given string of characters.

- Include or exclude files or folders that are locked, shared, system files, invisible, stationary, or aliases.

- Include or exclude files created by certain applications you designate (an easier way of applying the **Type/Creator...** filter).

- Include or exclude files or folders with a specific label. These can be the Macintosh default labels or any you or your users set up. It can also apply to files given *any* label at all.

How you use these filters is dependent on how you and your users work, so we won't even try to direct you on this. Here is how we do it in our office, but this might not be how you should do it. Filter selections can be seen and edited by choosing the **Show Filters** command from the **Customize** menu.

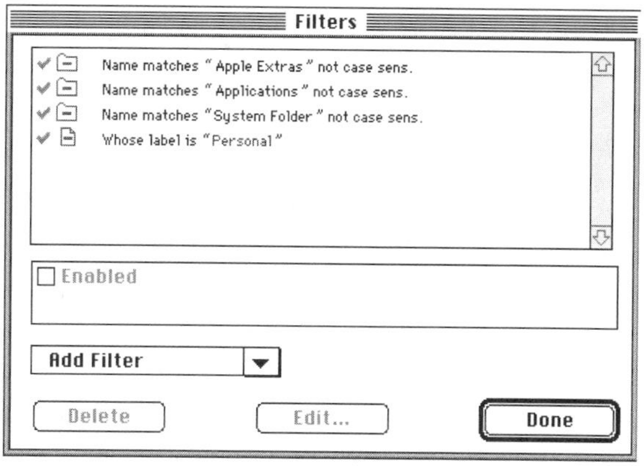

Viewing Filters

Long ago, we learned the value of basic folder standardization across a network, so all our users have and properly use their Applications and Documents folders. We chose to exclude the former and don't need to specifically include the latter. We chose to exclude the System Folders, which is not always a good idea. Although the System Folder's contents don't change often, the files in its Preferences folder do. We leave that to daily backups. We have also excluded the "Apple Extras" folder, created by some newer Apple software installers. Finally, we have agreed to exclude anything with the label "Personal."

Step 6: Set the Schedule

Establishing when your continuous archive will run is easy: continuously. This actually means at least daily.

449

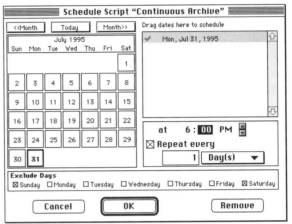

Archive Schedule

In the example shown in the previous picture, ARCserve kicks in at 6:00 P.M., giving it four hours to run before the daily backup executes. This is more than enough time in my circumstance. I told it to begin on the last Monday in July and to run every day excluding Saturday and Sunday.

Finished!

That's it. Each archive session will be added to the tape until you run out of tape or you put in a new one. If the amount of data that changes on your network is light, you could plan on changing the tape quarterly. Don't go longer than that.

RETRIEVING RECENTLY LOST FILES WITH ARCSERVE

The beauty of using ARCserve for continuous backups becomes readily apparent the first time one of your users announces that "something just happened" to a document, naturally avoiding all personal association with that "something." As long as what just happened, well, just happened (meaning since the last archive), you can recover the document. Better yet, since all your users have ARCserve on their computers too, your users can recover their documents themselves! Novel, eh? This assumes that the archive script isn't running at the time, of course. Here is what you can do or tell them to do.

Step 1: Create a Retrieval Document

There is nothing complicated about this—you just need to select the source media that contains the continuous archive and the destination hard drive of the workstation to which it is being restored.

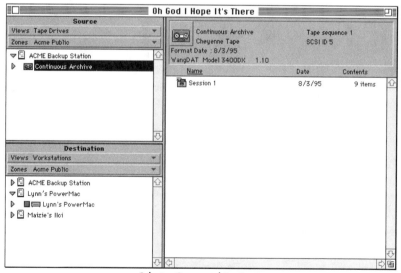

Selecting Source and Destination

It's a good idea to verify that the default **Restore into new Folder** checkbox is selected in the Script Settings window so the archived data doesn't overwrite the newer data. Sometimes, you find that the cure is worse than the ailment and that you have made too many changes to a document to make going back to an earlier version acceptable.

Step 2: Find the File

Finding the file you want to retrieve can be accomplished graphically, by browsing the sessions located on the archive tape in the same way you would navigate the Macintosh folder structure, or through the **Quick File Access** command, which works much like the Macintosh **Find File** function.

Browse Session Folder Structure

The **Quick File Access** command, located in the **Utilities** menu, is especially useful. It will search through all archive sessions for the file matching the search parameters you specify.

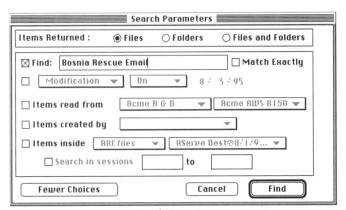

Search Parameters

You can then narrow it down from the information presented in the results window and click the **Restore** button to retrieve it.

Choose Version to Retrieve

Finished!

If you selected the **Restore into new Folder** script setting, you are prompted to create this destination folder. Otherwise, the retrieved files will be put right back where the user had left it previously, safe and sound.

Incidentally, we included the document "Bosnia Rescue Email" on the CD-ROM that comes with this book. If you are at all patriotic, give it a read. It illustrates the power and immediacy of the Internet even if it doesn't have a darn thing to do with backups.

PART THIRTEEN: THE ROAD WARRIOR'S GUIDE TO BACKUPS

This section is for the network administrator who needs to get the boss up and running (often literally) with a PowerBook or Duo. It is also aimed at technically savvy executives who need to get themselves up, running, and out the door. It focuses on what can be carried on a trip and what should you should do when you return to the office.

Somewhere in the annals of history there is going to be a Silicon Valley reference for the "digital nomad." It will point to two biographies, Andy Gore's and Mitch Ratcliffe's. These two define "road warrior." They are the PowerBook Pair: the Duo Duo. They wrote the now classic *PowerBook: A Digital Nomad's Guide* (New York: Random House, Inc., 1993). We have learned—and borrowed —much from that book, and we'll be borrowing from it again for this chapter to supplement our own information. Buy the book. It's wonderful.

Don't Bore Me with the Details . . .

- Identify the information you will need when you are on the road ahead of time. This includes applications and connectivity technology.

- Test your files on a different computer before you go on the road. You might have used resources available only to your own desktop when creating your presentations.

- Back up and restore your hard drive once before you leave. You can't do anything about it if you back up incorrectly when you are on the road.

- Back up often while on the road, either to floppies or to removable media.

- Create an easily identifiable folder and put the essential information inside this folder. It makes it so much easier to back up and synchronize.

- When on your home network, act like a full network citizen and use the network backups. Don't be a lone warrior. They survive only in the movies.

CHAPTER 31:
BACKUP PLANNING FOR
THE ROAD WARRIOR

Base your decisions about how you will protect your data while on the road on two factors: *tolerance to loss* and *weight*.

What Can't You Afford to Lose?

When we leave to go to a client site, we expect to be running every known network administration software product (some known only to us). We can't afford to lose much, so we carry spare hard drives. For other people, the situation is a bit different. Ask yourself this question: Why are you leaving the office?

Is it to make a presentation to a client or at a seminar? If so . . .

* Is the presentation on your PowerBook's hard drive?

* Should you make a duplicate presentation, or can you recreate it on the fly?

* Is the software with which you created the presentation in a standard package others have, or is it something you might not find in other places? In other words, can you run your presentation from a client's computer if necessary?

- What about fonts? Did you use fonts that are part of the standard set, or do you need to back up a copy of your special fonts, too?

- What about art? Are all the images used in the presentation embedded in the document or are they linked to files available only on your desktop Macintosh's hard drive. How about sounds and music?

- Do you have a paper copy, just in case?

Are you going far away? Will you need to connect remotely to your office e-mail system, America Online, CompuServe, or the Internet? If so . . .

- How long can you afford to be out of electronic information based contact?

- To which service can you reroute all your messages so you can limit your software to a single connectivity package?

- Can you reroute your e-mail messages to a fax machine at your destination hotel? If you can, do you *want* to?

- Can you receive e-mail file enclosures through your service? Do you need to?

How Much Do You Want to Carry?

Here's a reality check to help you with this decision. Forget about thinking you are going to create a single disk that holds both your system information and a single all-in-one application, like ClarisWorks. It won't happen unless you spend a lot of time fiddling with the disks and are endowed with the brain power and know-how of either an Andy Gore or a Henry Norr.

Floppy disks are great for the storage of information but not for applications, resources, *and* information.

If your drive dies and you need to boot off an external device, your choices are going to be a full hard drive, a Magneto Optical drive, a Bernoulli drive, or a SyQuest drive.

Note: To boot off an external hard drive, you need to be sure that it has system software installed on it and that the system software is the right software for your computer. If you're installing the system software onto an external hard drive from a computer other than your PowerBook, use the **Custom Install** option to ensure that you have software that will run a PowerBook.

There are battery-operated hard drives on the market. These kinds of drives free you from the burden of carrying a power supply (for a while). APS sells a good one for the PowerBook, called the APS Companion II drive. These drives come in sizes of 504 MB and 773 MB. They weigh in at about two pounds. APS also has a Parallel version for PCs, called the MobilStor, which is available in 340 MB and 520 MB sizes.

There aren't any MO drives really built for travel. MO drives hold either 128 MB or 230 MB in a disk size that *is* portable. They are slow, but then there isn't much that can ruin the data on an MO drive.

One of the most popular mobile storage devices to hit the market in a long time is the Iomega Zip drive. With an initial per unit cost of under $200 and 100-MB cartridges running about $15 each in volume, these Bernoulli-based devices are very appealing to a lot of people. They are easy to use, come in SCSI and Parallel versions, and weigh a tad over a pound. You should know this before you buy one, though: At the time of this writing, they have no battery-power option, and the power supply that comes with them is heavier than, and almost as big as, the drive itself! Iomega does offer a smaller universal power supply, but that's extra, as is an HDI adapter you need have to use its SCSI cable with your PowerBook.

Not to be outdone by Iomega and its cheap Bernoulli-based drive, SyQuest too is offering a device in the same price range, based on the SyQuest mechanism and using 135-MB cartridges. We don't yet know about the weight of the hardware associated with the EZ135, but be concerned about the same weight issue as with the Zip drives f you look into buying one: How portable is portable if the power supply dwarfs the drive?

APS's line of traditional SyQuest drives includes one it packs into its ultra-light SR1000 case. This drive isn't battery operated, but even with power supply and cartridge, it weighs just a little under 1.75 pounds. The cartridges can hold either 105 MB or 270 MB of data each. A MobilStor version of this for PCs is available as well.

Preidentify Your Files to Be Backed Up

When you back up, you can't always see which files are in the folders. It is therefore important to organize your drive so you have all your important files in one place. One way we do this for our clients is by setting up a folder called "!Essential" on the root directory. We put the exclamation point in front of the folder name to bring it to the top of the folder list when one is looking for information to back up. Another way is to use a *Documents* folder. This is created when you tell System 7.5.x that you want the default for all saved files to be a folder with such a name. This is set in the lower right of the General Controls control panel.

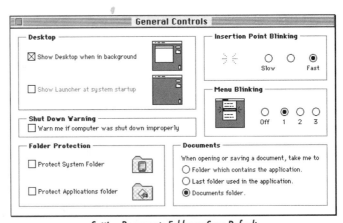

Setting Documents Folder as Save Default

We also recommend that you put your programs in a folder called *Applications*. It makes it much easier to find them and to select them for backing up.

Use Network Backups and File Synchronization

Our last bit of advice to you is on what to do when you return to the office. First, make your PowerBook part of the network backup. Although both Retrospect and ARCserve permit you to do immediate local backups, it is safer to make yourself part of the network's overall scripted backup. Second, synchronize your important and continually changing files. There are few things more annoying than to have all the work you did on the plane lost because you copied an older version of a file onto your PowerBook from your desktop when you returned.

EXERCISING VERSION CONTROL WITH FILE ASSISTANT

Apple was very thoughtful in bundling PowerBook File Assistant on the hard drives of its portable computers, as this utility eases the burden of version control. In other words, it makes sure that if one version of a file is on your PowerBook and an older version is on your desktop Macintosh (or vice versa), the older one is automatically updated. This process, called *file synchronization*, can be applied to both folders and files.

To use File Assistant most effectively, perform a little work ahead of time. Specifically, we suggest that you decide which files moving between your portable and desktop computers *need* to be synchronized and then create a folder just for them.

In my case, I have but one folder to worry about: Documents. This is where I keep a database of client contacts, a vendor database, a calendar file, and the chapters of the books I write. Being a writer and a consultant, I live out of my PowerBook. Unfortunately, I am limited in what I can do with my PowerBook, so on my desktop I also have a Power Macintosh from which I run most of the software I write about. I may do my writing at home or on the road with the PowerBook, but I experiment and take screen captures from the desktop. With all this moving back and forth, it is important that I keep up to date on the versions of the files with which I work.

On my hard drive, the Documents folder is used for files that change in substance but not in name. Other stuff is saved to the ever-messy desktop or in the "Files Received" folder that Farallon's Timbuktu put on my disk. In setting up File Assistant, I first created a folder called *Tom's PB Mirror* on a shared volume, called *Projects*, located on my desktop computer. This is where I dragged the Documents folder when setting up File Assistant, as illustrated in the following picture.

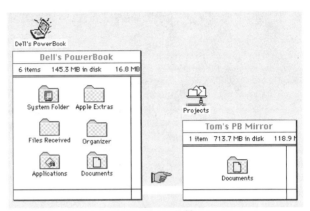

Copying Target Folder

When you are first setting up file synchronization, *the files or folders that are to be linked must be identical.* This is what we suggest. File Assistant *does* give you the option of synchronizing folders that have differing names and file contents. This is enabled by selecting the **Allow non-matching folder names** checkbox in the **Preferences** command from the **File** menu.

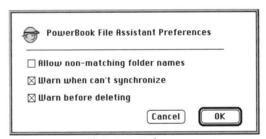

File Assistant Preferences

If you permit this, File Assistant will automatically copy files from nonmatching folders to each other until they do match!

Do one last thing before you synchronize your files. Make sure that the clock on your desktop Macintosh is synchronized with the one on your PowerBook. This is set in the Date & Time control panel.

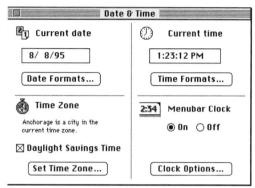

Synchronize Clocks

Remember to do this again later if you bring in your PowerBook after having been in a different time zone. (A different dimension is fine, too.)

To link the files and folders you have selected, launch File Assistant by double clicking on its icon or accessing its alias from the **Apple** menu.

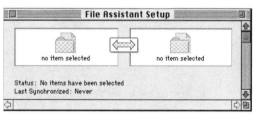

Empty Selection Window

Drag the folder you want linked from your PowerBook to one side of the file selection window.

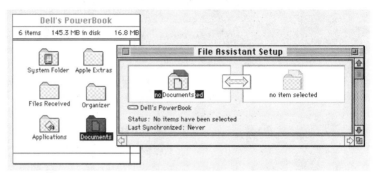

Drag Folder from PowerBook

Then drag the folder you want it linked to on the desktop Macintosh into the other side of the selection window.

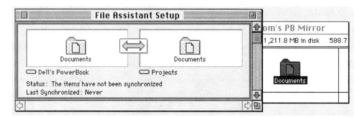

Drag Folder from Desktop Macintosh

The two linked folders and their parent drives will now be displayed in the Setup window. Scroll down to add additional folders to the window.

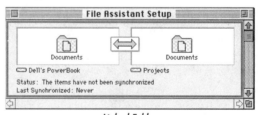

Linked Folders

Now that you have told File Assistant which folders you want synchronized, tell it *how* you want them synchronized. The commands for this are located in the **Synchronize** menu.

Set Link Direction

The best choice here is **Two Way**, which ensures that the contents of the folders you set up are up to date. If you were looking to stay current with a particular file on a file server, however, you could use a one-way option.

It's time to synchronize! Choose **Synchronize Now** from the **Synchronize** menu. This installs the link. Later, File Assistant will check the files in both folders to ensure that both contain the newest versions. If it finds that you have deleted a file from either folder, it will ask you whether you'd like to trash its corresponding files in the other folder as well.

Missing Files in Linked Files

File Assistant gives you two choices for when it will go to work. If you select **Manual** from the **Synchronize** menu, it updates the links when you launch File Assistant and choose the **Synchronize Now** command. If you choose **Automatic**, it updates the links when you launch File Assistant and every few minutes thereafter.

To really make it "automatic" requires more steps. First, make sure that the shared volume containing the desktop's linked folder is always available. Do this by choosing **Always** in the **Remount Shared Disks** option in the AutoRemounter control panel.

Using AutoRemounter

Second, put an alias of the File Assistant application in the Startup Items folder of the System Folder so it launches as soon as the PowerBook boots up.

CHAPTER 32:
CATCHING THE NOMADS
WHEN THEY RETURN

Remember what we said at the beginning of this section? While the nomadic users are on the network, they should be treated as regular network citizens. Well, now we are going to talk about how to capture the nomadic users *whenever* they come back to the network.

With the advent of Retrospect 3.x, you have the ability to create a full-time *backup server*—a server that runs 24 hours, 7 days a week, 365 days a year. That's pretty cool. As the backup server operations don't interfere with the normal scripted operations, there isn't any reason *not* to run the backup server full time if you have the machine to do it. What the backup server does, that none of the other scripts can do, is look for the source computers on a regular basis. If the source computers haven't been backed up lately, the backup server takes the initiative and grabs them whenever it can.

We'll walk you through the scripting process and then show you one extra thing the users can do on their own without a script.

CREATING THE BACKUP SERVER SCRIPT

To initiate the backup server script, tab over to the **Automate** section of Retrospect. Once there, click **Scripts** to create the new script.

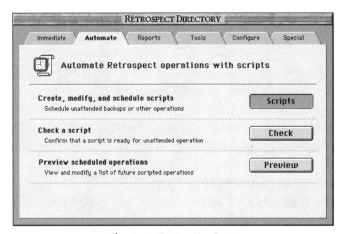

Choosing to Create a New Script

Step 1: Creating a New Script

A dialog box appears with the backup scripts you have already written. Click **New** to proceed with creating the new script.

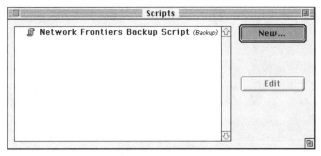

Creating a New Script

This brings up one more dialog box asking which kind of script to create. Since we are creating a backup server script, I guess you had better select that in the dialog box options. If you don't . . . well, then you are on your own.

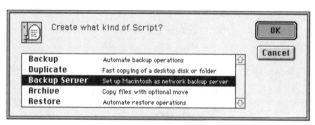

Selecting Backup Server Script

Retrospect next asks you to name the script. We called ours the *Nomad Catcher.*

Step 2: Selecting the Sources

Now it is finally time to group some of your sources. We have grouped our PowerBook users into a source group called *Consultants.* You can create groups from the **Volume** menu. When reading the backup reports and logs, we will realize that if they aren't backed up and they are a member of the Consultant's group, they are probably somewhere like Poughkeepsie or some other incredibly fun town.

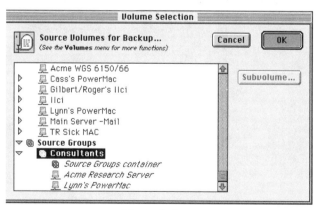

Selecting the Sources

Once we have set our nomadic PowerBook users as members in the source group, it is time to select the source group as the group to add to the backup server's script to be backed up on a regular basis. Select the group and click **OK**. The group is added to the Sources database. If for some reason you want to go back and add more computers to the database, Retrospect gives you that option in the Sources window. If not, click **OK** again to continue the process of setting up your script.

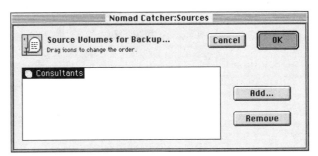

Consultants Group Added to the Sources Database

Step 3: Selecting the StorageSets

After you have selected your sources, select the StorageSets to which you want to back up. We've already created regularly scheduled backups being rotated to StorageSets A through C and are going to select these as our destinations.

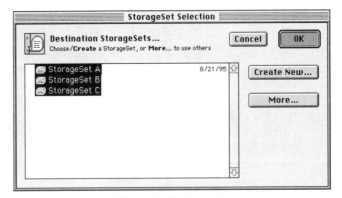

Selecting Existing StorageSets

Why not create new ones? You want your nomadic users backed up to the same tapes as your regular users. I have it on good authority (Pat Lee at Dantz told me, and he's never lied to me—yet) that the way the backup server works is that Retrospect examines which tapes are in the tape mechanism, and if it finds only one of them in the set, backs up to that StorageSet. If it finds more StorageSets in the backup drive, it backs up to the one backed up to *the longest time ago*. In other words, it tries to keep them all up to date. Pretty nifty, huh? Well, I think so.

Once you have selected your StorageSets, you are brought to the same type of window as when you selected your sources, a window that gives you the option to go back in and add a few more. Since you are using the same StorageSets as you use in your regular backups, there is no reason to do anything other than click **OK**.

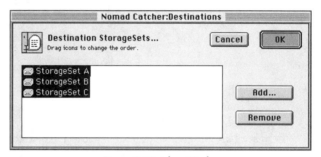

StorageSet Database Window

The ability to back up to any of the available StorageSets is both a blessing and a curse. It is a blessing in that it is probably the most elegant solution to finding an available StorageSet that I've seen. It flawlessly integrates the backup server into the normal backup routine. Very nice, very nice indeed. It is a curse, however, in that if you have multiple StorageSets loaded simultaneously (most of the real world won't be doing that), Retrospect picks the StorageSet with the least up-to-date information and then backs up to that one. While writing this very page, I decided to see how well the backup server worked, and instead of backing up a couple of pieces of information, I found that my PowerBook was being completely backed up to the server. This was because StorageSet C was loaded into the tape system (as well as A and B), and since C had nothing on it, the entire contents of the drive were backed up. Oops.

Step 4: Setting Your Options

Next, set some options. The backup server is almost set correctly (according to me, that is), but there are a few things to set that will make it "just right."

Backup Server Options

Early Backup The default options are that every computer should be backed up at least once per day and that verification is **On**. These are fine, but click the **Options** button to set additional options. Before you skip on to clicking the **More Choices** button to see the rest of them, ensure that the **Allow Early Backup** option is selected as well. This option allows the *users* to set a sort of "push" backup, putting them on the list to be backed up next by the server.

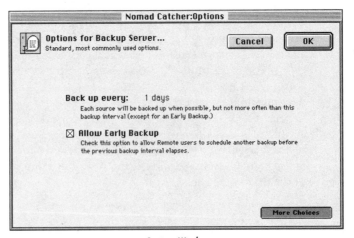

Options Window

Once a user sets his or her °Remote control panel to be backed up **As soon as possible** (shown in the next screen shot), the backup server recognizes this and gives the computer top priority for being backed up.

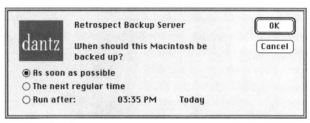

Schedule Feature Within the User's °Remote Control Panel

That's fantastic if you are a PowerBook user and you need to be backed up before you run out of town (or out for a consulting meeting).

Remote Countdown

The **Remote Countdown** option sets how long Retrospect displays a dialog box asking the user whether he or she wants to be backed up, before a server-based backup begins. The user may opt to defer the backup until later. If the user doesn't click *anything*, the dialog box remains on screen for a specified length of time or until the backup time comes around, and then the backup will proceed. Of course, if the user opts to click **OK**, the backup begins immediately.

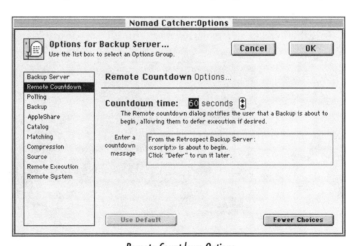

Remote Countdown Options

Remote Connections The next options are the **Polling** options. These tell Retrospect how long to wait before searching the network for the specified computers. The defaults here are fine, unless you want it to wait longer.

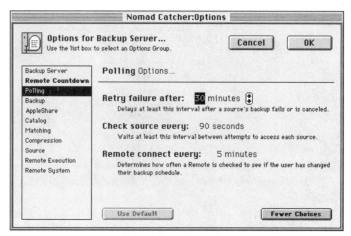

Remote Connection Options

Setting the Backup Bit One of the things Retrospect can set is each folder's and file's backup bit. This is a bit of information that, when set, can tell other programs that the computer has or has not been backed up. Programs like SaberLAN and Server Sleuth can check the backup volume's bit and each folder's backup bit. There is nothing right now that checks individual file backup bits, so don't set the source file's backup time.

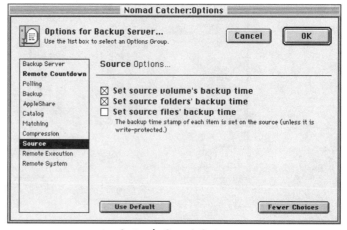

Setting the Source's Options

Step 5: Setting Your Schedule

One of the things I've found is helpful is to set a custom schedule.

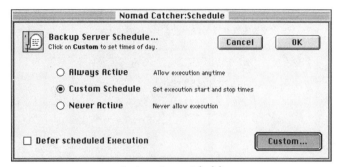

Setting a Custom Schedule

Clicking the **Custom Schedule** button brings you into the type of window that we described back on page 267. Instead of going through it again, I'll just show you the one we created.

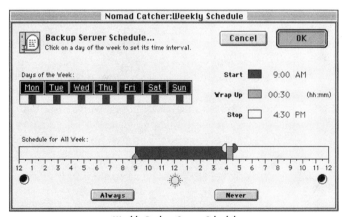

Weekly Backup Server Schedule

We set our schedule to run from 9:00 A.M. through 4:30 P.M., with a grace period of 30 minutes. This means that it will look for computers to back up until 4:00 P.M. These times are when the users will be in the office with their computers. After these times, the normal backup procedures should be taking place.

Step 6: Set the Server to Run

Your backup server script is saved and ready to go. The window displays what you have set and when it will run. The only thing left to do is to turn on the Backup Server from the **Run** menu.

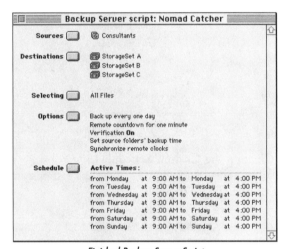

Finished Backup Server Script

Once you have set the Backup Server to run, you will see a window like the one in the following picture. It shows that it is running. It also gives the status for each computer you set to be backed up. The pop-up menu shows you other options as well, such as StorageSets and scripts. I like leaving the pop-up on this option because I want to see what's going on with each of the computers being backed up.

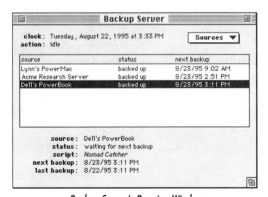

Backup Server's Running Window

APPENDIX:
DUTIES AND
RESPONSIBILITIES OF THE
BACKUP COORDINATOR

We want to give you the one thing you probably don't have right now—a job description for the *backup coordinator*. Along with the job description, we will give you a basic budget outline.

Setting Departmental Policy

Backup plan coordination should result in a departmental policy for backup and recovery. Therefore, the following paragraph should be at the forefront of the backup coordinator's job description. Here's a sample that conforms to Toigo's book (which we mentioned earlier):

> The Backup Plan Coordinator will develop the company policy for the protection of information assets for [whatever your department
> coordinator shall set a yearly budget which is approved by [v
> final say on budgets in your company or department].

Depending on the politics in your office, you may want to add some strong language to ensure the policy that you create is actually followed, such as:

> Failure by any [whatever your department is called] employee to perform assigned duties outlined in the company policy for the protection of information assets will be considered a severe breach of company security and may result in disciplinary action. [Refer to whatever section in your company employee manual deals with discipline and dismissal.]

Put this up front so there are no surprises for anyone.

Yearly Risk Analysis

The backup coordinator should conduct a yearly risk analysis. This consists of a critical workstation and server audit, threat evaluation, budgetary planning, implementation, and training procedures.

> The Backup Plan Coordinator will conduct a yearly risk analysis. This will consist of auditing all networking devices within the Coordinator's control. Following the risk analysis, a threat analysis will also be conducted. It is the responsibility of the Backup Plan Coordinator to work with [whomever] to create a backup plan budget and then to implement a backup and restoration strategy pursuant to the backup plan budget set for the year.

Training and Testing

A crucial part of the disaster recovery plan is the ongoing training of the coordinators and the periodic testing of the plan. A server that is backed up but has never been tested for restoration is a server waiting for a problem to occur at the worst possible moment. Therefore, you should have something in your backup plan stating that the coordinator is responsible for obtaining training and for testing the backup plan as well.

> The Backup Plan Coordinator is responsible for training himself or herself on new techniques and strategies. The Backup Plan Coordinator is also responsible for training [x number] of assistant coordinators on a yearly basis.

> The Backup Plan Coordinator is responsible for testing the restoration of each server being backed up at least [x number] times per year. This will be sched-

uled [x number] months in advance and users will be notified of impending tests. Tests should be conducted during [business or non-business] hours.

You should also provide some minimal level of training for users. Even if they play no role in the backup procedure, they did to know a bit about it. For instance, they need to know it *exists* so they don't waste personnel hours recreating what you could have easily restored. Maybe this is no more that a yearly "Backup and You" or "Backup Questions and Answers" meeting, but do provide something.

> The Backup Plan Coordinator is responsible for promoting user [awareness or understanding] of the company policy for the protection of the company's information assets.

Hardware Maintenance

Although the plan you create will protect your company's data from loss due to hardware failure, it is still better if you catch hardware problems before there is a failure. The coordinator or an assistant should visit all the hard drives on the network and run a utility to hunt down such things as bad blocks, conflicting SCSI addresses, and whacked-out directory structures. While they are at it, they can defragment the drives, which will speed up backup times.

> The Backup Plan Coordinator, or an assistant under the direction of the Backup Plan Coordinator, will conduct [monthly, bi-monthly, or quarterly] storage device maintenance. This will consist of auditing all storage devices within the Coordinator's control to seek out and correct faults up to and including the replacement of a given storage device. Storage devices that are not faulty will be optimized and defragmented for increased performance.

While you probably don't need to write this into the plan, it is a good idea to keep a database of information relating to storage devices on your network to permit fast troubleshooting and replacement. This should at least include the manufacturer, serial numbers, and exact model numbers. If you have PCs, it's a real good idea to jot down the BIOS information as well. A good time to gather this information is during the walk-through.

Support, Software, and Supplies

Establish the ability to obtain the tools needed to do the job. These tools could include backup software, software upgrades, and hardware (such as DAT drives). Plan for your consumable supplies also, such as tapes and cleaning cassettes. A final item to include might be an off site storage service, such as DataSafe.

> The Backup Plan Coordinator is responsible for the procurement of and budgeting for all software, hardware, services, supplies, and materials needed to execute the company policy for the protection of the company's information assets on a yearly basis.

Budget

To create a budget, simply plug in your best guess at costs for the categories we have just discussed. Again, politics may play a part here, but we strongly recommend planning for the "worst case." In backup management, the proverbial glass is always half empty.

Planning

Risk Analysis
Personnel hours in creation
Threat Analysis
Personnel hours in creation
Documentation
Ex: publishing or copying costs, if any

Training

Backup Plan Coordinator
Personnel hours in training
Classes, books, and other training materials
Assistant Coordinators
Personnel hours in training
Classes, books, and other training materials

Network Users
> *Personnel hours in training*
> *Classes, books, and other training materials*

Testing

Backup Plan Coordinator
> *Personnel hours in testing and training*

Assistant Coordinators
> *Personnel hours in testing*
> *User downtime (if applicable—**try to avoid this!**)*

Hardware Maintenance

Backup Plan Coordinator and Assistant Coordinators
> *Personnel hours for hardware maintenance*

Replacement Costs
> *For "X" number of devices, with "X" being the number you expect to lose*

Software, Support, and Supplies

Hardware
> *Ex: DAT drives*

New Software
> *Ex: backup and utility software*
> *Upgrades for existing software*

Services
> *Ex: PO Box and DataSafe*

Consumables
> *Ex: tapes and cleaning cassettes*

Backup Plan Coordinator and Assistant Coordinators
> *Personnel hours for procurement*

INDEX

NETWORK FRONTIERS FIELD MANUAL SERIES

NEW RELEASE CD-ROM

ENCLOSED

The **Network Frontiers Field Manual Series** consists of several excellent hands-on guides for designing, managing, and troubleshooting AppleTalk networks! Network Frontiers, Inc. is the developer of the Apple Certified Server Engineer (**ACSE**) program and each book in the series corresponds to an **Apple Certified Course**.

> "This series of books is focused on teaching networking professionals the ins and outs of the AppleTalk world . . . .Network Frontiers is highly qualified to write on the subject. They are the authors of the ACSE certification test, the designers of networks from coast to coast, and the authors and trainers of nationally acclaimed classes upon which both the book and the ACSE program are built. Their style of writing is technically accurate, lively, and straightforward."
>
> **—James J. Buckley,**
> **President of Apple USA,**
> **Apple Computer Computer, Inc.**

Developers of

Apple Certified
Server Engineer
Program

Electronic Updates

FRONTIERS IN NETWORKING CD-ROM

This quarterly CD-ROM update is the only way to stay on top of the latest topics covered in the **ACSE** tests. We all know that books written about technical materials outdate themselves within a year—that's why we publish this electronic journal. It contains updates for each book in the series, new and provocative insights & techniques into network design, management & troubleshooting issues, network demonstration tools, technical notes from vendors, potential test questions, and interactive training materials.

Special Introductory Offer: When you enter your annual subscription you'll receive the first CD-ROM update **FREE**. If you are not completely satisfied with the *Frontiers in Networking CD-ROM* write *CANCEL* on your invoice and you'll have no further obligation.

Available Fall 1995
ISSN: 1083-3501
All Countries: $89.95 (1996 annual subscription), 4 issues

TO ORDER YOUR ANNUAL SUBSCRIPTION:

AP PROFESSIONAL
Circulation Department
525 B Street, Suite 1900
San Diego, CA 92101-4495
1-800-894-3434
1-619-699-6742
e-mail: apsubs@acad.com
All prices are in U.S. dollars and are subject to change without notice.
Canadian Customers: Please add 7% goods and services tax to your order.

NETWORK FRONTIERS FIELD MANUAL SERIES

MANAGING APPLESHARE™ AND WORKGROUP SERVERS
Dorian Cougias & Tom Dell

Foreword by **James J. Buckley**, President of Apple USA

This book will show network administrators how to create and maintain multiple AppleShare file servers and set up personal file sharing across a network.

Key Features

- Learn all about the new PowerPC Apple Workgroup Servers.
- Get the most out of AppleShare and other server-based software.
- **RAID**—how to use it.
- Learn how to manage multiple servers remotely.
- Includes CD-ROM with network tools.

CONTENTS: Introduction. Building an AppleShare Server. Setting up an AppleShare Server. Preparing Users for Sharing Files. Managing AppleShare File Server. Managing AppleShare Print Server. AppleShare and the PC. AppleShare and the Internet. Managing Personal File Sharing. Who Owns the Data on Your Servers? Managing Multiple Servers with Server Manager. Server Accounting Management with Server Tools. Networking Database Information with Viper Instant-Access. Managing Group Scheduling with Now Up-to-Date. Maintaining Database Consistency with Now Contacts. Distributing Workstation Software with FileWave. Sharing Digital Documents with Acrobat. Conclusion. Appendices. Index.

In Bookstores **August 1995**
Paperback, c. 500 pp., $29.95
ISBN: 0-12-192568-4
Includes one CD-ROM.

NETWORK FRONTIERS FIELD MANUAL SERIES

MANAGING APPLETALK™ NETWORKS

Dorian Cougias & Tom Dell

Managing AppleTalk Networks will teach readers the basics of managing AppleTalk networks, including bridges, routers, gateways, router management, network numbering schemes, and network zone management.

Key Features

- Choose the best network management software for the job.
- Learn how to plan your network administration calendar.
- Easy management of your network from your desktop—software distribution, asset management, and more.
- Learn how to stay legal with your software and save money at the same time.
- Includes CD-ROM with network tools.

In Bookstores **October 1995**
Paperback, c. 400 pp., $29.95
ISBN: 0-12-192564-1
Includes one CD-ROM.

DESIGNING APPLETALK™ NETWORKS

Dorian Cougias, Tom Dell, and E.L. Heiberger

Learn how to update your current network design or create a new one that will successfully support its users. Gain a thorough understanding of AppleTalk from cabling-up through familiarity with TCP/IP to support Mac TCP Clients.

Key Features

- **CAT5** installations to support **10BaseT** and **100BaseX**.
- Where to put a hub, a switch, or a router to control network traffic.
- **TCP/IP** addressing and its integration with AppleTalk.
- How to design a network based upon your network service needs.
- Includes CD-ROM with network tools.

In Bookstores **November 1995**
Paperback, c. 400 pp., $29.95
ISBN: 0-12-192566-8
Includes one CD-ROM.

NETWORK FRONTIERS FIELD MANUAL SERIES

TROUBLESHOOTING APPLETALK™ NETWORKS

Dorian Cougias & Tom Dell

This book will provide the fundamentals and practical applications of network troubleshooting, from troubleshooting basic network components through network re-design concepts.

Key Features

- Troubleshooting Methodologies.
- Baselining Tools and Procedures.
- Problem Isolation, Correction, and Prevention.
- Includes CD-ROM with network tools.

In Bookstores **January 1996**
Paperback, c. 400 pp., $29.95
ISBN: 01-12-192560-9
Includes one CD-ROM.